Karl Albrecht, Ph.D., one of the pioneers in the development of stress-reduction training for business managers, is an organization development consultant in San Diego, California. He teaches at the University of California Extension and lectures widely on management, communications, human relations, and stress reduction. Dr. Albrecht is the author of a number of books on stress reduction and management.

STRESS

AND
THE MANAGER
MAKING IT WORK FOR YOU

KARL ALBRECHT

A TOUCHSTONE BOOK
Published by Simon & Schuster, Inc.
NEW YORK

First Touchstone Edition, 1986

Published by Simon & Schuster, Inc.
Simon & Schuster Building
Rockefeller Center
1230 Avenue of the Americas
New York, New York 10020

Originally published by Prentice-Hall, Inc.

TOUCHSTONE and colophon are registered trademarks of Simon & Schuster, Inc.

Designed by Maria Carella

Manufactured in the United States of America

10 9 8 7 6 5 4   Pbk.

Library of Congress Cataloging-in-Publication Data

Albrecht, Karl.
  Stress and the manager.

  (A Touchstone book)
  "A Spectrum book."
  Reprint. Originally published: Englewood Cliffs,
N.J.: Prentice-Hall, © 1979.
  Includes bibliographies and index.
  1. Job stress. 2. Executives—Psychology. I. Title.
HF5548.85.A43 1986   158.7   86-12256
ISBN 0-671-62823-2 Pbk.

Foreword

Occupational stress forms a major category in the International Institute of Stress library collection of more than 120,000 publications on stress and related subjects, but very few of these references are of any direct use to the driving force in business and commerce — the executive and the manager. Indeed, these individuals have been turning to us in great numbers for courses and guidance on stress reduction, but unfortunately we can only offer our help to a limited number of them. We would exhaust our fund of adaptation energy and, of course, stress ourselves beyond the limits of *our* stress tolerance if we even attempted to reach out to all of them. It is therefore very encouraging to see that a book has now been written that has captured and synthesized the very essence of our vast store of

v

knowledge about stress. The book you are about to read has
come at a time when it is needed most.

A respectable job is no protection against the stress of life
in the business world today. Stress is with us to stay, so we have
to learn more about it; through our knowledge we can harness
its energy positively to work for us in the best possible way.
That is, we must learn to adapt ourselves to enjoy a maximum
of eustress (good stress) and a minimum of distress.

Stress is "perception." It is the demands that are imposed
upon us because there are far too many alternatives, too many
choices. Stress is caused by being conscientious and hardwork-
ing; it is "being willing to labor under the pressure of deadlines,"
it is "being strong enough to face up to resolving difficult business problems," and, naturally, it is also rampant in the maze of
complex interpersonal business relationships.

Stress plays a decisive and integral role in every business
venture and in every business negotiation. Like heredity, high-
fat diets, and lack of exercise, it can contribute to coronary
heart disease, peptic ulcers, suicide, nervous disorders, migraine
headaches, insomnia, pill popping, cocktail hangups, marital
discord, child abuse, self-abuse, lack of confidence, allergies,
strikes, picketing, and labor violence. The causes of these losses
to business and industry are not immediately evident in stock
exchanges. We only see a bearish market, a drop in the value of
the dollar, economic crises, political imbalance, or a loss of
national identity. We see a stupendous loss of vital human
resources.

Karl Albrecht's analysis of "wellness" could be a powerful
stimulus to anyone who would like to know more about a
holistic approach to health. We tend to think that this concept
would be irreconcilable with the aims and aspirations of indus-
trialization. Not so. *Stress and the Manager* recognizes full well
that the manager, the executive, and the laborer are first of all
human beings, just as susceptible to the harmful effects of distress as anybody else. That is why the idea of "human resources
development" seems to us most appealing and useful, if not

indispensable, to arriving at a state of wellness, a state that would appear out of our reach.

We must now assume our responsibilities to ourselves and to others on an equal basis, and we must share and help one another to salvage our lifestyles and enlighten ourselves to the ultimate truth — that human resources are finite and must be used prudently with minimal destruction of our environment, both internal and external. The efforts we have to put in require much discipline and belt-tightening. It is now necessary for managers to face up to their physical and mental limitations if they truly wish to enjoy their triumphs and successes. They must even learn from the harsh realities of indecision, wrong decisions, and bad policy. If they cannot appreciate the lessons afforded by this exposure, they cannot really appreciate life, that great abstraction which we scientists are trying so hard to study.

These are all the things that Karl Albrecht has succeeded in explaining in *Stress and the Manager*. His description of the stress concept is wonderfully well-presented. Simplicity and style of prose are the telling hallmarks of this volume. The end product is a well-balanced book, written with an astute understanding of the complexities of the stress mechanism and the distress factor in business today.

I would not hesitate to support this book and will give it a place of prominence among recommended reading in the library and documentation service of our International Institute of Stress, for all those concerned with management.

HANS SELYE, M.D.
International Institute of Stress
University of Montreal

Contents

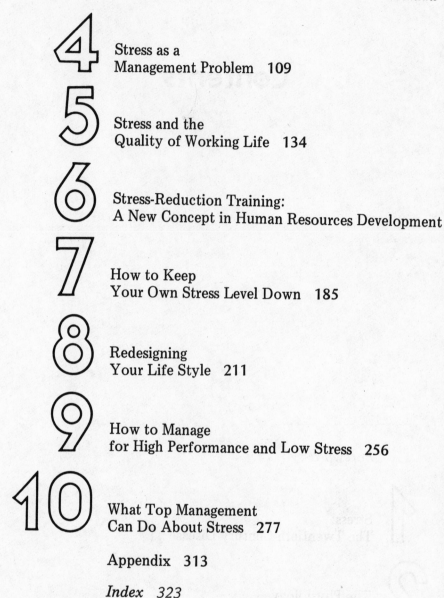

1

Stress:
The Twentieth-Century
Disease

A strange new disease has found its way into the lives of Americans and into the lives of people in other highly industrialized nations of the world. It has been steadily growing, affecting more and more people with ever more serious consequences. It is now reaching epidemic proportions, yet it is not transmitted by any known bacterium or other microorganism. The range of symptoms is so broad as to bewilder the casual observer and to send the typical physician back to the textbooks. The symptoms range from minor discomfort to death, from headache to heart attack, from indigestion to stroke, from fatigue to high blood pressure and organ failure, from dermatitis to bleeding ulcers. This disease is exacting a steadily increasing toll of human health and emotional well-being. It is not really a disease in itself but, rather, a runaway condition of a normal body physiological function, namely, *stress*. We now know that chronic stress causes diseases of various sorts, complicates others, and induces discomfort and misery in those who suffer from it.

Although stress as a chemical process within the body is a normal manifestation of the body's adaptation to the demands of its environment and can be caused by physical *stressors* such as severe injuries or bacterial invasions, most of the chronic stress experienced by twentieth-century Americans comes from anxiety. Apprehension, conflict, crowding, upheaval in personal life, rapid and unrelenting change, and the pressures of working for a living are inducing stress in people at levels that threaten their health and well-being.

In a broad sense, this book is about human *wellness* — what it is, how and why we've been steadily losing it, and how we can get it back.

THE EXPONENTIAL CENTURY

The period from 1900 until the present stands apart from every other period in human history as a time of incredible change. Mankind, at least in the so-called "developed" countries, has lost its innocence entirely. The great defining characteristics of this period — the first three-quarters of the twentieth century — have been change, impermanence, disruption, newness and obsolescence, and a sense of acceleration in almost every perceptible aspect of American society.

Philosophers, historians, scientists, and economists have given various names to this period. Management consultant Peter F. Drucker (1968) has called it the Age of Discontinuity. Economist John Kenneth Galbraith (1977) has called it the Age of Uncertainty. Media theorist Marshall MacLuhan (1964, 1968) called it the Age of the Global Village. Writer and philosopher

Alvin Toffler (1970, 1975) called it the Age of Future Shock. Virtually all thoughtful observers of America, Americans, and American society have remarked with some alarm about the accelerating pace with which our life processes and our surroundings are changing *within the span of a single generation.* And this phenomenon is spreading all over the industrialized world. I call this the Age of Anxiety.

Not only are our lives changing, but most of the variables that define the change are moving at ever-increasing speeds. We not only have change, we have *acceleration.* A large portion of the change has occurred within recent history, largely since World War II. This suggests that the next 25 years will see even greater changes if this trend continues. The quickening pace of these change variables describes what mathematicians call an exponential curve, illustrated in Exhibit 1-1. Just looking at such a curve, showing for example the number of new inventions or processes, or the number of people in the world, or the rate at which consumer products come into being and die, gives

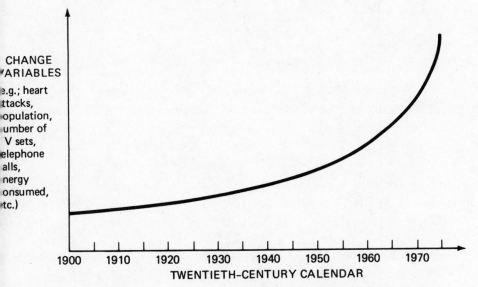

EXHIBIT 1-1. Many aspects of American life follow this exponential change curve.

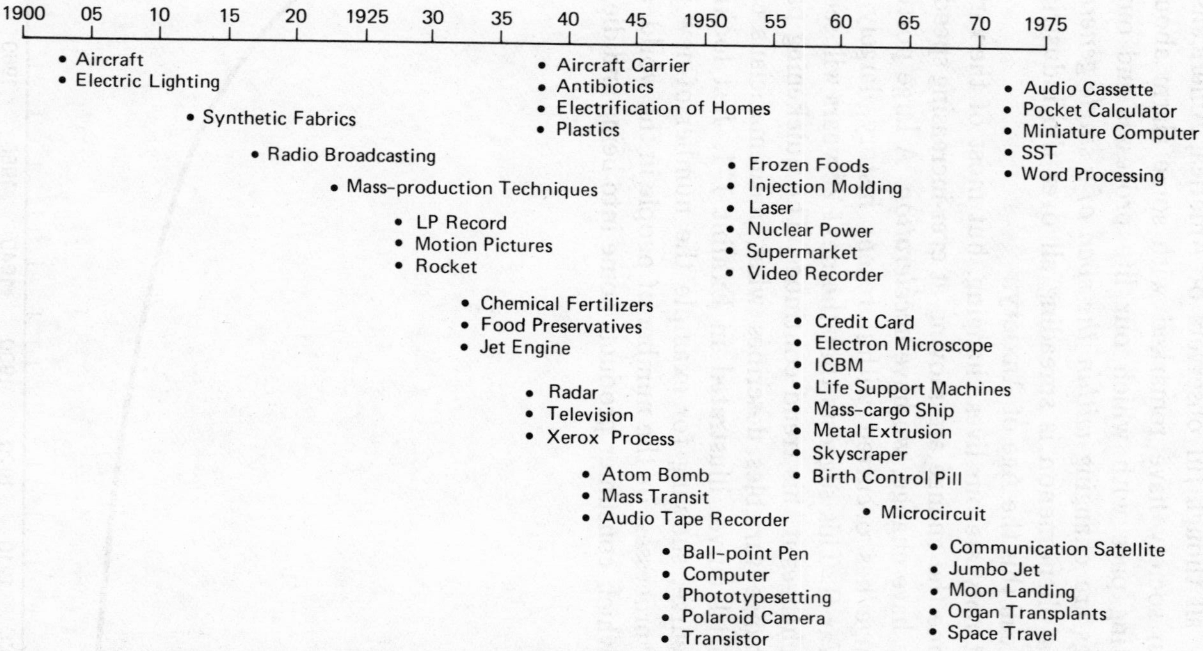

EXHIBIT 1-2. Many significant technological events have occurred within a single lifetime.

Timeline axis: 1900 05 10 15 20 25 30 35 40 45 1950 55 60 65 70 1975

- Aircraft
- Electric Lighting
- Synthetic Fabrics
- Radio Broadcasting
- Mass-production Techniques
- LP Record
- Motion Pictures
- Rocket
- Chemical Fertilizers
- Food Preservatives
- Jet Engine
- Aircraft Carrier
- Antibiotics
- Electrification of Homes
- Plastics
- Radar
- Television
- Xerox Process
- Frozen Foods
- Injection Molding
- Laser
- Nuclear Power
- Supermarket
- Video Recorder
- Atom Bomb
- Mass Transit
- Audio Tape Recorder
- Ball-point Pen
- Computer
- Phototypesetting
- Polaroid Camera
- Transistor
- Credit Card
- Electron Microscope
- ICBM
- Life Support Machines
- Mass-cargo Ship
- Metal Extrusion
- Skyscraper
- Birth Control Pill
- Microcircuit
- Communication Satellite
- Jumbo Jet
- Moon Landing
- Organ Transplants
- Space Travel
- Audio Cassette
- Pocket Calculator
- Miniature Computer
- SST
- Word Processing

one a feeling of apprehension. The intuitively felt questions are: "Can this continue indefinitely?" "Where are the limits?"

Exhibit 1-2 shows a number of selected events of the first three-quarters of the century, each of which has touched off shock waves of social, technological, and economic change throughout American society and indeed the world. With the events arrayed on a linear time scale as in Exhibit 1-2, we can grasp the awesome intensity of the change process that is underway. The more significant new arrivals include:

Aircraft
Aircraft carrier
Antibiotics
Atom bomb
Audio recording cassette
Ball-point pen
Birth control pill
Chemical fertilizers
Communication satellite
Computer
Credit card
Electric light
Electrification of all homes
Electron microscope
Electronic calculator
Food preservatives
Frozen foods
Injection molding
ICBM (Intercontinental Ballistic Missile)
Jet engine
Jumbo aircraft
Laser
Life-support medical machines
Mass-cargo ship
Mass-production techniques
Mass transit

Metal extrusion
Microelectronic circuit
Miniature computer
Moon landing
Motion pictures
Nuclear power
Organ transplants
Phonograph record
Phototypesetting
Plastics and other synthetic materials
Polaroid photography
Radar
Radio broadcasting
Rockets
Skyscrapers
Space travel
Supermarket
Supersonic transport plane
Synthetic fabrics
Audio tape recorder
Television
Transistor
Video tape recorder
Word processing machines
Xerox process

Although these changes have had far-reaching noticeable effects, it may be that some of the most important effects have so far gone undetected. For example, we know of the fantastic power of the computer and its omnipresent influence in many areas of our lives, but you may find it a challenging mental task to list as many direct influences as possible that the advent of the computer has had on your own life. You'll surely find the idea of the computer so intimately interwoven with many other aspects of society that it will be impossible to separate it out as a single distinct influence. Similarly, sociologists still argue about the influence on our society of television as a cultural communication mode. All agree that the impact has been enormous, but not all agree on the exact form of the impact.

We know that many of these change modes have served to put people into closer contact with one another by transferring information faster, with greater density, and with greater psychological impact. Rapid long-distance travel by jet aircraft has fostered a "mobicentric" society in which many people relocate about the country but stay in physical contact with families and friends. The airplane, as well as long-haul trucking and to some extent railroads, has made commerce a nationwide process. Goods manufactured in one corner of the country travel to all other areas for retail distribution. Multibillion-dollar food distributing corporations such as Safeway Stores, Incorporated move the products of American farms and factories about the entire country. A national telephone system puts Americans in electrical contact with one another across the continent, and indeed around the world, within seconds and at an amazingly low direct cost. Abundant electrical power for lighting keeps people active and busy much later at night than was the case in 1900.

The chronicle of these changes could go on and on. Suffice it to say that we are surrounded by change, we are imbedded in change, and change permeates virtually all of our lives as members of this exploding society. Truly, this has been so far the *exponential century*, and it shows no signs of stabilizing or coming to equilibrium. The disconcerting facts are that we simply do not know where we are going as a society or what will happen next. To try to predict with any confidence the developments of the last quarter of the century is a laughable exercise in fantasy which, if set down on the record, would probably prove to be ridiculously conservative when viewed from the perspective of the year 2000.

For example, take a moment to review the previous list of new events and count those that people foresaw before the beginning of the century. Only a few were even dreamed of in wildest speculation. Leonardo da Vinci and Jules Verne forecast heavier-than-air flight, but most of their contemporaries considered them hopeless visionaries. Just before Orville and Wilbur Wright demonstrated their airplane at Kitty Hawk, the U.S. Army had cut off all funds for the development, on the conviction that it was theoretically impossible.

Charles Babbage's "calculating engine," a contraption of gears and shafts, foreshadowed the digital computer, but no one predicted the development of the electronic technology that made it more than a curiosity. Nuclear power, television, electronics, radar, space flight, motion pictures, the Xerox process, the Bomb — all these revolutionizing changes burst into existence in a relative flash along the time scale of the twentieth century. The present-day profession of *technological forecasting* is more an exercise in logical possibilities, with a strong philosophical flavor, than an attempt to say what will be.

This is the nature of our world as we enter the last quarter of the twentieth century — bewildering change, ever-increasing demands on us as creatures to adapt to newness, and a growing sense of awe and apprehension about what it all means and where it all is leading us. Whether we like or not, we are all citizens of the exponential century.

THE NEW AMERICAN LIFE STYLE

Americans have become exponential creatures forced to adapt to exponential change. And, as we see later, it is taking its toll of their psychological well-being and their physical health.

One consequence of the bewildering variety of changes taking place within this exponential century has been a complete metamorphosis in the typical American life style. Most Americans living at the three-quarter mark of the twentieth century are no more like their turn-of-the-century ancestors than those ancestors were like their own ancient cave-dwelling forebears. A citizen of the 1900s suddenly transplanted into the 1970s would find himself utterly bewildered by that world. He would encounter so many things, processes, and social norms entirely beyond his imagining that he would probably remain confused and disoriented for months or even years. Similarly, a citizen of the 1970s taken back to the world of 1900 would surely find himself groping for familiar things and processes in a world that would seem incredibly primitive and decentralized.

To understand the psychological impact of the changes that have taken place within a single lifetime and to appreciate the vastly increased levels of stress that Americans now experience, we must look at the major changes in life style that have transformed 1900 man into 1970s man. Five areas of change seem to me most significant in assessing what has happened to the American creature. Although these categories may not cover all significant changes within this century, nevertheless I believe they constitute the primary reason why this period has become the age of stress.

The five significant areas of change are as follows:

1. From rural living to urban living.
2. From stationary to mobile.
3. From self-sufficient to consuming.
4. From isolated to interconnected.
5. From physically active to sedentary.

Let's look at each of these changes in turn to see what kinds of pressures and demands for adaptation they have placed on the typical American.

In 1900 most Americans lived on farms or in rural areas.

Only 40% of them lived in urban areas. However, with the rapid development of technology, transportation, and big corporations, as well as the concentration of large manufacturing operations in the cities, a steady migration brought most Americans to the cities. By 1975 almost 75% of Americans lived in urban areas. And of the remaining rural 25%, only about 4% could be classified as farmers. Many of the others made their livings by working in cities or urban areas. This has revolutionized the style of living for a large fraction of the American population, making them much less self-sufficient and much more dependent on the logistic systems that serve the cities.

The city dweller usually eats, sleeps, and lives within a few yards of other people whom he knows only casually. He is usually confined to a small plot of territory, with the necessities of life carefully condensed into living quarters and storage spaces. In some ways, the typical city apartment or condominium is reminiscent of the ancient cave. The primary difference is electricity, hot and cold water, and indoor toilet facilities. City dwellers usually spend a large fraction of their waking hours in fairly close proximity to other people, especially if they work for organizations.

A typical city worker will get up at a fixed time in the morning, drive a car to work on a crowded freeway or busy street, go into a densely populated building, ride up a crowded elevator, and work all day as a member of a social unit. He may eat lunch in a crowded restaurant and walk to and from lunch along a crowded, busy street. Living in the presence of large numbers of people induces a relatively high level of alertness in the city dweller. Everyday activities such as sprinting across the street to avoid oncoming traffic, or jamming on the brakes to avoid a scurrying pedestrian, all require the city dweller to stay alert and act quickly.

And, of course, crime and violence are frequently on the mind of the city dweller. He wonders from time to time what the chances are of being robbed, mugged, or assaulted by those who lurk insanely at the edges of the social structure, unable to meet their needs in socially acceptable ways. Larger and older cities, which some politicians like to term "our 'mature' cities," generally have fairly large slum areas, which tend to breed crime and antisocial behavior as well as continued poverty. Former Mayor Lindsay is said to have listened to astronauts Borman, Lovell, and Anders describing the moon by saying, "It's a forbidding place . . . gray and colorless . . . it shows scars of a terrific bombardment . . . certainly not a very inviting place to live or work," and to have remarked that for a chilling moment he thought they were talking about New York City.

The entire setting of the city as a sociologistic operation demands a much higher level of alertness and responsiveness than the quiet, rural setting in which challenging events come much less often and with much less severity. This combination of crowding and reactivity seems to induce a much higher nominal level of stress in the city dweller than that experienced by the rural person. We can readily understand the effects of the on-your-toes orientation in keeping a person aroused for a full working day, but the effects of crowding have not been so widely recognized.

Although people vary in their tolerance and appetite for contact with other humans, every person has a comfort level that can be exceeded. Having even one person within your "near zone" — a spatial area surrounding your body out to a radius of three to five feet — will make you somewhat more aroused than simply being alone. As a creature, you react in a very basic biological way to the presence of others in your near vicinity. Prolonged close contact, without means for retreat and relaxation, can be extremely stressful for most people.

From time to time, I have noticed in myself a "crowded" feeling when I have had to drive my car on a busy Los Angeles freeway during the rush period. Sometimes, while waiting for a traffic jam to clear on the "world's biggest parking lot," I have looked around at the surrounding sea of cars and drivers and have begun to feel a vague sensation of imprisonment. I often watch other drivers as they hunch forward, hands gripping their

steering wheels, faces fixed in expressions of intense concentration and anticipation. I watch as they "jack-rabbit" away as
soon as an opening clears. Moving along at 55 miles an hour in a
small steel and glass conveyance and seeing four others surrounding me at a distance of less than 10 feet away is for me a
somewhat stressful experience. I believe city driving induces a
low-grade level of anxiety in all drivers, although many of them
have been driving for so many years they have come to see
themselves as being perfectly calm. When tempers flare in very
heavy traffic, the stress of driving shows through dramatically.

These two key factors, *crowding* and *pace,* induce an almost unremitting arousal within the body of the typical city
dweller. This form of stress was almost completely unknown to
the rural dweller of 1900, and it is to a great extent unknown
even to today's farmer or resident of a tiny out-of-the-way
American town. Clearly, the migration from farms to cities was
a migration from tranquillity to anxiety. Although most city
dwellers seem to have learned to live in the city environment,
and even to prefer it, nevertheless it has been taking its gradual
toll of their health and well-being.

Second, Americans have become the most "mobicentric"
people on earth. The automobile and the airplane have extended the reach of virtually all people and have cut them loose
from their places of birth. Large numbers of people travel about
the country on business and on vacations. They change jobs
much more frequently than ever before. Some estimates hold
that the typical professional person changes jobs on the average
of every three to five years. Other estimates suggest that the
typical family relocates to another home on the average of
every six or seven years.

The typical pattern for 1900 was to be born in a community, to grow up there, to work there, to marry and raise a
family there, and to grow old there. The typical late-twentieth-
century style is to be born somewhere, to grow up in several
different somewheres, to be educated somewhere else, to
move from place to place as part of one's career, and to get mar-

ried and divorced and remarried. The American of the 1900s
who could afford a vacation to Europe would have had to be
quite wealthy indeed, but by the 1970s almost any typical
middle-class family could manage to fly to Europe for a week
or two.

The American love affair with the automobile led to a
1975 ratio of one registered automobile for every two people,
counting infants, children, the aged, and the insane (and
accounted for 50,000 highway deaths a year). A great portion
of the American economy revolves about the automobile.
About a million people are employed directly in the manufacture of cars, and they work for a few large companies. Several
million others manufacture the vast array of parts, components,
materials, and spare parts needed to make the cars and to keep
them operating. Hundreds of thousands of others produce and
distribute the petroleum products throughout the land that
enable a citizen to drive his car from one end of the country to
the other end without fear of running out of gas or oil.

Virtually every teenager longs for—and soon gets—his
own "wheels." This is the big growing-up event—emancipation
from the home and physical liberation through mobility. The
development of the fast-food industry, paced by enormously
profitable firms like McDonald's, has supported and capitalized
on this mobility phenomenon.

Whereas the typical citizen of 1900 worked within a 10-
to 15-mile radius of home, Americans of the fourth quarter of
the century think little of driving 30 to 50 miles to and from
work each day. And for more and more working people, travel
has become at least an occasional part of their jobs. It is difficult to find an adult American who has never taken an airplane
ride. The large megalopolis areas on the east and west coasts
have shuttle flights between their larger cities that operate many
times each business day. I can leave my office in San Diego,
take a half-hour flight to Los Angeles, and be conducting business in a client's office before the morning is half over. I can
reach San Francisco in slightly more than an hour.

The citizen of 1900 would have considered the idea of moving across the country to take a new job an upheaval of the first magnitude; the late-century citizen sees it as a logical step in a career pattern. Of course, the industrial society of 1900 had so few large organizations that such a move would not have been even appropriate.

The biological phenomenon of jet lag did not exist in 1900, even in imagination. Traveling at 600 miles an hour for five hours puts one in a different time zone, where people eat, sleep, and work on different schedules. A great deal of study has shown that jet lag is primarily a disorder caused by desynchronization of basic biological cycles within the body and that it causes physical stress as well.

The primary form of anxiety arising from the new mobicentric life style is the loss of a sense of permanence. In his book *Future Shock*, Alvin Toffler (1970) demonstrates that too high a rate of change for a person produces the physical stress reaction in his body and leads to a reduction in emotional well-being, severe degradation of physical health, and a general decline in the quality of life. Without some regions of stability in one's life, Toffler says, one loses the sense of continuity and predictability that makes life relaxing and assuring. Too much change destroys this feeling of stability and causes chronic anxiety.

Third, Americans have become *consumers*. In 1900 the majority of families grew at least some of their food, raised animals, and made many of their own necessities, but by the 1970s the usual family had become almost wholly dependent on a small number of farmers and on factories for the goods they consumed. And by the 1970s the style of consumption had become so opulent, compared to the 1900 style, as to be readily classifiable as vulgar. The enormous surge in the manufacture of consumer products of all kinds, spurred by advancing industrial technology and the mass brainwashing capability of the highly sophisticated advertising industry, has produced a generation of eager and obedient consumers.

The function of advertising has been to teach Americans in mass numbers to want, need, and buy the products of American industry. Americans buy almost any product that appears on the market provided it is well packaged and has sufficient advertising exposure — from microwave ovens to citizens' band radios to pet rocks. The proverbial visitor from Mars would surely remark about the apparent compulsion of most middle-class Americans to own *things*. Acquisition and consumption of the fruits of American industry have become ends in themselves — a form of proof and self-assurance of one's economic security and standing. The annual buying spasm every Christmas season, when Americans purchase an enormous variety of gift items, including elaborate and costly toys that their children promptly toss into the closet and forget, testifies to the fierce preoccupation with getting things.

News magazines such as *Time, Newsweek,* and *U.S. News & World Report* occasionally carry articles pointing up the economic distress of the middle-class American. There is always an interview with the Joneses, a suburban couple with two children, two dogs, two cars, and two jobs. "It's getting terrible," say the Joneses. "Our taxes are going up, our medical bills are going up, and Jane has had to go back to work just so we can make ends meet." But making ends meet for the Joneses means replacing their four-year-old car with a new one, buying a camper or other recreational vehicle, buying a continuous stream of consumer articles and gadgets, buying an extra television receiver for the children's room, and upgrading the family television set to a version with an extra large screen. Jane has to have her clothes, and John has to have his fishing equipment and golf clubs. Compared with over 80% of the world's citizens, the Joneses are wealthy beyond belief. The average farmer in India or Brazil or China or Africa could no more conceive of a style of living like theirs than he could conceive of personally flying to the moon. Yet, to the Joneses, times are tough.

It is a time when middle-class buying power has shaped virtually the entire landscape of the country. Advertisers court the discretionary income of the American family with every variety of gadget, toy, pastime, and "labor-saving" device imaginable. American industry gave the world the electric carving knife, a device so moronically simple that the user has only to hold it steady (presumably the average housewife can still do that), push the button, and let the oscillating blade do the work.

Because of the need to sustain the buying boom and to create and maintain demand for the products of American factories, a "throw-away" mentality has steadily crept into American life. In his book *Future Shock*, Alvin Toffler (1970) observes:*

Nothing could be more dramatic than the difference between the new breed of little girls who cheerfully turn in their Barbies for the new improved model and those who, like their mothers before them clutch lingeringly and lovingly to the same doll until it disintegrates from sheer age. In this difference lies the contrast between past and future, between societies based on permanence, and the new fast-forming society based on transience.

The child soon learns that Barbie dolls are by no means the only physical objects that pass into and out of her young life at a rapid clip. Diapers, bibs, paper napkins, Kleenex, towels, non-returnable soda bottles — all are used up quickly in her house and ruthlessly eliminated. Corn muffins come in baking tins that are thrown away after one use. Spinach is encased in plastic sacks that can be dropped into a pan of boiling water for heating, and then thrown away. TV dinners are cooked and often served on throw-away trays. Her home is a large processing machine through which objects flow, entering and leaving at a faster and faster rate of speed. From birth on, she is inextricably embedded in a throw-away culture [p. 53].

Toffler goes on to enumerate a variety of other throw-away

*From *Future Shock* by Alvin Toffler. Copyright © 1970 by Alvin Toffler. Reprinted by permission of Random House, Inc.

articles, each suggesting by its very existence that American life
is fundamentally a process of consumption. He especially notes
the arrival of the paper wedding gown, an artifact of an "advanced" culture that has some interesting implications.

The apparent effect of this compulsive consuming and of
the transient nature of the things acquired has been to create in
the back of the American mind a general impression that
nothing lasts — or even should last. Although the value implications of this idea lie outside the range of this discussion, nevertheless this unconscious attitude carries with it a vague feeling
of anxiety about loss of permanence. The citizen of 1900 believed in thrift, saved scraps of clothing, wood, and other useful
materials, repaired functional objects that had broken down,
and purchased only what he could not conveniently make. But
the citizen in the fourth quarter of the century throws away the
sock with a hole in it, throws away the broken tool and buys
another, throws away leftover food, puts table scraps into the
garbage disposal, and throws away the lawn chair with the
broken webbing. Toffler believes that the fourth-quarter citizen
has so little permanence left in his life, that he experiences an
unconscious anxiety about it. Perhaps this explains the enormous interest of many city dwellers in buying antiques and
"funky" articles with an air of nostalgia about them. Many
Americans pay high prices for horse collars, chipped dishes, coal
scuttles, old brass ornaments, and ancient faded photographs of
strangers, possibly trying to recapture a feeling of the stability
and realness of the past. I believe these aspects of the changing
American life style — consumerism, disposalism, and transience
— have deprived many Americans of much-needed feelings of
stability and permanence and have contributed heavily to the
rising levels of environmentally derived chronic stress they feel.

The fourth factor, *interconnectedness,* has probably done
more to change the lives, beliefs, values, aspirations, and habits
of Americans than any other. And it has probably led to a
greater share of the increasing stress load than any other factor.
Whereas the citizen of 1900 got most of his news from

local gossip channels and the town newspaper, and his main interest was what was happening in his own community, the citizen of the fourth quarter is literally deluged with information about the community, the state, the country, and the world. Most Americans experience constant information overload and don't know it. They wallow about in morbid and distressing accounts of crime, disaster, political machinations, and international tension, euphemistically called "The News." The function of the television news broadcast, and indeed of all commercial television programming, is to deliver predictable numbers of pliable viewers of the proper demographic make-up, to advertisers who pay for the opportunity to insert buying directives into the viewers' uncritical fields of attention. Semanticist Irving J. Lee (1941) has referred to this century as the Age of the Organized Lie [p. xiv].

The incredibly efficient and high-capacity media that transfer information and persuasion throughout the land have the effect of connecting every American with every other one, in some way or other. An event taking place in one part of the country can be known within minutes in all other parts of the country. Hundreds of millions of people watched a live television broadcast in 1969 as Neil Armstrong stepped out of the *Eagle* and walked on the surface of the moon. Both processes — a moon landing and world-wide television coverage of it — were utterly inconceivable to the general public of 1900.

With television, radio, nation-wide newspapers and magazines, and the extremely efficient telephone, Americans have come to conceive of themselves as interlocked with one another and interlocked with all other countries of the world. As mentioned earlier, sociologist Marshall MacLuhan (1964, 1968) has advanced the notion of the world as being a "global village," shrunk by our highly efficient communication media.

Many media experts believe the relatively recent sense of disenchantment and dissatisfaction Americans feel about their national leaders comes from simply knowing too much about them. In Lincoln's time, they reason, most citizens had only heard of "honest Abe" and had perhaps seen paintings or photographs of him. But Americans of the twentieth century had the dubious privilege of seeing Lyndon Johnson holding his dog by its ears and cheerfully showing his surgical scar for all to see. They watched the details of Richard Nixon's final agony as he was forced out of office by the Watergate affair, and they watched as congressmen debated and investigated at excruciating length on the misdeeds of the Nixon underlings involved in the episode. They watched Gerald Ford bump his head and stumble getting out of a helicopter. The high-speed visual media have had the effect of demystifying our national leaders. We see them in various stages of undress and in varying exposures of their normal humanity. It may be that Americans need to believe in their leaders as being somehow more than human, a bit unreal and mystical. Television has swept all that away and has stripped them of their charisma.

The generation that came of age at the three-quarter mark of the century was the first subculture of human beings raised and socialized primarily by the television set. Researchers calculate that, by the time the typical American child reaches the age of 18, he will have spent more hours watching and listening to the television set than in school, and far more hours than in high-quality contact with his parents.

The A. C. Nielsen Company, by whose statistics many television programs live or die, estimates that 97% of all American households have television sets (*U.S. News and World Report*, 1977, pp. 20–23). Nearly 77% of these are color sets. Almost 45% of American homes have more than one set. The company estimates that adult women, the heaviest viewers, spend over 30 hours each week in front of the TV set. Young children, ages two to 11, average over 25 hours each week. Adult men come next, with over 24 hours, and teenagers watch over 22 hours a week.

Other experts estimate the average television time as high as four to six hours a day, seven days a week. This is an enormous length of time for human beings to spend in a trance-like stupor, uncritically absorbing the values, subtle messages, and outright directives transmitted to them by production script-writers and advertising copywriters.

To grasp the significance of this mode of socialization, try a brief experiment for yourself. With a note pad beside you, watch about two or three hours of the most popular television programs during prime evening time. See how many episodes you can identify in which some particular social value is stated, implied, or suggested by the way in which the story unfolds.

For example, how many times does the hero use violence, physical force, or intimidation to achieve his ends? How many separate incidents of violence or threatened violence do you count within two to three hours? What values are implied in the typical program with respect to sex and the part it plays in human relationships? What is the function of sex in the story? What common stereotypes do you see reinforced — the passive housewife, the dumb blond, the dumb cop, the beautiful and charming career girl, the crooked politician, the masculine detective, the hip black person with lots of rhythm and the latest slang, the calm and cool doctor? How do the protagonists deal with their problems? For what do they strive?

A short session using this kind of analysis may convince you that the *primary* means by which American children learn the values they adopt is by seeing them implied and modeled on the television screen and in the movies. In a very real sense, television and motion pictures tell our children what the "facts" are. They tell children what kinds of behavior are plausible, feasible, and desirable, and what their likely consequences are.

One of the "facts" learned by American children — and their parents, too, apparently — is that the world is a dangerous place. Several studies have shown that the typical heavy television viewer believes the incidence of violent crime and robbery to be much higher than the occasional viewer does and estimates it to be much higher than it really is. Heavy viewers believe there are many more doctors, lawyers, executives, and other professionals than there actually are in the real world.

They also tend to see other people as being less trustworthy than do occasional viewers. They overestimate their chances of encountering violent crime substantially — much more than do occasional viewers.

Researchers George Gerbner and Larry Gross (1976), reporting in *Psychology Today* magazine, observed:

> . . . those of us who grew up before television tend to think of it as just another medium in a series of 20th-century mass communications systems, such as movies and radio. But television is not just another medium. If you were born before 1950, television came into your life after your formative years. Even if you are now a TV addict, it will be difficult for you to comprehend the transformations it has wrought.
>
> Television is different from all other media. From cradle to grave it penetrates nearly every home in the land. Unlike newspapers and magazines, television does not require literacy. Unlike the movies, it runs continuously, and once purchased, costs almost nothing. Unlike radio, it can show as well as tell. Unlike the theater, it does not require leaving your home. With virtually unlimited access, television both precedes literacy and, increasingly, preempts it [p. 41].

Not only does television portray highly unrealistic, stereotyped versions of life, but it frequently shocks and horrifies the viewer. A steady diet of TV violence keeps the heavy viewer in a semiagitated state of arousal, which is occasionally relieved somewhat by commercials and light comedy. Watching television news, one gets an impression of a world where violence and unrest are rampant, where everything goes wrong, and where catastrophe strikes every day. By its very nature, the news must disturb people in order to capture their attention. Radio news operates in exactly the same way. I believe the essential psychological process of newscasting is to capture the attention of the viewer with a report of something going wrong in the world, thereby arousing in him a distinct feeling of anxiety and apprehension. Then, by packaging the horror story up nicely, promising more details later, and sandwiching it between several items of national news and football scores, the newswriter says to the viewer: "There! Wasn't that terrible? But you can thank your lucky stars it wasn't you!" And the viewer can heave a little sigh, cluck his tongue, and muse about what the world is coming to. I believe this one–two punch of arousal followed by relief is the primary mode by which television news captures and influences the viewer.

In his provocative book *De-managing America*, executive Richard Cornuelle (1975) comments on the lopsided view of life in America that television and newspaper organizations gather and sell as "news." He quotes Charles Kuralt, the TV commentator who traveled all over America filming his *On the Road* features:

> To read the papers and to listen to the news, . . . one would think the country is in terrible trouble. You do not get that impression when you travel the back roads and the small towns. . . . You find people who are courteous and neighborly and who really do care about their country and wish it well. . . . You do not get the feeling of a country on the brink of revolution or torn apart by hatred — the kind of impression you might get if you only read the page-one stories [p. 28].

The effect of heavy television viewing, in my opinion, is to create in the viewer a gradually accumulating feeling of anxiety and apprehension about the world in which he lives. The omnipresent threat of nuclear war, of inflation, of racial unrest, of higher taxes, of malfeasance in political office, and of neighborhood crime all add up to make the heavy viewer a more anxious person than the person who watches television seldom or not at all.

It is my opinion that the high-speed communication media *within* which we live have the effect of overloading us with information about problems beyond our control, of alarming us with incidents far removed from our immediate experience, and of helping us to worry vaguely and without focus. This is an extremely important component of the twentieth-century stress diet experienced by the typical American.

The fifth important change factor, the shift from a physically active life style to a sedentary one, more or less sums up the other factors previously mentioned. Not many Americans work *hard* for a living any more. Some labor statisticians estimate that fully 50% of the work force now engages in "knowledge work" — the production, processing, and handling of information. The fraction of the work force engaged in heavy physical labor is steadily declining, as automation and new machinery take the place of muscle power. Instead of walking to his job and spending 12 hours a day at strenuous but healthful work, the typical American now spends about eight hours a day at sedentary work, one to two hours sitting in a car driving to and from work, and four to six hours parked in front of the television set. This repetitive daily routine has deprived Americans of the activities that oblige them to use their muscles and to stay trim and fit.

American housewives, "emancipated" by a variety of labor-saving devices, have lost the sense of working productively at keeping up a home. In 1900 a wife worked as hard as her husband did, helping with crops, raising animals, churning butter, preserving fruits and vegetables, raising children, and caring for the house. She also walked considerable distances on the farm or in the town, doing her daily chores. Now the middle-class wife — if she doesn't work at a sedentary job outside the home — merely rattles around inside the house, with the children away at the baby-sitting center euphemistically called a "school," and struggles most of the time against a gnawing feeling of boredom, lack of challenge, and meaninglessness. The most meaningful activity of the day is watching five or six soap operas on TV.

Alcoholism and the abuse of socially acceptable drugs and medications has been skyrocketing among suburban wives over the last decade. More than a few of them start the day with liquor and carry through with tranquilizers. Just as an underworked factory worker can become restless, uneasy, and anxious, so can the underworked and underchallenged housewife. It is ironic but true that lack of work is just as stressful as overwork. Add to this the frequent messages the housewife gets from television, magazines, and books telling her that today's woman is a feminist. She should make a career for herself, get an education and a good job, and join the world of the free-spirited women who have been given so much attention by the media. Having been raised and fully socialized with the belief that the only fulfilling life for her is marriage and a family, she now feels swindled, defensive, unsure of herself, and angry. A great deal of the stress she experiences arises from her adjustment difficulties.

The American child has also become a sedentary creature. More and more children are overweight, inactive, and physically weak. In the early 1960s, President Kennedy's Council on Physical Fitness detected a dramatic downtrend in the fitness levels of American children. Although many programs have attempted to reverse this trend, the child of the fourth quarter of the century is still considerably less physically able and less fit than his counterpart of 1900.

Apparently, the hypnotic effect of staring at the television set makes this form of activity addictive for most children. Those who spend the daylight hours after school watching television simply lose the opportunity and the incentive to engage in normal, child-type play activities. We have raised a generation of children who are almost as sedentary and out of condition as their parents. It is very likely that a sedentary child will carry this habit pattern into his adult years, living in a style that promotes poor health, low vitality, overweight, and susceptibility to major diseases such as heart attack, stroke, and other degenerative disorders.

A direct consequence of this shift from active living to sedentary living is that many Americans have become fat. Over-

weight is a primary preoccupation of many people in this country, but few of them are willing to change their life styles and
habit patterns in order to get into good condition and lose
weight. So they buy diet books and weight-loss pills and answer
mail order advertisements for the latest magic way to lose
weight "without exercise and without feeling hungry." They go
on crash diets until they have punished themselves enough and
dissipated their guilt feelings, and then they revert to their overeating habits, which they had merely set aside for a few weeks
or months.

Unfortunately, the sedentary person, especially after the
age of 40, lives at great risk of health breakdown because his
body cannot maintain itself at a high level of efficiency and
biological performance. The sedentary person is more susceptible to colds, flu, minor disorders, and digestive upsets and is
much more strongly predisposed to the killer diseases of heart
attack, high blood pressure, stroke, and related disorders. And,
even worse, it seems that the sedentary person handles stress
much less effectively than the active, physically fit person does.
Whether this reflects a difference in psychological make-up, in
overall living patterns, or in body physiology is not yet clear,
but the facts show that the sedentary person succumbs sooner
and more severely to major stress diseases than does the
healthy, fit person.

All these factors taken together portray a new American
life style — one of affluence, material comfort, and security but
also one of rapid and unsettling change coupled with a steadily
growing feeling of gnawing uncertainty. Americans are the most
comfortable and yet the most uneasy people in the world. The
effects of crowding, of frequent major changes in their life situations, of constant acquisition and disposal of physical articles,
of moving at an ever-increasing pace, and of experiencing more
frequent and intense episodes of pressure and conflict in their
jobs are steadily adding up on most Americans. These effects,
added to the steadily declining level of physical conditioning
and health habits, make Americans subject to stress-derived

disorders more than ever before. We are in the middle of a national epidemic of stress disease, and the statistics of death and health breakdown show it clearly.

Apparently, the new American life style is not the final answer. We must find a reasonable modification of that life style that gives us back our physical health and our emotional well-being.

FUTURE SHOCK

Writer and sociologist Alvin Toffler (1970) coined the term *future shock* to describe the *feeling* of vague, continuous anxiety that arises in people who are subjected to a rapid pace of change. Americans in particular, who live in an environment of social, technological, and logistic acceleration, feel the psychological effects of impermanence. It is, says Toffler, as if we feel the future rushing upon us, and there is nothing we can do to stop it or even slow it down. The present gets replaced by the unfamiliar future at such a rapid rate that we are forced into a state of *continuous adaptation*. And this adaptation, Toffler believes, produces an underlying feeling — largely unconscious — of apprehension and longing for stability. In his research of the future shock phenomenon, Toffler visited many organizations, interviewed many people, and examined a great deal of research results dealing with expected futures and with human adaptation to change. He concludes:* ". . . future shock is no longer a distantly potential danger, but a real sickness from which increasingly large numbers already suffer. This psychobiological condition can be described in medical and psychiatric terms. It is the disease of change [p. 2]."

*From *Future Shock* by Alvin Toffler. Copyright © 1970 by Alvin Toffler. Reprinted by permission of Random House, Inc.

In describing the potential of humans for adapting to rapid change, Toffler further observes:

> . . . I gradually came to be appalled by how little is actually known about adaptivity, either by those who call for and create vast changes in our society, or by those who supposedly prepare us to cope with those changes. Earnest intellectuals talk bravely about "educating for change" or "preparing people for the future." But we know virtually nothing about how to do it. In the most rapidly changing environment to which man has ever been exposed, we remain pitifully ignorant of how the human animal copes [p. 2].

Toffler offers a dramatic perspective on the rate of change that American society has experienced, with his concept of the "eight-hundredth lifetime." Dividing the past 50,000 years of human history into lifetimes of about 62 years gives us about 800 human lifetimes to use as a kind of historical time line. The first 650 of these lifetimes, Toffler observes, were spent living in caves. Writing has been available only for the past 70 lifetimes, making it possible to preserve information precisely from one lifetime to the next. The wide-scale use of print has happened only within the last six lifetimes. We have been able to measure time accurately for only the last four. The electric motor is a phenomenon of the last two lifetimes.

Toffler observes that the overwhelming majority of the material goods we use and the technological processes that shape our lives so powerfully have emerged within the short period of the last lifetime. The pace of change has been quickening for the last 150 lifetimes, and we are now seeing the sharp rise of the exponential curve caused by the mutually compounding effects of technological changes and "advancements." Because one invention or technological process tends to beget or enable many others, change is a self-reinforcing and self-accelerating process.

Toffler believes that the effect of this accelerating change is to force upon virtually all people who experience it an inescapable level of *physiological stress* — a form of tangible biological arousal that makes them more vulnerable to other pressures and events in their lives. Future shock can itself make people physically sick, and it predisposes them to becoming sick as a general matter.

If we are to deal effectively with future shock, says Toffler, we must find ways as individuals to adapt psychically to an increasing rate of change and to engineer our lives to create our own islands of stability and sanity to which we can occasionally retreat in order to find feelings of security and to reduce anxiety.

Toffler's book may well turn out to be not only one of the most prophetic but also one of the most famous and unsettling books of our time. For me, simply rereading it and paging through some of the key portions is an unsettling experience. The word pictures Toffler uses to describe the headlong rush of the future into our present-day lives engender in me a feeling of anxiety, apprehension, and a desire to retreat. Simply reading *Future Shock* is a stressful experience. And more than once, in writing the manuscript for this book, I have found myself beset with anxious feelings and sensing the need to put it aside for a time. It seems that even thinking about stress for any length of time can be stressful.

Although not all forms of stress arise from the future shock phenomenon, it is important to understand that future shock causes in most people an underlying "bias level" of anxiety and stress, which predisposes them to loss of emotional well-being and health breakdown when combined with the other stress loads caused by everyday living and working.

THE DECLINE IN AMERICAN WELLNESS

Over the first three-quarters of this century Americans have enjoyed a dramatic increase in health and a dramatic decline in wellness. I offer this paradoxical-sounding statement to draw a sharp distinction between the medical view of "health" and the broader, holistic view of the well-being of the total person.

Although medical research and the competent treatment of patients by physicians has virtually eliminated most infectious diseases, there has been a simultaneous increase in a number of other diseases, known broadly as degenerative diseases. Diseases such as tuberculosis, diphtheria, pneumonia, and various other general infections have virtually disappeared from the charts as the most prominent killing diseases, but others such as heart attack, hardening of the arteries, stroke, cancer, kidney failure, and cirrhosis of the liver have increased dramatically. This second category of diseases, now known to be stress-related, has become the new health menace of the twentieth century. Exhibit 1-3 compares these disease categories for the two benchmark years of 1900 and 1970. Notice especially the dramatic increase in heart diseases.

The commonly accepted definition of "health" among American physicians is *the absence of any substantial symptoms which would suggest an underlying disease process.* This means that you can have frequent severe headaches, chronic indigestion, diarrhea, constipation, intestinal cramping, sleeplessness, and frequent feelings of fatigue, and so long as you don't have all of them at the same time, your doctor will probably pronounce you healthy.

And he is right from the medical point of view. But from a broader point of view — your own — you are not well. You would like to feel better, but to the physician your subjective comfort is not really a goal of the medical treatment. The goal is to locate and eliminate any concrete disorder. If you complain enough, the physician will probably prescribe some medication that will eliminate the symptoms and mask the underlying source of your unwellness — the stress process within your body. Nutritionist Carlton Fredericks comments acidly, "The typical doctor's definition of good health is the ability to remain upright in a strong wind."

I advance this point of view, not to demean the medical

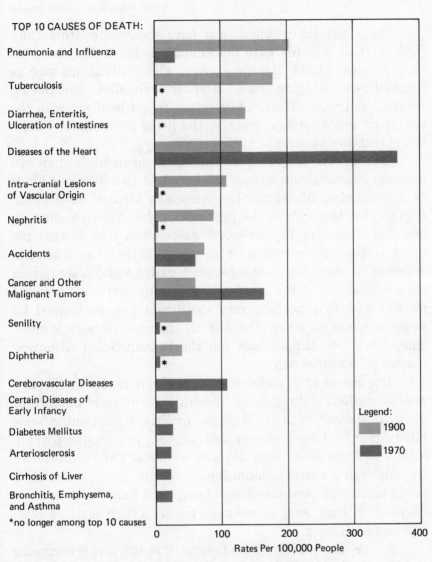

TOP 10 CAUSES OF DEATH:

Pneumonia and Influenza

Tuberculosis

Diarrhea, Enteritis,
Ulceration of Intestines

Diseases of the Heart

Intra-cranial Lesions
of Vascular Origin

Nephritis

Accidents

Cancer and Other
Malignant Tumors

Senility

Diphtheria

Cerebrovascular Diseases

Certain Diseases of
Early Infancy

Diabetes Mellitus

Arteriosclerosis

Cirrhosis of Liver

Bronchitis, Emphysema,
and Asthma

*no longer among top 10 causes

Legend:
1900
1970

Rates Per 100,000 People

EXHIBIT 1-3. Stress-related diseases have emerged as primary causes of death in the late twentieth century. Adapted from "The Ills of Man" by John H. Dingle, *Scientific American,* September 1973. Reprinted with permission.

profession, but to assert as emphatically as possible that so far most physicians have almost entirely overlooked the primary basis of most twentieth-century disease — namely, the emotions and health behaviors of the patient himself.

Many practicing physicians have commented that fully 80% of their patients have emotionally induced disorders, yet they go right ahead "treating" them with medications such as tranquilizers, sleeping pills, stomach remedies, muscle relaxants, and pain killers. They refuse to get involved with the *causes* of the disorders, namely, the living processes and emotional reaction patterns of their patients.

One of the tragedies of American medicine is that two separate organizations educate and control two different kinds of practitioners of health. The American Medical Association tells us that the body is the province of the physician–chemist, and the American Psychological Association tells us that the mind is the sole province of the psychiatrist. This historical semantic blunder leads most people — patients and practitioners alike — to act as if the mind and the body were two separate entities and that nothing very significant can be learned by studying them together. The original theorists of holistic medicine, the Greek Hippocrates and the Roman Galen, disproved this many centuries ago.

The broad term *wellness* is increasingly replacing the outmoded medical definition of "health" as the mere absence of physical disease entities. Wellness implies a continuum scale rather than a binary sick-or-well choice. It includes psychological wellness along with physical wellness. The World Health Organization's current definition of health reads, "Health is physical, psychic and social well-being, not only freedom from disease." A high level of wellness means a high level of total human functioning.

In the last quarter of the twentieth century, it is becoming embarrassingly obvious to most scientists — but not especially to physicians and psychiatrists — that *all disease has both psychic and physiologic components.* But subdividing professional practitioners along the arbitrary lines of "mind" and "body" makes it virtually impossible for them to develop an integrated methodology for treating the entire person. In this respect, American medicine may be at least 50 years behind such countries as Japan, where physicians treat the patient, not the disease.

Organizations such as the Association for Holistic Health have been promoting an integrated view of human well-being, and a slowly growing number of doctors has been beginning to learn and practice this approach to treating their patients. More physicians are beginning to understand the enormous health benefits of exercise and to promote stress reduction techniques. These doctors seem to take a strong interest in their own health and to practice the living techniques they preach.

However, while more and more doctors are moving toward a holistic, person-centered, total-systems approach to wellness, the vast majority of them still treat symptoms and dispense medication, with little appreciation of the personality patterns of the patients or of his style of living. Psychiatrists are probably more adaptable in dealing directly with stress as an emotionally based disorder, but it is not yet clear how the small number of such professionals can effectively help the huge numbers of Americans whose health is in danger from stress overloading.

The key principle underlying the entire holistic health concept is *responsibility.* This is the notion that one's health is almost entirely a function of what one does with one's body and one's thoughts. Poor health behaviors lead to poor health. Immature thinking and reacting lead to negative emotions and unnecessary stress. Overeating, oversmoking, overuse of tobacco, abuse of recreational drugs or patent medicines, and sedentary living are *choices* that one can make or unmake. By taking complete responsibility for your health, you become obligated to yourself to act and live in ways that will guarantee your own total wellness.

I believe that the total wellness concept will emerge as one of the most significant advances of our age and that many people will eventually adopt it as a guiding principle for living in the exponential century. Until that happens, however, we will continue to be plagued as a society by stress-influenced disorders and by a low level of vitality and general wellness, although we will have what the physician considers acceptable health.

STRESS IS KILLING PEOPLE

Most medical researchers now believe that the chemical stress reaction within the human body is a causative factor in most contemporary health breakdowns and that it is at least linked to many other disorders. This theory makes sense from the physiological point of view because we know, for example, that bacterial invasions or physical injuries actually trigger the stress syndrome. And over the past 10 to 15 years it has become starkly clear that emotional reactions not only trigger the body's stress response, but they prolong it for as long as they themselves last. Hormone flows within the body are a direct physical consequence of emotional arousal, anxiety, and worry. Chapter 2 offers a more thorough description of the physiology of stress.

The list of diseases that medical researchers now recognize as being caused by stress or aggravated by stress reads like "Who's Who in American Disease." The ulcer has long enjoyed a dubious reputation as a mark of high-pressure living. The overstressed business executive who developed an ulcer formerly saw it as a status symbol. Now, perhaps, many ulcerated business people see their trademark as a sobering symptom of a style of living and feeling that is taking them down the road toward a much more serious health breakdown.

Authoritative research has now linked the heart attack firmly with stress. Other factors such as heredity, diet, overweight, and smoking play a part. Nevertheless, many researchers consider chronic, unrelieved stress to be the primary factor in heart attack and other major cardiovascular disease.

Over 1,000,000 Americans each year have heart attacks. About half of them die immediately, or within a few hours.

This works out to about one heart attack somewhere in America every 32 seconds. Of those who survive, half will probably die of a second heart attack within two or three years. One out of three heart attack victims is younger than 65.

For most people, the period of convalescence following the heart attack changes them into permanent patients. Most victims live in more or less continual fear of the next one. They slow down their living processes, they tend to engage in fewer activities, they often become less assertive and less enthusiastic, and they often lose much of their commitment to achievement. And their colleagues often inadvertently reinforce the image of a permanent cripple by treating them cautiously, kindly, and with great concern for not arousing them. For many patients, the period of years following the attack becomes a time of psychological capitulation and even of waiting for death as an inevitable event.

Men in the United States have heart attacks at three times the rate of women. Heart attacks in men 35 and 40 years old are not highly unusual. Some statisticians estimate that the average "healthy" male has one chance in five of having a heart attack before he reaches age 65.

Strokes and similar cardiovascular accidents compete with cancer for the Number Two position as the most frequent cause of death among adult Americans. The same stress factors that give rise to heart attack also give rise to strokes, embolisms, and related circulatory diseases. Over 300,000 people die every year from strokes, and the number seems to be climbing.

Cancer, in fact, may have a stress-derived component. Some researchers claim to have identified a "cancer personality" — a pattern of attitudes and behavior that correlates more highly than any other with the incidence of cancer. Over 300,000 people die each year from cancer, and the disease is diagnosed in over 650,000 new patients a year. The United States has one of the highest rates of cancer incidence in the world, and virtually all the so-called "developed" nations experience much higher rates of cancer than do the underdeveloped or "developing" nations.

Another disease clearly linked to stress is *hypertension,* or high blood pressure. In most cases, this particular disease has no direct organic basis — it simply sets in. Most cases of hypertension are what physicians call "essential hypertension," which means that they don't arise from any medically correctible malfunction. Although other factors such as overweight, diet, and smoking surely play a part, many researchers now believe that stress is the primary cause of hypertension. This disorder kills over 60,000 people a year, most of whom would not have to die if they received early medical treatment. Hypertension also leads fairly directly to other kinds of degenerative diseases, such as kidney failure and malfunction of other organs. It is also often found in precardiac patients and those who experience strokes.

Hypertension is not evenly distributed across the population. More city dwellers seem to have it than rural people. Men suffer from it more than women. And inner-city blacks seem to have the highest incidence. Elevated blood pressure seems to be connected with elevated levels of anger, frustration, and other emotions that the individual feels incapable of expressing or actualizing. Some estimates place the incidence of high blood pressure among ghetto black people as high as 30%. Medical authorities generally agree that, in the overall population, about 20% to 25% of adults have dangerously high blood pressure.

Some medical researchers believe that sudden, acute stress can actually kill a person whose health has been weakened either by prolonged stress itself or by degenerative factors such as age or circulatory disease. George Engel (1977), professor of psychiatry at the University of Rochester, studied 275 case histories of sudden death, as well as many historical accounts of deaths of famous personalities. He identified four main categories of sudden stress:

1. A traumatic disruption of a relationship with a loved one or the anniversary of such a happening.
2. A situation of physical danger, struggle, or attack.

3. Extreme sense of failure, defeat, disappointment, humiliation, and loss of self-esteem.
4. A sudden moment of triumph, public recognition, or reunion with loved ones [p. 114].

In these cases, Engel believes, the people involved expired as a result of a sudden stress overload that their bodies could not handle. Heart attacks, strokes, blood clots and embolisms, and various indistinct physical effects precipitated their deaths.

Many other forms of physical disorder constitute the catalog of human discomfort. Many malfunctions that physicians classify as vague symptoms of "nothing in particular" can degrade the quality of life for people, and in many cases these symptoms can disable them. To the doctor, a headache is simply something the patient reports and must learn to live with. To the patient, a headache is a problem, a disorder in itself. It may not be interesting to the doctor, but it is extremely interesting to anyone who wants to build and maintain a high level of total wellness. Digestive upsets, muscle aches, chronic fatigue, and a lump-in-the-throat feeling can all originate in extraordinary levels of stress within the body that are sustained for too long.

Although one must probably tolerate a certain amount of minor stress discomfort, it is clear that chronic stress, prolonged beyond reasonable bounds, not only creates intolerable levels of discomfort, but it can steadily degrade one's health to the danger point. Once the health level has reached the danger point, continued chronic stress can precipitate a major health breakdown. It is indeed a fact of life for twentieth-century Americans that *stress can kill.*

HOW STRESS AFFECTS BEHAVIOR

Although stress as a physical and chemical process within the body is entirely normal to our functioning as living creatures, the individual experiences tangible discomfort when the stress reaction remains "turned on" at high levels for long periods. This discomfort is a whole-body sensation, because the flow of stress hormones affects every cell within the body. Given occasional periods of escape from the troubling situations that induce the stress, such a person will usually live fairly effectively and be comparatively healthy. However, if the person has no escape routes, if the situation is a long-term, unresolvable dilemma, if the pressure load continues without letup for a long period, then he will automatically seek whatever forms of stress relief are available.

The chronically stressed person will behave in ways calculated to escape from or overcome this uncomfortable whole-body feeling. Much of our stress-avoidance behavior is unconscious, but it nevertheless serves the same useful purpose. Unfortunately, however, many of our available avenues for stress avoidance have undesirable side effects. The most popular forms of escape from stress are:

1. Drinking liquor.
2. Frequent or heavy eating, especially sweet foods.
3. Smoking.
4. Drinking coffee, colas, or other high-caffeine drinks.
5. Using marijuana, heavy drugs, or mind-altering pills.
6. Using prescription drugs such as tranquilizers and pain pills.
7. Using patent medicines to suppress specific symptoms.
8. Using sleeping pills.
9. Withdrawing psychologically; robotizing one's behavior; self-destructive behaviors.
10. Lashing out at others, displacing anxiety and anger onto other people.

In virtually every case of stress-reactive behavior, the individual unconsciously substitutes a known pleasant feeling for the unpleasant stress feeling. The person who eats many sweets, for example, focuses on the good taste and the voluptuous sensation of eating as a form of anesthesia for the stress feelings. The drinker anesthetizes his central nervous system with the chemical depressant effects of alcohol. The person who takes tranquilizers does exactly the same thing.

Those who use tobacco, caffeine, and other stimulants unconsciously hope to elevate themselves out of the discomfort. This tactic seldom works, because the chemicals they choose have the effect of further aggravating the stress reaction. An oversupply of caffeine, for example, stimulates further the already overstimulated adrenal glands, producing subjective feelings of further arousal. The person who uses sleeping pills, tranquilizers, or psychological withdrawal patterns is simply trying to escape from awareness of anything, let alone of the stress feeling. Worshipers of TV often escape into a passive world of synthetic experience. Attendance at movies usually increases significantly during economic downturns.

For those who are decidedly lacking in maturity and social adjustment, chronic stress can lead them into antisocial behavior or even violent crime. Crime rates frequently rise somewhat during times of economic turbulence. The number of people who cannot carry out the social struggle for achievement and material security probably becomes larger in times of extreme social stress. More of them slip into the desperate category. Most hard-core criminals show the effects of very poor social adjustment, and they experience the mind-breaking stress of alienation and loss of self-worth.

Still other people who have been stressed far beyond their limits choose insanity as a means of escape. They go crazy in order to drop out of the terrifying, unrewarding, hateful, stressful microworld in which they have been living. There is a certain peace in insanity.

At the extremes of maladjustment and misery, suicide provides the ultimate means of stress reduction. Suicide rates often go up in times of economic crisis or extreme social turmoil. Men kill themselves at about 2½ times the rate at which women do, although the rate for women has been steadily rising. Suicides are often teenagers, students, people in financial crisis, or those whose lives have fallen into a shambles. The 25,000 people a year who commit suicide elect to blast out their brains rather than learning new ways of dealing with their world.

The drawback to all these behaviors lies in their side effects. Alcohol dulls the senses, creates dependence, and eventually damages the drinker's health. Tranquilizers rapidly create dependency and interfere with the normal high-level mental functions the person needs to live a challenging and rewarding life. Withdrawal creates a sense of detachment and unreality, and it tends to isolate the individual from high-quality human contact.

Only a few consciously selected forms of stress avoidance have the potential for constructively reducing stress. One is to learn to relax one's body physically, thereby de-escalating the stress response to manageable levels. Another is re-engineering the pressure situation or simply departing physically from it for long enough periods to relax, unwind, and achieve a peaceful frame of mind. No chemical escape route has been shown to be truly effective in reducing the stress response itself, and none is without significant undesirable side effects. As we see in Chapter 8, creative low-stress living requires a conscious approach to arranging one's activities and experiences to produce an acceptable balance between the stresses of living and the rewards of living.

THE "RESPECTABLE" AMERICAN DRUG CULTURE

Far and away the most popular form of stress escape for Americans and increasingly for citizens of other "developed" countries is the use of anesthesia — chemical agents that suppress the stress signals being transmitted by the body. Middle-class American parents frequently express shock, disbelief, and flat disapproval of the extent to which their teenage children use drugs for teenage purposes. Yet, the stunning irony of the situation is that the parents of drug-using children have usually modeled for them the very kinds of drug-using behavior the parents so piously condemn. We have in the United States a middle-class drug culture whose proportions and effects on people stagger the imagination. The only difference between the adult drug scene and the teenage drug scene, besides the sheer difference in magnitude, is that adult drugs are socially acceptable. They have the establishment stamp of approval, and they form an integral part of daily living for a large number of Americans.

Jimmy and Jane find it hard to understand what's wrong with their use of "reds" and "goof-balls," when dad comes home every day with liquor on his breath and has a few beers after dinner in front of the TV set, when mom is so hooked on her Valium she can't remember whether she's coming or going, when mom and dad both smoke heavily and get nervous and irritable when they run out of "cancer sticks." The kids can't understand why mom and dad go out to parties and come home drunk, yet disapprove of a little "harmless" teenage recreation like "popping uppers." The children see the family medicine chest stocked with the fruits of the pharmaceutical industry, such as aspirin and more powerful pain pills, antacids, laxatives, sleeping pills, cold medicines, and various prescription drugs.

The message the children get is that we have a pill for just about everything. All you have to do when life gets a little rough is to reach for the right bottle, pop a pill, and everything will soon be all right. A generation of overstressed escapists has raised another generation of overstressed escapists. A popular teenage expression of the late 1970s is, "Oh, wow! I just can't handle that right now." More and more teenagers and young adults are turning to the drug route as a way out of a confusing, threatening, unrewarding world they don't understand and don't know how to change.

The typical 14-year-old boy or girl knows exactly how and where to get almost any form of drug. Those who choose not to indulge, sometimes against enormous peer pressure, still know what it's all about and how to get it if they want it. The typical junior high school in the United States is a veritable supermarket of drugs, and the product line ranges all the way from cough syrup to "pep" pills to cocaine and heroin. School administrators and parents prefer to deny the existence of, and refuse to deal directly with, a situation schoolchildren accept as a "normal" part of their everyday lives.

The single best-selling prescription drug in America is Valium. Close behind it are Darvon and Librium. These tranquilizers, classed pharmaceutically as central nervous system depressants, operate on the body by chemically interfering with the normal function of nerve pathways, including those of the brain, in such a way as to deaden the stress response. Pharmaceutical manufacturers admit they do not know precisely how drugs such as Valium work, but they market them enthusiastically to doctors who prescribe them for patients suffering from anxiety and a host of other stress-derived disorders.

Americans spend well over $3 billion a year for packaged nonprescription drugs, with almost $1 billion of it going for analgesics such as aspirin and for cough and cold "remedies" (*Scientific American*, 1977, p. 121). They spend well over $4 billion a year for prescription drugs. Drug firms invest at least one-fourth of that revenue — $1 billion — in marketing and promotion targeted almost exclusively at doctors. This amounts to about $4,000 per physician per year.

However, alcohol still holds a solid lead in sales and consumption as the Number One form of stress escape. Americans spent nearly $11 billion in 1975 for retail purchases of liquor and probably that much again as consumers in drinking establishments. Liquor is one of the few products that sells predictably well no matter what happens to the economy. In fact, alcohol consumption usually rises during hard times. Per-capita consumption of hard liquor rose almost 20% between 1960 and 1975, and per-capita consumption of beer rose by over 25%. Certainly not all liquor consumption should be considered to be an escape from stress, but in fact a great deal of it is. And a steady increase in drinking suggests a clear trend of increasing stress.

The American Hospital Association places the level of bona fide alcoholism in the United States at about 10 million people, or nearly 5% of the entire population. This means that almost one adult in every 10 is hooked on alcohol, according to the medical definition of addiction, except that nearly one million of the alcoholics are teenagers. Fully half the alcoholics in the United States are women. This is one case in which the stress of living shows up in female behavior just as strongly as in male behavior.

Cigarette smoking, another socially acceptable drug habit, has increased dramatically over the years. Although production of tobacco products that are not inhaled, such as snuff and cigars, increased modestly or not at all from 1900 to 1975, production of cigarettes increased by an incredible 14,000%! This works out to the consumption of nearly 10 cigarettes a day—half a pack—for every human being in America, including infants, the aged, and the insane. When the U.S. Surgeon General declared cigarettes a health hazard and succeeded in having cigarette advertising excluded from television, tobacco consumption declined slightly and then continued its steady climb. It seems virtually impossible to frighten the heavy smoker out of his suicidal habit. As a form of self-stimulation that helps to anesthetize stress feelings, inhaling nicotine is one of the most popular pastimes in the United States.

Americans also have a national addiction to cola drinks, attributed to largely by enormous advertising campaigns by manufacturers such as Coca-Cola, Pepsi Cola, and Doctor Pepper. Coca-Cola has been one of the most profitable businesses in the world, with a product that has been steadily displacing coffee and milk consumption. The combination of caffeine and sugar in cola drinks is recognized by researchers and physicians as being habit forming by means of the "lift" it imparts to the nervous system. The lift is followed by a mild sense of depression, which creates a desire for another lift. Per-capita consumption of cola drinks *tripled* between 1960 and 1975, reaching a level equivalent to 1½ eight-ounce cans every day for every single man, woman, and child in the United States (*Today's Living*, 1976, p. 16).

These statistics make it obvious that the use of mood-altering chemicals in America, and to some extent in other developed countries, has completely run wild. Cultures we are pleased to label "primitive" all without exception reserve the use of tobacco, drugs, and intoxicants for special occasions such as celebrations and rituals. Only in the so-called advanced cultures do we use these chemically induced altered states of awareness as routine means for escaping reality. This social process gives grim testimony to the accumulating effects of chronic stress in the bodies, minds, and souls of our people. The exponential century is exacting its price.

THE PRICE BUSINESS PAYS FOR STRESS

Executives and managers in all kinds of organizations are becoming increasingly concerned about the human costs of doing business. Most managers understand and accept the fact that human resources constitute the most costly form of capital for any organization, but they are now beginning to see rising costs from human breakdown. When absenteeism increases, when turnover increases, when more and more employees begin to have health problems that affect their job performance, when alcohol and drug abuse creep into the organizational setting, and when anger and frustration begin to play a heavy role in labor–management relationships, executives begin to worry about the underlying pressures that may be causing all this.

It is now clear that many of the employee problems that cost money and performance as well as employee health and well-being originate in physiological stress. Stress directly and indirectly adds to the cost of doing business, and it detracts from the quality of working life for a very large number of American workers.

Dr. Michael Smith (1977), Chief of Motivation and Stress Research for the National Institute for Occupational Safety and Health (NIOSH) in Cincinnati, believes that most organizations are paying higher prices than their top managers realize for occupational stress. He cites machine-paced workers in particular, such as postal employees who operate keyboard letter-sorting machines, as having very high incidences of health breakdown, emotional disorders, and missed-time incidents. Other stress-producing occupations, says Smith, include those that require dealing with distressed clients (such as is the case in health services and welfare work), and those jobs in which the employee feels a high level of obligation but lacks the sense of having the control necessary to meet expectations (such as is the case with a psychotherapist or air traffic controller) [p. 34]. Says Smith:

> Stress affects all workers to some extent and some more than others. In addition to the stresses the individual experiences in his or her private life, the job itself can induce certain "set-up" stress levels, which bring the worker close to the danger point. Then, all it takes is some precipitating event or problem, and the person gets pushed beyond the limits of adaptation, and he or she simply breaks down.

A preliminary NIOSH study of 130 job classifications identified 40 of them as being high-stress jobs. A review of health clinic data among a variety of organizations in Tennessee identified 10 jobs as involving the highest incidences of reported stress disorders. This does not mean that these are necessarily the highest stress jobs, but it does indicate a strong connection between the job and stress. These jobs were:

Health technicians.
Waitresses.
Practical nurses.
Assembly line inspectors.
Musicians.
Public relations officials.
Clinical laboratory technicians.
Dishwashers.

Warehousemen.

Nurses' aides.

It is, of course, impossible to separate out the effects of individual life styles and pressures outside the job situation. However, Smith (1977) notes, four of the 10 occupations on the list are in the health professions. In addition, a large number of the jobs are female-dominated occupations. These studies found that females reported a vastly higher percentage of stress disorders than males did.

Other studies seem to suggest that shift workers have a greater incidence of minor health problems, lost time from work, and less satisfaction with the quality of their overall lives. Dr. Donald Tasto, of the Stanford Research Institute in Palo Alto, California, reports greater incidence of ulcers, digestive upsets, eating problems, and disruption of sleeping patterns, especially among workers who rotate through various shift-work schedules. Tasto believes shift-work stress diseases will increase as energy-intensive manufacturing companies move into night shift operations to take advantage of cheaper, off-hour electricity rates.

In addition to job-induced stress, American workers also experience higher levels of stress due to events in their private lives and due to increasing difficulties in personal adjustment within the changing fabric of their society. Business organizations are having to deal with alcoholism and drug abuse much more than ever before. The problem is becoming increasingly severe and costly.

Dr. James W. Schreier (*Behavioral Sciences Newsletter*, 1977), assistant professor of management at Marquette University, surveyed the problem of chemical dependency among workers in 89 companies in the Midwest, comparing results in 1977 with results in 1971. He concluded that the problem has worsened, despite counteractive programs in the organizations. He estimates that alcoholism alone costs American society about $15 billion a year — $10 billion for lost work time, $2 billion in health and welfare costs, and $3 billion in property damage, medical expenses, workmens' compensation, and insurance. He believes that the abuse of various other drugs costs an additional $15 billion, making a total societal cost of $30 billion for the effects of chemical dependency.

We have probably detected only the tip of the iceberg in terms of the consequences of stress for human health and for organizational effectiveness. We still have to add in the effects of executive health breakdown, which can be much more costly on a person-for-person basis and which is often much more severe for the individual, than in the case of line-worker health problems. When the executive "crashes," he usually does it dramatically and often irreversibly.

We now know without doubt that business organizations of all kinds pay an enormous price for human stress, and the price is increasing. We also know that the people who experience the stress are paying an enormous personal cost in their physical health and emotional well-being. It is time to swing our organizational problem-solving resources around to this emerging problem and to make the changes necessary to bring this twentieth-century disease under control.

REFERENCES

"The Corporate Problem That Didn't Go Away." *Behavioral Sciences Newsletter* (Special Report). Glen Rock, N.J.: Behavioral Sciences Newsletter, 1977.

Colligan, M. J., M. J. Smith and J. J. Hurrell. "Occupational Incidence of Mental Health Disorders." *Journal of Human Stress*, September 1977.

Cornuelle, Richard. *De-Managing America: The Final Revolution.* New York: Random House, 1975.

Drucker, Peter F. *The Age of Discontinuity.* New York: Harper & Row, 1968.

Engel, George. "Emotional Stress and Sudden Death." *Psychology Today*, November 1977.

Galbraith, John Kenneth. *The Age of Uncertainty*. Boston: Houghton Mifflin, 1977.

Gerbner, George and Larry Gross. "The Scary World of TV's Heavy Viewer." *Psychology Today*, April 1976.

Lee, Irving J. *Language Habits in Human Affairs*. New York: Harper & Row, 1941.

MacLuhan, Marshall. *Understanding Media: The Extensions of Man*. New York: McGraw-Hill, 1964.

MacLuhan, Marshall, and Quentin Fiore. *War and Peace in the Global Village*. New York: Bantam, 1968.

"Life and Death and Medicine." *Scientific American*. San Francisco: W. H. Freeman & Company, 1973.

"Beware of Soft Drinks!" *Today's Living*, October 1976.

Toffler, Alvin. *Future Shock*. New York: Random House, 1970.

Toffler, Alvin. *The Eco-Spasm Report*. New York: Bantam, 1975.

"TV's New Pitch." *U.S. News & World Report*, September 12, 1977.

2
The Physiology of Stress

THE DIFFERENCE BETWEEN PRESSURE AND STRESS

In our discussion, we must draw a very important distinction between the terms *pressure* and *stress*. Throughout this book, the term *pressure* refers to those features of a situation that may be problematic for the individual and that amount to demands for adaptation of some kind. *Stress*, on the other hand, refers to a specific set of biochemical conditions within the person's body — conditions that reflect the body's attempt to make the adjustment. In short, pressure is in the situation; stress is in the person.

One thing we know for sure is that different people can react differently to the same pressure situation. For example, one person might find an invitation to give a short talk before a large audience to be a challenging and enjoyable experience. Another might be virtually paralyzed by fear and apprehension as the time draws near to stand up and speak. Conversely, the first person might become upset and distraught in an emergency in which someone requires first aid treatment, whereas the second might operate calmly and efficiently.

Neither of these people, in either of the hypothetical situations, would be so placid and unaroused that his body would exhibit the peaceful physiology of sleep or daydreaming. Each would be aroused to some some particular extent, with the stress response underway to some level of intensity, but the effect on the person's performance in the situation would be characteristic of that person as an individual. Because of one's personal history of experience and learned reactions, he will "convert" pressure into stress in his own distinctive way.

Given this distinction between pressure and stress, we can analyze situations and responses somewhat more carefully. We will no longer say, "I'm under a lot of stress lately," but rather, "I'm under a lot of pressure lately." When we say, "I'm experiencing a great deal of stress," we will be talking about our physiological reactions and feelings, rather than about the situation we're trying to cope with.

This distinction also opens up some significant avenues for stress reduction. For example, you can choose to remove yourself from a pressure situation in which you've been developing an unacceptable level of stress. You can also act in such a way as to re-engineer the situation, if possible, to eliminate or reduce the level of pressure. And you can teach yourself to react less intensely to many situations, thereby limiting the level of stress you feel. All three of these strategies are effective and useful and receive further treatment in following chapters.

The notion of an individual's converting pressure into stress points up sharply that the ability to handle pressure varies widely among people, and it is very much a learned skill. Some people seem to become disabled by even small upheavals in their lives and routines. Others seem to thrive on pressure, complexity, ambiguity, and challenge. This characteristic pattern of response to pressure — sometimes referred to as *reactivity* — usually correlates fairly well with the individual's general level of personal adjustment, maturity, and problem-solving skills.

Highly reactive people seem to meet even the most minor disturbances as if they were crises. They often react just as strongly to minor frustrations as they do to fairly major provocations. Those who have learned less reactive patterns of dealing with challenging situations seem to reserve the panic mode for situations of true crisis proportions. They can usually adjust the level of intensity of their reactions to the relative gravity of the situation. This strategic form of reactivity is an important skill for personal stress management, and one can consciously learn it. Chapter 6 describes in some depth stress reduction training and the associated skills.

Equally important, we need not consider either pressure or stress to be intrinsically bad or undesirable. Stress is a natural part of human functioning, and pressure is a normal aspect of human interaction. As Exhibit 2-1 shows, a person functions

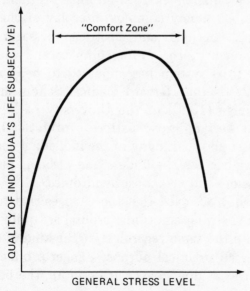

EXHIBIT 2-1. Quality of life is highest at moderate levels of stress.

best at moderate levels of stress. We must learn to tell the difference between a reasonable level of stress and too much stress, between a reasonable amount of pressure and too much pressure. A zero-stress condition is impossible. A no-pressure situation is impractical and unworkable in human endeavors. We must search for acceptable levels of pressure and stress that contribute to our performance and achievement and do not threaten our well-being.

THE PHYSIOLOGICAL STRESS REACTION

When we speak of the stress reaction, we are speaking of a definite, clear-cut, and well-defined electrochemical response pattern within the human body. A fairly thorough description of the stress reaction will help us to understand the profound effects of stress on human functioning and to gain a great deal of respect for the body's adaptive mechanisms.

Scientists since the turn of the century have studied in great detail the human body's internal "terrain," trying to understand the extremely complex interplay of chemical secretions, physical functions, and electrical messages. The more they have studied it, the more complex and incredible the design of the total system has appeared to be. Dr. Walter B. Cannon (1932) of the Harvard Medical School and more recently Hans Selye (1956) of the University of Montreal have suggested that certain gross patterns form the basis of the body's responses and that many of the individual changes physiologists observe can best be understood as being parts of these coordinated whole-body response syndromes.

Selye (1956) observed that the changes that take place in the body during strong emotional arousal are quite "standard," that is, they are the same regardless of the kind of emotion experienced. For all practical purposes, anger produces the same chemical changes as does fear. Furthermore, the body exhibits these same change processes in response to extreme pain, injury, disease, and even hunger. Selye identified the pattern he called the condition of "just being sick." He noted a great deal of similarity in the appearance of sick people, independent of their particular disorders. He considered this similarity to be a basic underlying pattern — the body's characteristic response to all forms of disease.

Cannon (1932) had earlier theorized that any challenging condition, such as hunger, extremes of heat and cold, noise, pain, loss of blood, or emotional arousal, caused the body to mobilize its electrochemical systems and to adopt a "war footing." He referred to this arousal condition as the *fight-or-flight* syndrome. It was, Cannon observed, as if the body had prepared itself quickly, efficiently, and comprehensively for physical battle or for energetic flight to escape the problem situation.

Later Hans Selye (1936)* elaborated these concepts within his theory of hormone chemistry and coined the term *stress response.* Selye showed that the stress syndrome is fundamental to virtually all higher forms of animals, and he developed a comprehensive theory of the body's adaptive processes, based on a three-stage general adaptation syndrome. He was the first theorist to clarify the primary glandular secretions and interactions making up the stress response and to identify the key organs and hormones involved in the response.

Both Cannon and Selye agreed, and other researchers have confirmed, that the human body possesses a life-saving reaction pattern — the stress response — which comes into play in a variety of pressure situations. What follows is a layman's description of this stress response or the fight-or-flight syndrome.

Picture yourself in some kind of intense pressure situation. Imagine, for instance, that you are about to deliver an address to an audience of about 1,000 people in a large auditorium. They are members of a professional society, and you have been invited to present some new and important informa-

---

*This was the first publication of the stress concept.

tion to them. Or perhaps you're about to give a briefing to the board of directors of your company, or you're about to testify in court concerning a complex legal matter in which you have been involved. Use your memory of similar situations to picture — *and feel* — what's happening in your body.

While you're waiting to go up to the platform to deliver your address, the master of ceremonies is introducing you. You suddenly realize, with full impact, that he's talking about *you* and that within less than one minute you'll be the object of the attention and scrutiny of over 1,000 people. Your attention span narrows down to the speaker's voice, the first few words of your opening remarks, and — most of all — an intense preoccupation with performing well and making a good impression.

Your field of vision narrows to take in only the path between yourself and the lectern. If you take a few seconds to "read" your body, you'll probably find that your heart is racing at something like 100 beats or more a minute, compared to a normal 60 to 70. You may notice that your hands have grown cold and clammy, that your underarms are beginning to perspire, and that your breathing is deeper but somewhat constricted. Your palms may sweat, or they may remain cold and dry. Your hands will probably tremble somewhat as you assemble your papers to begin. Unless you're an accomplished speaker, your face has probably taken on a serious, concentrated expression, with a smile or a laugh just about the farthest possibility at this instant. Your body has probably taken on a kind of readiness posture, with all major skeletal muscles somewhat tense. You are probably beginning to move your center of gravity forward, transferring your weight onto the balls of your feet and preparing to rise to a standing position. All your attention is concentrated on what you are about to do. This is your normal, whole-body fight-or-flight stress reaction. In this particular instance, you want the flight option. The primitive part of your mind wants to absent itself from the situation; this is its naive, unvarnished strategy for ridding itself of this challenge to its well-being.

If we could examine the microscopic processes going on inside your body, we would find an amazing assortment of happenings. By a process scientists still do not fully understand, your thought processes—your mostly unverbalized statements to yourself about what you fear may happen—trigger a chain of events within the structure of your *central nervous system.*

Your *sympathetic nervous system,* which is one of the two main branches of the autonomic nervous system, comes fully into play and activates a virtual chemical orchestra of hormone secretions. The small portion of your brain called the *hypothalmus* triggers the *pituitary gland,* which is located nearby at the base of your brain. The pituitary gland releases its characteristic hormone, ACTH (adrenocorticotropic hormone) into the bloodstream. When the ACTH reaches your *adrenal glands,* located just above your kidneys, it sets off a characteristic reaction in them. The adrenals intensify their output of *adrenalin* into your bloodstream, along with a family of related hormones called *corticoids.* It is this family of hormones, but particularly adrenalin, that brings your body up to a highly aroused state. Because the bloodstream is the common communication and transport system for the entire body, these stress chemicals soon reach every cell in your body. And they make the journey to the farthest point in less than eight seconds. Simultaneously, commands traveling throughout your nerve pathways alert your heart, lungs, and muscles for increased action. Exhibit 2-2 illustrates the physiology of the stress reaction.

The activation of your sympathetic nervous system produces some very useful effects. It is as if some ingenious designer had optimized you as a creature for fight or flight. Your muscles become more richly supplied with blood, as the tiny blood vessels constrict and raise your blood pressure, meanwhile diverting blood away from your extremities. This is why your fingers and toes become cold, and this is the working principle of the popular but slightly misnamed "mood ring" that was briefly popular. The liquid crystal substance inside the ring changes color dramatically as your skin temperature changes.

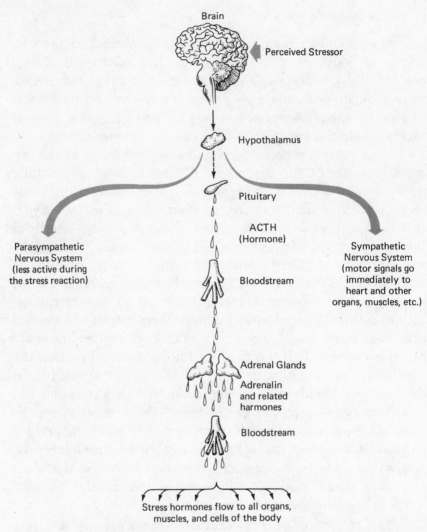

Brain

Perceived Stressor

Hypothalamus

Pituitary

ACTH
(Hormone)

Parasympathetic
Nervous System
(less active during
the stress reaction)

Bloodstream

Sympathetic
Nervous System
(motor signals go
immediately to
heart and other
organs, muscles, etc.)

Adrenal Glands

Adrenalin
and related
harmones

Bloodstream

Stress hormones flow to all organs,
muscles, and cells of the body

EXHIBIT 2-2. The stress response mobilizes the entire body for "fight-or-flight."

Your muscle tone quickly increases, making muscular action more immediate and more efficient. Your liver immediately begins working to convert its stored *glycogen* into *glucose*, which your brain and muscles need in greater supply. Your breathing becomes more rapid and intense, increasing the amount of oxygen in the blood so your muscles and your brain can burn the glucose efficiently. Your heart pumps more rapidly and intensively, sending an abundant supply of blood to those portions of your body that need it. The distribution of the blood throughout your body is radically changed, according to a suddenly revised system of priorities. The plentiful supply of blood your stomach and intestines enjoyed, especially if this is an after-dinner speech, is quickly reduced in favor of higher priority needs (one reason why your digestion suffers when you experience intense or prolonged stress).

Blood rushes to your head, and your brain's electrical activity intensifies as it optimizes its processes for conscious control of your body's actions. A great deal of your brain's attention is given over to the preparation for violent physical action, which may be one reason why you can't think very effectively on abstract levels during a panic state.

Other interesting changes take place in your body when it adopts this "war footing." Your hearing becomes more acute. The pupils of your eyes dilate, making your vision more sensitive. You can easily appreciate the survival value of these various changes. Indeed, even the concentration of a certain clotting agent in your bloodstream increases! Many other second-order changes have been discovered or postulated, all of which seem to be closely connected with the stress syndrome.

Changes in electrical resistivity of the skin, for example, give a fairly reliable indication of stress. A drop in the skin's surface temperature, especially at the extremities, is also a fairly reliable clue. The polygraph, or so-called "lie detector," relies on changes in skin resistivity, blood pressure, and breathing to give clues to the subject's emotional response to the questions of the interviewer.

Clearly, the *stress reaction is a coordinated chemical mobilization of the entire human body to meet the requirements of life-and-death struggle or of rapid escape from the situation.* The intensity of the stress reaction depends on the brain's perception of the severity of the situation.

Of course, the modern businessman or industrial worker as a social creature has a third possibility, namely, to stay within a stressful situation, neither fighting nor fleeing. For example, in a heated business conference involving conflict or hard feelings, the protagonists often continue to deal with one another in self-controlled ways, overcoming their more primitive tendencies to fight or flee.

Other human examples of a situation in which one can neither fight nor flee, Hans Selye observes, include being imprisoned—especially in solitary confinement—or being otherwise physically restrained from freedom of action. These situations induce stress, but they permit no effective avenues for resolving it.

The response syndrome is a completely normal process within the body. Selye (1956) described it as the *alarm reaction*, and he considered it the first stage of a three-stage process that takes place if the human being continues to experience the problematic situation or stimulus (i.e., the *stressor*) for an extended period of time. In the example given, you may feel that your body is overreacting, that your emotional response is more intense than called for. You probably wish you could have just a little kick of adrenalin to help you stay on your toes and to do a good job. Instead, you find yourself helpless to control your body's activation level, a miserable feeling that we all experience in certain situations at certain times.

Of course, if you have delivered the same talk dozens of times to similar groups and if you are confident of getting a warm and positive reaction from the audience, your reaction will probably not be nearly so intense as it was during your first experience. The primitive, nonrational side of you recognizes the situation and can accommodate it more easily.

From the purely utilitarian point of view, we could say that although our bodies are mobilized for fight or flight in these pressure situations, we generally choose to do neither because of our adherence to cultural norms of social behavior. If your boss or one of your colleagues chooses to berate you in front of others, your authentic, natural, creature impulse will probably be to want to physically attack him. However, your social conditioning tells you this impulse is not appropriate to the situation, so you may decide to keep still or at most to trade verbal messages in a lively exchange. Ironically, your body knows nothing of your rational decision-making process. It merely takes the trigger signal from the brain and sets off the standard chain of automatic chemical events called the stress response. Indeed, you may find yourself trying to suppress the physical evidence of your anger and hostility by remaining immobile, clenching your teeth, controlling the expression on your face, and modulating your voice carefully. The great physiological dilemma of stress is that *we so often mobilize our bodies involuntarily for fight or flight and that we so seldom carry through the process in physical terms.* This amounts to "stewing in our own juices," a process which, if long continued, can have very serious consequences for health and well-being.

Once the reason for the arousal has disappeared, or once you have re-evaluated the probable outcome of the situation and revised your estimate of the relative threat to your well-being, the stress reaction begins to subside. After you have finished giving your presentation and you realize the audience has reacted well, and — above all — that the ordeal for you is finished, a different set of chemical events occurs. Your body continues to metabolize the stress chemicals, and the *parasympathetic branch* of your nervous system becomes activated as the sympathetic branch becomes less active. The parasympathetic system has the effect of demobilizing the body (i.e., of restoring its inner workings to the original low-arousal state). The various features of the arousal process begin to reverse themselves. Breathing becomes slower and more shallow, the heart rate gradually diminishes, blood pressure drops, the blood gets redistributed, and a host of other variables begin to return to their previous baseline levels and even briefly below baseline. This *parasympathetic rebound* enables your body to repair the effects of its previous excitement.

The sympathetic and parasympathetic branches of your nervous system thus operate in a seesaw fashion, first escalating

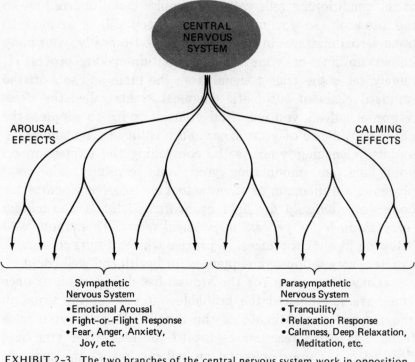

CENTRAL
NERVOUS
SYSTEM

AROUSAL
EFFECTS

CALMING
EFFECTS

Sympathetic
Nervous System
• Emotional Arousal
• Fight-or-Flight Response
• Fear, Anger, Anxiety,
   Joy, etc.

Parasympathetic
Nervous System
• Tranquility
• Relaxation Response
• Calmness, Deep Relaxation,
   Meditation, etc.

EXHIBIT 2-3. The two branches of the central nervous system work in opposition, alternately raising and lowering the body's excitation level.

and then de-escalating your body as the situation demands. Exhibit 2-3 illustrates this complementary relationship between the two divisions of your autonomic nervous system.

From the neurological standpoint, the nervous, chronically tense, overreactive person has lost the ability to mobilize his parasympathetic nervous system fully. Having spent so much time in the anxious state, his body has more or less "forgotten" how to recover and relax. Relearning this parasympathetic response — a neurological skill — is the basis of deep relaxation training, as described in Chapter 7.

Actually, the stress response is not an on–off phenomenon but, rather, a continuing process that varies in its level of intensity. While you are asleep or very calm and relaxed — daydreaming, for example — your internal *activation level* will be at a minimum. If someone walks into the room and engages you in conversation, the activation level will intensify somewhat. Your body will activate itself sufficiently to deal with the changed situation. If you decide to get up from your chair and move about, your body will meet this further increase in your involvement with your surroundings by intensifying its stress response a little more. If you were to read your body signals at this point, you would discover an increased heart rate, slightly stronger breathing, greater concentration, and perhaps a slight drop in skin temperature. The stress response is a finely tuned process, keyed closely to the level of the demand being made on your body.

To carry this observation process further, let's consider your body's response to a strong physical demand. Suppose you decide to devote your lunch break today to a jogging session. You change into your jogging suit, go out to your favorite nearby jogging area, and begin to "pick 'em up and lay 'em down." Within a few seconds after you break into a jog, your internal activation level will begin to increase. Your heart will beat faster, your breathing will intensify, your blood pressure will increase somewhat. *Even exercise produces the same activation of your sympathetic nervous system as was produced by the fear situation described earlier.* This coordinated chemical mobilization process is a standard reaction pattern which your body needs to meet the normal demands made upon it.

Indeed, Selye (1956) refers to it as a *stereotyped response.* Selye's working definition of stress is *the nonspecific response of the body to any demand made upon it.* By "nonspecific" he means that the response pattern is independent of the actual stressor. Although each stressor, such as heat, cold, bacteria, physical injury, or an externally perceived threat, produces its own specific changes in the body, they all produce additional nonspecific effects. The sum total of these nonspecific effects — that is, effects common to all stressors — is what Selye labeled stress. Selye's great contribution to human physiology was the concept of stress as a nonspecific, stereotyped bodily syndrome. In Selye's words (1974):

> From the point of view of its stress-producing or stressor activity, it is immaterial whether the agent or situation we face is pleasant or unpleasant; . . . It is difficult to see how such essentially different things as cold, heat, drugs, hormones, sorrow, and joy could provoke an identical biochemical reaction in the body. Nevertheless, this is the case [p. 16].

We can add a variety of other examples to the stressors Selye mentions. Bacteria, for example, elicit the stress reaction in your body when they make you ill. Intense noise does the same thing. So does a physical injury, such as a sprain, a bruise, or a burn. These produce what is termed *somatic* stress (i.e., stress induced by direct trauma to the body rather than stress triggered by an internal emotional reaction). Yet somatically induced stress and psychologically induced stress are biologically identical.

Another way to look at the stress reaction is to consider the body as a self-regulating system that brings various chemical processes into play to oppose any changes in its internal equilibrium. Cannon (1932) applied the term *homeostasis* (coined by 18th-century physician Claude Bernard) to this powerful self-regulating capability. Cannon contended that it was the basis of all disease reactions. Selye (1956) showed that the stress response is indeed the basic mechanism of homeostasis.

THE STRESS OF LIFE

In his writings, Hans Selye has often emphasized that stress is a normal part of the body's functioning and that it is a consequence of the business of living. Although too much stress can be dangerous to health and well-being, he says, this does not mean that we should — or even can — strive to eliminate stress altogether. Even happiness and joy cause stress, and very few of us would want to live a life without them. In his recent book, *Stress Without Distress*, Selye (1974) contends, "Stress is the spice of life [p. 83]." Complete freedom from stress, he observes, comes only in death. Selye has founded the International Institute of Stress in Montreal, an organization intended to advance our understanding of stress phenomena and provide for the exchange of new information.*

Selye (1974, 1978) uses the two separate terms *eustress* and *distress* to distinguish between positive and negative life consequences of stress for the individual, even though chemically the two forms of stress are exactly the same. Eustress, he says, is the stress of achievement, triumph, and exhilaration. All of us to some extent, and some of us to a great extent, welcome certain stressful experiences and situations because of the positive feelings we get from them. The accompanying eustress is a natural part of effectively meeting challenges such as those in a managerial job or in any other professional job. Eustress is the stress of winning.

Conversely, stress becomes distress when for any reason we begin to sense a loss of our feelings of security and adequacy (Selye, 1978). Helplessness, desperation, and disappointment turn stress into distress. Distress is the stress of losing. Exhibit 2-4 illustrates the relationship between pleasant experiences and eustress, as well as between unpleasant experiences and distress.

Our purpose in learning to deal more effectively with stress is not to avoid the challenges and triumphs of life but to capitalize on them. We also want to reduce, as far as possible, the unpleasant distress that can sometimes result from difficult situations and from ineffective strategies of living and striving.

*The address of this organization is: International Institute of Stress, University of Montreal, 2900 Boulevard Edouard-Montpetit, Montreal, Quebec, Canada H3C 3J7. Telephone: (514)343-6379.

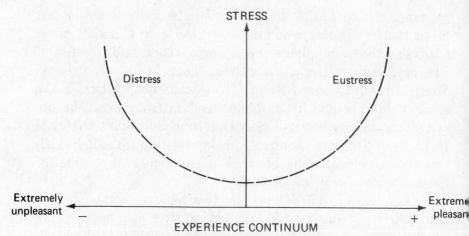

EXHIBIT 2-4. Stress is a natural consequence of both pleasant and unpleasant experiences. Based on material in Levi, L., *Stress: Sources, Management, and Prevention,* New York: Liveright Publishing Corporation, 1967. Reprinted with permission.

Obviously, we need to focus attention in this book on concepts and techniques for reducing distress, but we must always keep in the back of our minds the fact that eustress is fundamental to creative and effective living. Hereafter, references to chronic high levels of stress may be taken to mean that the individual is experiencing distress, not eustress. This is somewhat like our habit of referring to someone as "running a temperature," when what we really mean is a temperature high enough to cause concern.

As Exhibit 2-5 shows, each person experiences at any one moment a certain set of stressors, both physical and psychological, and each person also has a certain momentary level of reactivity. This reactivity level, which may have been influenced by recent stress experiences, determines how the individual will respond to the momentary level of challenge. By following the person's experiences and stress reactions over a certain length of time — say, a few weeks or months — we can estimate roughly the total stress score he has built up.

The internal stress meter will have a high score if the stress experiences have been frequent and intense and if the person has had few opportunities for physical relaxation and prolonged escape from pressure. The score will be low if the stress input has been low and if the amount of relaxation and readjustment has been ample.

As twentieth-century people, we must find individual workable answers for ourselves to the question: "How much stress is enough?" This translates into a variety of related questions, such as "What kind of life do I want to live?" and "How can I learn to deal with my life's challenges in such a way as to minimize stress while still deriving fulfillment from living?" Insofar as work life in the business organization contributes to life's challenges and life's stresses, the purpose of this book is to extend these questions to deal with new possibilities for management practice.

We must now ask, for example, "What kind of total organizational environment should we create, so that twentieth-century people can gain their livelihoods (and thereby contribute

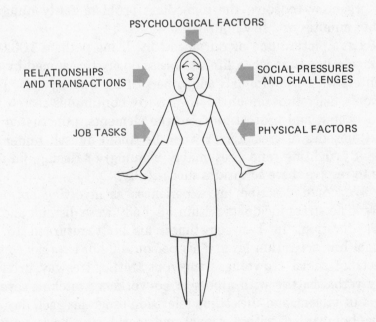

EXHIBIT 2-5. Each individual experiences a total stress level due to all environmental demands.

to the survival of their organizations) while experiencing levels of stress that are reasonable for them and gaining personal fulfillment in doing so?"

Twenty-five years ago, that question would have seemed absurdly philosophical, idealistic, and even fatuous. Now, as we enter the last quarter of the twentieth century, it is much more plausible and compelling.

EPISODIC STRESS VERSUS CHRONIC STRESS

The great enemy of human health is not the occasional crisis, or dangerous situation, or emotional upheaval. It is the prolonged, unrelieved state of worry, anxiety, and arousal that many people experience and cannot escape. The stress reaction in the body operates to mobilize its functions for *short-term crisis situations*. Generally, the fight-or-flight process enables the organism to solve the immediate problem fairly quickly, within minutes or a few hours at most.

Let's picture one of our ancestors, living perhaps 100,000 years ago in a time when life was occasionally threatened by encounters with wild animals and others of his own species. This person's daily life amounted to a fairly continuous search for food, water, and protection from the elements, punctuated by short episodes of great terror when he found himself under attack. By fighting (and presumably winning) or fleeing, he was able to resolve these situations successfully.

We could describe his experiences as involving *episodic stress*. The stress incidents within his body were distinct and of short duration. In between times, his body returned to its normal low activation level. This person did not experience the effects of social crowding, dangerous traffic, freeway driving, daily verbal battles with a boss or co-workers, watching several hours of violent and unsettling television programs each day, or being bombarded with national and world-wide news reports designed to make him anxious and uneasy about his world.

Through the process of evolution from this condition, our twentieth-century bodies have become optimized for dealing with episodic stress very effectively.

However, we no longer have such a simple life situation, in which we can expect a relatively low-stimulus pattern of experience, punctuated with occasional demands for fight or flight. We have today all the twentieth-century "extras" described in the preceding paragraph — and many more. Many people in the United States experience continuous, unrelieved, high stress levels for a large portion of their waking day. In medical terms, this means *chronic stress* — continuous, low-grade arousal without substantial relief. Medical researcher Kenneth Pelletier, who has studied health effects of stress, believes that our bodies can handle episodic stress quite well, having spent many centuries of evolutionary "learning" and adaptation. However, says Pelletier (1977), *"chronic stress leads to serious health breakdown* [p. 35]."

These facts make a strong case for an individual to learn to monitor his internal arousal level and to find ways to relieve the stress frequently and completely allowing the body to carry out its chemical repair work. This principle of stress management forms the basis for organized programs of environmental engineering within business organizations, as well as for training programs for individuals in personal stress reduction.

HOW STRESS ATTACKS YOUR BODY

As we've noted, chronic, unrelieved stress presents the most significant problem for human health. Throughout the remainder of this book, we deal with this form of stress from the point of view that we need not try to escape from stress altogether. We must simply find ways to balance the episodic stress we experience with substantial periods of recuperation and repair, in order to protect our health and well-being.

It's important to understand something of the physical

deterioration process that occurs within the body under prolonged stress. To get a brief picture of this process, let's review
some of the key findings from Hans Selye's (1936) early experiments with laboratory animals.

In his early experiments with hormone chemistry, Selye
(1936) was trying to isolate the effects of individual hormones
in their purest form on laboratory rats. He believed that if he
could find out precisely how each individual chemical affected
the rat's body, he could isolate various body processes for detailed study. He injected various prepared extracts from endo-
crine glands into a number of test rats. After some period of
exposure to the chemical, the rat was sacrificed, and Selye performed a detailed autopsy. His experiments produced a very
confusing result. Despite the many different kinds of hormones
or even other chemicals he used, he found an identical form of
internal damage in every one of the rats' bodies. Extensive
attempts at purifying the injected chemicals had no effect. The
result was always the same.

Selye found three rather dramatic effects within the body
of each test rat. First, he found an extreme enlargment of the
rat's adrenal glands. They were greatly swollen from over-
activity, and the adrenal *cortex*, or covering, was considerably
thicker than in a normal rat. Second, he found a substantial
shrinkage of the rat's *thymus* gland and atrophy of the associated *lymph nodes*. Third, ironically, he found that the rat had
developed ulcers in its stomach and intestines. This stereotyped
damage syndrome occurred so reliably in the test rats that Selye
began to wonder about the whole basis of his approach to hormone chemistry. He became quite discouraged for a time,
almost abandoning this line of research. Then, in one of those
historic flashes of scientific insight, Selye seized on the possibility that he had been observing, not the effects of any one
particular hormone (because the results were identical), but the
consequences of the rat's homeostatic *response to the dose
itself.* Selye theorized that the injection of any substance into
the rat constituted a massive challenge to the chemical equi-

librium of its body and that if the process were continued over a substantial time, the stress response itself would do the damage, not the injected chemical. Selye was saying, in effect, that any *stressor*—presumably anything that challenged the rat's chemical equilibrium—might produce the same stereotyped damage syndrome.

He tested this hypothesis by presenting his test rats with nonchemical stressors. He immobilized a group of rats by clamping them securely to a level surface, so they could not move their paws, heads, or even their tails. This turned out to be an extremely stressful experience for rats (and probably humans, too). After a test period, Selye sacrificed this group of rats, conducted autopsies, and found exactly the same three damage mechanisms. From this and a number of confirming experiments with other stressors, Selye reached an historic conclusion. He postulated the stress response as the body's *nonspecific reaction to demands made on its internal equilibrium.* He referred to the three effects as the stress–damage "triad" resulting from prolonged exposure to the stressor.

Selye (1936) postulated a time-extended, three-stage process of stress damage he called the *general adaptation syndrome.* The three stages were:

1. The *alarm reaction*, which we have described in detail.
2. The *resistance* stage.
3. The *exhaustion* stage.

The alarm reaction, Selye said, was the initial mobilization stage of the overall process by which the body meets the challenge posed by the stressor. After some time, such as the initial period of sickness caused by infection, the alarm reaction subsides, and the stage of resistance ensues. During this stage, the body's resistance capability actually increases, and the battle for survival is on.

However, if the body does not win the battle (e.g., if the person cannot escape from a terrifying situation or cannot defeat the life-threatening enemy, or if the body's chemical processes cannot overcome the injury or infection), then the resistance level progressively weakens and the stage of exhaustion sets in. In this stage, says Selye, the body has simply run out of adaptive energy, and the organism dies.

In one case, we can say that a person was killed by the bacteria or virus or injury that the body could not overcome. But in the case of emotionally induced stress that was intense and prolonged, we can say that the person was *killed by stress itself.* His body ran out of adaptive energy and died because it didn't "know" that its reaction was inappropriate and too intensive.

Selye published his findings in medical literature (1936), as well as in a landmark book titled *The Stress of Life* (1956), triggering a world-wide medical interest in stress phenomena and causing many isolated research findings to fall into place. Many medical experts consider the idea of the stress response to be one of the most significant organizing concepts in scientific history. It has enabled researchers to integrate many of their findings and to direct much of their work within an organized framework.

For example, a long-standing medical curiosity fell into place when it was considered within the context of the stress syndrome. Physicians who had treated people for extremely severe burns had occasionally noted the development of stomach ulcers in these patients. Selye's theory (1936) would explain these as the consequence of the stress response of the body to the damage it had sustained. The physiological connection between stomach ulcers and job pressures became obvious. Thereafter, the whole emotional basis for stress and health breakdown immediately came under scrutiny.

Medical researchers have found the same triad of organ degeneration in human beings that Selye found in test rats. Enlarged adrenal glands reveal the same oversecretion of adrenalin. Ulcerated stomachs and intestines show the same effects of overstimulation and chemical irritation. Shrunken thymus glands and lymph nodes show essentially the same degeneration in man as in rats. Researchers are only beginning to understand the immense significance of this process in human health. The thymus, for example, operates as part of the body's immunity system, helping to mobilize an extremely complex array of chemical countermeasures to deal with bacteria of many kinds. This finding clarifies the factual basis of the old folk wisdom that one is more prone to get sick if he is fatigued or distraught. Many of the complex and subtle chemical changes that take place in the overstressed body tend to disrupt the effectiveness of digestion, assimilation of nutrients, vitamin balances, sleep cycles, and even brain function. We presently have only an inkling of the extent to which stress undermines the body's functioning, but the evidence is mounting rapidly as research proceeds.

One of the simplest and most familiar consequences of stress is the aging process. One of Selye's (1956) alternative definitions of stress is "the rate of wear and tear on the body caused by living" [p. 274]. Selye seems to consider each human body as having a characteristic amount of total adaptive capability. When this is used up after an accumulated demand of many years, the body is ready to die. We could paraphrase Selye's point of view as contending that no one dies of old age; everyone eventually dies of stress.

Unfortunately, many people seem to die of stress much sooner than others and perhaps much sooner than they should. An increasingly familiar way to die in America is a health breakdown caused by—or linked to—a continued, unrelieved overdose of stress. Over the past 20 years, medical researchers have discovered an increasing number of links between stress and health breakdown. A comprehensive listing of these diseases is not practical here, but it is enlightening to examine a few of the better known disorders.

A word of caution is in order before we look into disease physiology, however. Very few, if any, diseases are "caused" in isolation by one factor. Because of the body's incredibly complex and interconnected system of chemical feedback loops, many of its parts and processes usually feel the effects of the disease process and of the medical interventions used to deal with it. We need to maintain a multiple-cause viewpoint in looking at disease. Rather than conclude that any disorder is "caused" solely by stress, we should think of stress as being one of the important variables in the body's operation.

Ulcers are a well-known example of stress-related disorders. We have known for many years that stomach and duodenal ulcers occur much more frequently in individuals who live fast-paced, intensive, high-pressure lives. The ulcer has lately lost much of its status value as an executive badge of achievement. Other factors predisposing one to ulcer conditions include a family history of ulcers and digestive disorders, excessive drinking, consumption of rich foods, excess stomach acidity (possibly stress-related), and possibly even blood type. Some medical researchers believe that people with Type O blood are more susceptible to ulcer development than others.

Heart attack, as we said in an earlier chapter, is an infamous stress-linked disorder. Actually, we should consider the whole range of cardiovascular disease, including coronary thrombosis, arteriosclerosis (hardening of the arteries), atherosclerosis (fatty deposits within the arteries), and stroke. Smoking, drinking, poor diet, and other health behaviors probably play a key role in establishing susceptibility to these disorders. Heredity may also play a part. Stress almost certainly aggravates the conditions that bring about cardiovascular disease, probably in a wide variety of ways.

Some investigators have theorized that prolonged stress causes cholesterol and other fatty substances to deposit themselves on the artery walls at abnormal rates, paving the way for thrombosis (obstruction of the arteries), which leads to life-threatening cardiovascular accidents. Heart attack is primarily a disease of men. Men in the United States have three times as many heart attacks as do women. The incidence of heart attack correlates dramatically with occupation and life style. Chapter 3 deals with the heart attack behavior pattern found among many business people.

High blood pressure, although not technically a disease, leads directly to a number of degenerative diseases, most of which can kill. Heredity may play a role here, as well as a variety of possible factors yet to be discovered, but stress almost certainly plays a key role in hypertension. The effect of high blood pressure is for the heart to force blood through constricted arteries and into organ tissues more violently than it should. Kidney failure often results from untreated hypertension, partly because of the overabundant supply of blood the kidneys receive as they carry out their cleansing function. Liver diseases often result for the same reason. Obviously, blood pressure that is too high will tend to aggravate conditions of arteriosclerosis and atherosclerosis, making a cardiovascular disorder much more likely. A weakened blood vessel can bulge and rupture under the pressure of the blood supply. The resulting *aneurysm* may result in spillage of blood into the tissue area. Such a condition can be fatal if it occurs in the brain tissue.

A number of other diseases, notably diabetes, are severely aggravated by stress. Still others, of a less threatening nature, can arise from or be aggravated by inappropriate levels of stress. Most physicians consider migraine headaches, for example, to be closely connected to stress. Digestive disorders such as colitis, spastic colon, gastritis, and chronic diarrhea and constipation are very sensitive to stress levels. And a variety of vaguely experienced aches and pains, feelings of fatigue and exhaustion, sleeplessness, and hyperactivity have their roots in the body's stress response when it is inappropriately mobilized. A number of general practitioner physicians have contended that as many as 80% to 85% of the patients who come into their offices arrive with emotionally induced disorders — diseases caused primarily by stress.

Although this listing of stress-linked diseases could go on and on, this brief summary makes a very strong point: *that the human body — your body — is capable of literally destroying itself when it is forced to maintain a high-stress, "alarm" state for long periods without relief.*

Consider the analogy of a large office building as representing your body. Imagine that the building has a system of sprinkler devices on each floor that has the function of dousing each room with water in the event of a fire. Now suppose the sprinkler system were to trigger itself by accident, without any signal from the smoke or flame detector. Imagine this happening several times each day, for a period of a year or so. You can easily picture the results of such a false-alarm process. The carpets would soon be soaked, and they would begin to rot and mildew. The walls would weaken and lose their strength for supporting the ceiling. The floors would begin to weaken and sag. The building would be virtually destroying itself from the inside out.

And this is precisely what happens within your body when your stress reaction triggers off too often and too intensively. Without any means for relieving the effects of the false alarm, your body will simply accumulate the effects of the stress chemicals. In such an extreme case, if you have no outlets for relaxation, demobilization, exercise, and internal repair, your health will be in danger. Whichever organ forms the weakest link in your particular body will give out first, and you will have a major health breakdown. This explains why human beings experience such a wide variety of disease modes triggered by stress. Stress attacks your whole body—it's merely a question of which part breaks down first.

A striking confirmation of this reality lies in the dramatic prediction made by a physician about the probability of Richard Nixon's having a health breakdown after his resignation from the presidency. Dr. Samuel Silverman (in Butcher, 1977, p. 25) associate clinical professor of psychiatry at the Harvard Medical School, followed Nixon's medical history and predicted that he would have a health breakdown after leaving office. Silverman contended that Nixon's habit of controlling his emotions tightly would produce physical consequences, probably in his legs and his lungs because of a previous history of disorders at those sites. Within two months after the resignation and the pardon by President Ford, Silverman's prediction came true exactly.

STRESS AND MENTAL HYGIENE

The stress reaction can have a curious self-reinforcing effect on one's thinking processes and, indeed, on one's overall mental health. This becomes clear once we realize that various thought processes can trigger anxiety and that the resultant stress chemicals actually permeate the tissue of the brain as they flow along in the bloodstream.

Think of some recent situation in which an alarming idea suddenly came to your mind, and a split second later you became quite aroused, anxious, fearful, or desperate. For example, suppose you've been sitting quietly at your desk, playing with some creative task and deeply engrossed in thought. You look up and gaze blankly at the wall, sensing something tickling at the edges of your consciousness. Suddenly, it bursts upon your conscious field of thought! You're supposed to be at an extremely important special meeting! You glance at your watch and realize that it's exactly time for the meeting to begin and that you still have to cover the five-minute walk over to another building!

What's happening inside your body at that instant? You guessed it—the stress reaction is soaring, producing rapid heartbeat, tense muscles, radically altered hormone flows, increasing blood pressure, and the beginnings of sweaty palms and cold extremities. The remarkable thing is that this entire reaction came into play as a result of a single thought that flashed through your mind. No bacterial infection, no injury, no intense heat or cold—just a thought. To grasp the significance of the profound effect of your thoughts on your body, imagine that you doublecheck your calendar and discover that the meeting is actually scheduled for this time tomorrow. What happens then? You feel a sudden and very welcome new thought: "I'm saved!"

You heave a sigh of relief, which is one of the first stages in your body's demobilization process. Your chest muscles begin to relax, your breathing begins to ease up, and the entire parasympathetic nervous system comes into play to de-escalate your internal arousal level. In this instance, your body was mobilized by a single thought and subsequently demobilized by another thought. This is really quite a remarkable process. It holds the key for an understanding of emotional well-being and points the way to some very inviting possibilities for self-management and a high level of emotional tranquility.

But let's return for a moment to the original problem situation and imagine that you really have the problem of getting to the meeting. Take a moment to develop a vivid mental picture of yourself in the situation and *feel* the arousal as you have in many similar situations in the past. Imagine that this is a very important meeting and that your presence there is essential. Imagine that a group of very high-ranking executives will be expecting you to give a short extemporaneous talk about a project of interest.

You probably lunge for your portfolio and discover you've neglected to assemble all the papers and reference information you need. Some of it is in the file cabinet, some is on your desk, and some will result from a brief calculation you've forgotten to make. Having abandoned all your aplomb, you scurry about your office, seizing various items you think you might need, jamming them into a folder, trying to put on your jacket at the same time, and you rush out the door cursing yourself for having let this happen. It's a miserable feeling of desperation, frustration, and anger. It's your stress reaction in full swing.

And deep within your brain a cruel thing has happened. The electrical activity of your brain has intensified enormously as it leaps to its primary function of commanding the muscles of the body in violent action to meet what it mistakenly believes to be a threat to your survival. The primitive, "ancient" part of your brain (which scientists believe evolved first in man) has most of the action, as it brings the entire skeletal muscle system to the ready, starts reading sense inputs more rapidly, and sending various commands to your muscles. Unfortunately, this portion of the brain seizes priority; your conscious, verbal, analytical, linear, and logical faculties get pushed aside somewhat in favor of the more primitive brain functions. Even though you can handle the situation and you do not find yourself psychologically disabled by it, nevertheless your intense arousal causes your brain to snap into this primitive mode, which is compatible with the "war footing" of the rest of the body.

It is as if entire portions of your brain actually shut down or "go off the air." As you stop to check your papers, trying to decide whether you have everything you need, you sense a kind of desperate blockage in your reasoning faculties. You can barely tear your attention away from the main problem — that you are late for the meeting. Your anxiety about what may happen as a result of being late is competing for your conscious attention, and it tends to dominate. You struggle to calm your inner processes, and you succeed to some extent. You may even stop for half a minute to close your eyes, heave a sigh, and remind yourself that the world is not coming to an end. If you do this, you probably find you can think more effectively.

Indeed, as you bitterly remind yourself, if you had taken a few minutes earlier to plan for the meeting, you could have assembled all the information when you were calm and thinking very clearly, and you could have made fairly sure you didn't forget anything. As it is, you wonder whether you'll arrive at the meeting to find you've forgotten to bring some item that is absolutely crucial to making your point.

The important message we can derive from reviewing this example of a normal stress situation is that a person's higher level mental faculties are substantially impaired by extreme stress and that they function more effectively when he is comparatively calm and not highly aroused. To some extent, you as a human being are the victim of the chemical processes within your body, although you virtually always retain a measure of abstract reasoning ability that can help you deal with the stress itself. This chemical fact has extremely important implications for mental hygiene in general and for individual personal adjustment in particular.

For example, we know from many experiences that a person who has become extremely angry may say things that are irrational, childish, and perhaps highly rationalized. He may do things he will sorely regret after he has calmed down. We even use the expression, "after he has come to his senses." From the standpoint of rational behavior, extreme anger amounts to a touch of temporary madness.

Similarly, a person who is extremely frightened may do things that in more rational moments he would not have advised himself to do. Some people are virtually paralyzed and immobilized by extreme fear. One possible explanation for this is that their brains simply switch off when the stress reaction sets in, and they cannot summon enough of their rational faculties to deal with the situation effectively. The term *panic* is almost synonymous in our language with distraught, ineffective, over-reactive behavior.

However, this chemical tyranny need not completely dominate us as human beings. We can overcome its effects to some extent. If you can retain even a fragment of your abstract mental faculties during arousal, you can train yourself to expand those faculties by reprogramming techniques applied while you are in a calm and more rational state. This is one of the elements of stress reduction training, as described in Chapter 6.

STRESS AND SEX

Another cruel consequence of chronic stress is a reduction in levels of sex hormones, both in men and women, which acts to reduce sex drive and probably plays a significant part in marital difficulties and in relations with the opposite sex among single people. It may well be that the post-war divorce explosion in the United States is thus interlinked with the increasingly stressful environment we live in, as well as with the more obvious changes in social values.

In men, a prolonged stress condition sharply decreases the level of the primary male hormone, *testosterone*, which directly influences the sex drive. Men who have experienced a continuing state of even moderate anxiety, such as concern over losing a job or a business reversal, tend to lose interest in making love. In addition to being distracted by the problems and pressures challenging them in their lives, they simply *don't want to* have sexual relations.

Dr. Robert Rose (in Lamott, 1975) at the Boston University School of Medicine studied soldiers in combat situations in Vietnam. Rose actually had urine samples taken from soldiers who were waiting to carry out attack operations, and he found abnormally low levels of testosterone. He also conducted tests among soldiers in training at Officer Candidate Schools. He found depressed levels of testosterone and other stress effects during the first few weeks of the training program. Later, after the soldiers had passed the screening point in the training cycle and were no longer anxious about being washed out, testosterone levels — and interest in the opposite sex — rose dramatically [p.51].

According to Kenneth Lamott (1975), stress apparently also slows the production of sperm cells in the male [p. 50]. The general effect of stress is to diminish the overall functioning of the male sexual apparatus, making intercourse a relatively uninteresting proposition and an unsuccessful one as well. When a man's sex drive is low or diminished due to prolonged stress, he is likely to experience occasional impotence, which can be a devastating occurrence. For most men, raised in the American tradition of John Wayne toughness and superstud sexuality, a loss of sexual function is an ego crisis of first magnitude. Unfortunately, this experience usually produces great emotional disturbance and anxiety for the man, further increasing his stress level. His anticipation of failure makes it more likely that he will fail, and he finds himself caught in a cruel self-reinforcing spiral of anxiety and misery.

Some researchers have even suggested that prenatal stress

experienced by mothers and early-life stress experiences of the child may cause disorders in sex hormone balances, thus predisposing the individual to homosexuality (Lamott, 1975). This hypothesis needs a great deal more exploration, but it seems to have some merit. It does appear that a marked increase in homosexual behavior may be linked to the generally higher levels of pressure in American society.

San Francisco, sometimes known to Californians as "the gay area," (formerly "the bay area") is indeed a busy, crowded, fast-paced city. Other large American cities also have substantial homosexual populations. Although it may simply be that newer social norms permit more open display of homosexual behavior than in the past, nevertheless it does appear that more and more people — especially males — who have made rather fragile adjustments to their sexuality are being pushed into these forms of behavior.

Women also experience a reduction in important sex hormones during prolonged stress. Progesterone, the principal female hormone, diminishes sharply under these circumstances, producing a general disorientation of female functioning. Frigidity is a common result of protracted stress, and the emotional difficulties usually associated with sexual dysfunction provide the woman with extra obstacles to reducing the stress she feels.

Given the traditional Victorian guilt programming with regard to sex that most women in America have experienced in their early years, together with the relatively high levels of pressure characteristic of American life, it is small wonder that so many marriage counselors and physicians report sexual dysfunction in so many marriages. Some have estimated that as many as 50% of American marriages involve substantial deterioration in the sexual relationship between husband and wife.

Decreased levels of progesterone also cause menstrual irregularities, which can be quite troublesome for a number of women. Most women find the monthly cycle of menstruation uncomfortable at best, with a certain amount of depression and irritability to be expected. Under conditions of high stress, emotional upset and anxiety along with irregularity make the experience even more difficult.

Inasmuch as sex is one of the natural human appetites, and a satisfying heterosexual relationship is beneficial to good mental health — and physical health, for that matter — then a stress problem can be a sex problem, which can be a happiness problem. Curing the stress problem and adopting a straightforward, guilt-free attitude toward one's sexuality can play a great part in health, happiness, and personal adjustment.

THE INABILITY TO UNWIND

As we have seen, a reasonable amount of stress can be the spice of life, but constant, unrelieved stress can kill. Many people in the United States today seem to suffer from chronic, low-grade anxiety about themselves, their lives, and their surroundings. And most of them seem unaware of their stress, because they've had it for so long. The stress of this continued anxiety steadily takes its toll of health and well-being.

We are beginning to understand now that one of the most important survival skills for human beings in twentieth-century America is a *neurological skill* — the ability to physically relax, unwind, and demobilize the body for long enough periods to allow it to recuperate and repair itself. Chapters 7 and 8 show that you as an individual can manage your own personal life and your psychological reactions to your circumstances in such a way as to maintain your body's average stress level in the spice-of-life zone and to protect your health over your entire lifetime.

Some people seem to have relatively little difficulty with pressure situations and seem to cast off the effects of episodic stress. For these people, life seems to be merely a series of propositions to be dealt with — some stressful, some pleasant, but all transient. The person who has learned to manage his own stress level seems to take things as they come and to dispatch life's problems without storing up an inappropriate level of anxiety.

Others, unfortunately, seem to have lost the ability to unwind. For these people, life seems to be a series of crises. The chronically up-tight person seems to meet even a small problem or provocation as if it were a critical incident, as if somehow his survival were in jeopardy. A sudden call to come to the front office, a snag in a project schedule, a conflict with a co-worker, or a problem with a teenage son or daughter all take on the same apparent magnitude for the up-tight person. Such a person meets even the smallest problem situations with an unnecessarily intense reaction.

If you observe the motions and bearing of such a person, you will usually see someone who carries his body as if braced to meet some imminent physical attack. This person may sit down in a chair but not actually relax. He may react quickly, interrupt others, express impatience or exasperation with others who talk slowly or deliberately, walk in a beeline at a somewhat quicker than average pace, and may carry out manual tasks with jerky, rapid-fire motions. Such a person may also rush through a meal, not enjoying it or even being very much aware of eating as an experience. He may have frequent digestive problems, including constipation. This person may have difficulty in falling asleep at night. Other signs of the chronically up-tight person include impatience with small obstacles, general irritability, and a distinct lack of a sense of humor. The ability to laugh —long and enthusiastically—is a hallmark of the person who can unwind easily.

The chronically up-tight person may try to unwind from time to time but feels he simply can't. From the point of view of the stress response, such a person has learned, neurologically speaking, a pattern of dealing with life's processes by inappropriately mobilizing the stress reactions within his body. Letting go of the up-tight pattern and learning to function at a more reasonable level of arousal requires that the person learn a new set of *neurological skills*. These are the skills of self-monitoring, voluntary de-escalation of the internal arousal level, and occasional deep relaxation. Stress reduction training, as described in Chapter 6, offers specific methods for learning these all-important survival skills.

REFERENCES

Butcher, Lee. "It's Called 'Hurry Sickness.' " *Holiday Inn Magazine*, January 1977.

Cannon, Walter B. *The Wisdom of the Body*. New York: W. W. Norton, 1932.

Lamott, Kenneth. *Escape From Stress*. New York: Berkeley Medallion, 1975.

Pelletier, Kenneth R. "Mind as Healer, Mind as Slayer." *Psychology Today*, February 1977.

Selye, Hans. "A Syndrome Produced by Diverse Nocuous Agents." *Nature*, July 4, 1936.

Selye, Hans (interviewed by Laurence Cherry). "On the Real Benefits of Eustress." *Psychology Today*, March 1978.

Selye, Hans. *The Stress of Life*. New York: McGraw-Hill, 1956.

Selye, Hans. *Stress Without Distress*. New York: J. B. Lippincott, 1974.

3

How People
Stress Themselves

MOST STRESS IS SELF-INDUCED

We can divide the causes of stress into two general categories, with the second occupying most of our attention for the remainder of this book. They are as follows:

1. *Physically induced stress* — stress that comes from a direct disturbance to one's body by the immediate environment.
2. *Emotionally induced stress* — stress caused by a person's own thought processes, without any physical stressor coming into contact with the body.

Agents that physically induce stress in the body include bacteria, viruses, extreme heat, extreme cold, high exposures to ultraviolet or infrared radiation from sunlight, nuclear radiation, high doses of X rays, physical injuries such as cuts, bruises, broken bones, sprains, and pulled muscles, poisons, near-poisons (caffeine, nicotine, and other social drugs), and physical exercise. In fact, any outside agent that presents a strong challenge to the homeostatic equilibrium of the body will evoke the stress reaction. This is the *somatic* stress previously referred to.

Emotionally induced stress does not stem from a stressor per se but, rather, from an electrochemical trigger signal originating in the higher portions of the brain which — by a process not yet fully understood — excites the hypothalamus and sets off the entire chain of chemical events described in Chapter 2. We can think of the stressor as a perceived event or process or an anticipated happening that the individual believes will bring very unpleasant results. Examples include a person who threatens to attack another, an impending automobile accident, an angry dog who gets free of his leash, a verbal attack by one whose goodwill another values and wants, the sudden news of the death of a loved one, and so on.

In every case of emotionally induced stress, the common feature is *expectation — the belief that something terrible is about to happen.* Whereas the physically induced form of stress arises from a physical affront to the body's equilibrium, emotionally induced stress arises from one's imagination. An impending automobile accident has no reality. There are only the car, the road, the individual driving the car, other cars, the rain, and so on. The accident is not real unless and until it happens. Nevertheless, the stressed person's body adopts the fight-or-flight response solely on the strength of his abstract thought processes — his estimate of what is about to happen.

Of course, certain forms of emotionally induced stress have great value for a person's survival. If one were indeed being attacked by a large and angry dog, some physical solution would be necessary. A full and automatic mobilization of one's body processes would be appropriate and useful in taking violent action. Avoiding an automobile crash calls for close attention and quick response, both of which are facilitated by the stress response.

On the other hand, we probably have to classify certain instances of emotionally induced stress as "useless," or at least unnecessary. For example, the stress you experience as you wait to give your speech to a large audience does not particularly help you to do a better job. If you haven't had much experience in those kinds of situations, your nervousness may cause your voice to tremble and break, your hands to shake, your breathing to become intense, and your chest muscles to become constricted.

In addition, you may not be able to think on your feet very well because your brain will be largely given over to the maintenance of your body's readiness for fight or flight. Since the probability that the audience will actually attack you is very remote and you do not choose to run away, your body will have mobilized itself for no good reason. In this case, anxiety is clearly your enemy rather than your friendly helper. The often-heard statement, "The butterflies in your stomach help you do a better job" is little more than a rationalization. Butterflies can and should be reduced to a practical minimum.

As twentieth-century citizens of the world's wealthiest country, most of us live in a highly controlled, physically benign environment. We experience disease from time to time and occasional environmental discomfort, but for the most part our technology has given us a relatively comfortable environment. Yet the fact that we have the world's highest proportion of stress-induced illness and stress-linked behavior patterns forces us to the conclusion that most of our stress is self-induced. Our national health problem is anxiety, not any kind of environmental discomfort. And our national need is to *learn* new modes of thinking and behavior that can enable us to avoid killing ourselves from the inside out.

The objective of stress reduction training is to enable an

individual to use his logical faculties to prevent the stress reaction from escalating beyond a practical minimum level in any situation and to acquire new neurological skills that help to regulate the body's activation level at will.

So far, we have not found the answer to eliminating "useless" stress, but I believe the answer is not very far in the future. I believe that one day we may discover or develop a training technique — probably a simple one — that will give an individual virtually total control over self-induced stress. Until then, we can only apply those techniques we have available. The available techniques are highly effective, and the current state of the art in personal stress reduction methods is sufficient for any individual to prevent major stress-related disease, probably to extend his lifespan, and to maintain health and well-being.

SOURCES OF SELF-INDUCED STRESS

The stressors that lead to self-induced stress, or emotional stress, simply serve as situational triggers to which we as normal human beings respond. In this sense, we speak of stressors as those aspects of our environment that we consider grounds for becoming anxious. Clearly, these psychological stressors will vary from person to person. Whereas your body and mine react essentially the same to a bacterial invasion, we may react quite differently to a confrontation with a snake, or to a loud thunderstorm, or to having a co-worker yell at us across a conference table.

Each of us brings to a situation his own peculiar history of involvements and reactions with various psychological stressors, and each of us has his own characteristic pattern of *reactivity*. A highly reactive person finds more of life's experiences stressful than does a less reactive person. Similarly, as we see in more detail in a later chapter, each of our bodies has its own characteristic "signature" of physical symptoms and sensations that gives evidence of high stress levels and that tells us about the state of our internal workings.

Here we deal with those situations, events, processes, and perceived possibilities found stressful by most of us. We emphasize those leading to strong stress reactions, but we must bear in mind that "normal" stress is always with us. We need not worry too much about levels of stress caused by everyday interactions, minor difficulties and frustrations, and occasional upsets. Well-adjusted people can handle the everyday stress of life and even thrive on it. We are mostly interested in levels of stress that present significant problems in peace of mind and overall well-being.

We can classify emotionally induced stress in four general categories as follows:

1. *Time stress* — anxiety reaction to the abstract concept of time, including the feeling that one "must" do something (or a number of somethings) before some deadline; also the general feeling that time is "running out" (whatever that may mean) and that something terrible will happen when it does.

2. *Anticipatory stress* — commonly known as "worry"; a feeling of anxiety about an impending event; sometimes a generalized anxiety, with little or no specific basis; in extreme cases of "anxiety attack," a diffuse feeling of dread, a fear that some horrible but unnamable catastrophe is about to befall one; sometimes called "free-floating fear."

3. *Situational stress* — anxiety as a result of finding one's self in a situation that is threatening and at least partially beyond one's control; the expected terrible happening may involve physical injury or danger; more often it involves loss of status, significance, or acceptance in the eyes of others.

4. *Encounter stress* — anxiety about dealing with one or more people whom one finds unpleasant and possibly unpredictable; a vague but intense feeling of apprehen-

sion when one discovers that the conventional rules for social interaction no longer govern the behavior of others, such as in an encounter or "sensitivity" group.

In the foregoing definitions, I have used the term *anxiety* more or less interchangeably with the term *stress*. This usage presents no particular problem if we remind ourselves occasionally that the stress reaction can also arise because of the influence of a purely physical stressor. In the case of emotionally induced stress, the term *anxiety* will serve just as well. It has the additional advantage of conveying the impression of arousal and internal activation.

The following sections deal with each of these four types of emotionally induced stress in greater depth.

Time Stress

To the proverbial Martian visitor just arrived on our planet, an interesting feature of each individual culture would probably be the relative sense of permanence, predictability, and stability of relationships and processes as displayed by common artifacts and typical human activities. Such an observer might notice that Oriental peoples such as the Japanese devote great attention to methods for structuring and conserving physical space, that Mediterranean peoples devote great attention to the fabric of interpersonal relationships and networks, that so-called "primitive" peoples such as Australian aborigines devote great attention to their relationships with the tangible and intangible forces of nature, and that Americans seem to devote great attention to structuring *time*.

Eric Berne (1972), psychotherapist and author, believed that all human beings need to have an appropriate degree of time structuring in order to overcome existential anxiety and to gain feelings of assurance and adequacy. Without at least some sense of the predictability of events in one's surroundings, Berne said, one will become anxious and disoriented. The relative thoroughness with which various people structure their time depends on their early life experiences and "programs," and on the culture in which they operate. [p. 22]

More than any other people on the face of the earth, however, Americans seem obsessed with time. There is a very old business adage, "Time is money." We say, "Time and tide wait for no man." We speak of "taking time," "saving time," "killing time," "making up for lost time," "having time," "losing time," and "gaining time." The fact that virtually every American home has a clock, that there are clocks in just about every business office, schoolroom, movie theater, shop, restaurant, and church, and even in automobiles and on highway billboards, makes it very difficult for us to visualize a culture that has no clocks and that does not conceive of time as a *commodity* — a "substance" that is to be bought, sold, measured, manipulated, and structured. Most of us have heard anecdotes about the "mañana" concept in Latin American countries, where hurrying is considered a peculiar behavior. Cultural differences can be much more profound than this, however.

Benjamin Whorf (1956), in studying the American Hopi Indians, was intrigued to find that their language contained no word for *time*. They had no way of stating — and therefore no way of intellectually perceiving — what we consider a fundamental aspect of reality. Nor did Hopi verb forms have the past, present, or future tenses that we consider essential for accurate discourse. However, said Whorf, in a number of ways the Hopi language served to describe the speaker's "reality" more effectively and more accurately than did English and other languages within its parent Indo-European language stem. Whorf found that the concept we call *time* was inseparably built into the basic definition of individual Hopi words. For example, he found a word for "house which stands now," a word for "house which stood long ago but is no more," a word for "house which I will build," but he found no isolated word to represent "house." To speak of a house without informing the listener of its relative temporal reality would seem to the Hopi an absurd way to try to talk [p. 57].

Whorf's contemporary, the late Alfred Korzybski (1933), who founded the study of general semantics, believed that our English language has a number of *structural flaws*, such as the illogical, elementalistic way of trying to describe an abstraction such as *time* as if it were a substance. However, this is precisely the way we as Americans have learned to think. And our behavior is largely governed by our mental reactions to this abstraction. The ingredients for time stress are built right into our culture and into our language.

In the business world, the principal stressor that gives rise to time anxiety is the deadline. This is our traditional and effective way of getting things done. The combination of a person's total workload, the relative severity of the deadlines involved, and his own personal level of reactivity will determine how much is enough.

Each employee has a fairly well-defined comfort zone or sense of urgency and time pressure within which he works effectively and gains a sense of accomplishment. Beyond this zone of reasonable time pressure, deadlines threaten, time seems to run out, there is not enough slack time for pressure relief or change of pace, and the individual begins to feel overstressed. Time stress, although physically the same as all other forms of stress, has its own special mental aspects. One feels desperate, trapped, miserable, and often rather helpless. In cases of very high time stress, one can even begin to feel depressed and hopeless. If one cannot step back and look at the situation and narrow down the required accomplishments to something reasonable, then one is caught like a helpless rat in a trap of his own making.

The key to freeing one's self from time stress is to take a new view of time or, rather, to pay less attention to time and more attention to *accomplishment*. To work effectively and happily, one must settle on a workload that one can accomplish reasonably well within the time available. The skill of *time man-*

agement offers a very effective avenue for reducing time stress and at the same time improving one's effectiveness in accomplishing the important things. Chapter 8 explains the basic concepts and techniques of time management more fully. Another important skill, discussed further in Chapter 8, is the mental skill of "de-obligating" one's self from situations and finding a sense of assertive freedom that immediately reduces the feeling of time stress.

Anticipatory Stress

The primary agent for anticipatory stress is the abstract concept of an upcoming event or experience that the individual conceives of as being at least partially or potentially unpleasant. For example, a sales representative may have an appointment with a very important customer late one afternoon. Although he hopes and probably expects to make an important sale and to have a very rewarding experience as a result, nevertheless he may spend most of the day dreading the appointment. Why so? Because all the things that could possibly go wrong loom up just as strongly, and possibly more strongly, than the potential good feelings.

It seems that each of us has a primitive, silent, "other person" inside us who reacts in terms of very basic feelings of fear and joy. This silent partner seems, for most of us, to have a way of seeing the worst side of a situation and of arousing the fight-or-flight reaction even though our conscious minds know it is uncalled for. Some people find themselves almost paralyzed and disabled by this anticipatory stress, but most of us have learned to overcome it by imposing a conscious control over our actions. Nevertheless, we all experience anticipatory stress to some degree or other, and our bodies pay the price if we cannot find sufficient escape and emotional relief from it.

In his book *What Do You Say After You Say Hello?*, Eric Berne (1972, p. 260) defined the useful term *reach-back*. Reach-back, in Berne's lexicon, is a period of time during which an impending event begins to influence one's behavior (and, we could add, his stress level). For people who have unusual difficulties with anticipatory stress, the reach-back of an event such as a major vacation trip or a wedding may be several weeks or even months. For others, who have learned to take life's disruptions fairly well in stride, the reach-back period is much less, possibly even just a few days. This does not mean that one should not plan well ahead for an important event or that one should not begin to do certain key things ahead of time. However, when one's activity consists simply of worrying about the upcoming event to the extent that the anticipatory stress interferes with other normal activities, then reach-back presents problems for that person.

One can learn to reduce the reach-back of an upcoming event by applying some of the stress reduction techniques discussed in Chapter 6. Stress reduction is partly a philosophical approach and partly a mental skill. This brings to my mind a hilarious scene from the motion picture, *A Funny Thing Happened on the Way to the Forum.* During one hectic scene, Zero Mostel (playing a scheming slave) had discovered that the master and mistress of the house were returning unexpectedly from their trip. The other slaves involved in his lucrative secret brothel became alarmed, running about in terror. When Mostel's Number One henchman rushed up, babbling incoherently and wringing his hands, Mostel shouted, "Calm down, will you?! I'll tell you when it's time to panic!" As we see in later chapters, this is a key attitude in reducing anticipatory stress.

In one sense, we can consider anticipatory stress as being merely a form of *worry.* Some people worry chronically about improbable happenings that never come true. Others seem to worry only occasionally and for short periods. We can take some food for thought from the old slave lady in the motion picture *Gone With the Wind.* She seemed to have worked out a constructive approach to anticipatory anxiety, saying, "Thursday's muh worryin' day. Ever' Thursday, ah sets down fo' a little while, and ah worries about things. Then ah don't have to worry no mo' for the rest of da week." There's something to be said for this philosophy, too.

Situational Stress

We can define situational stress as anxiety about what might happen next in a situation that one finds potentially unpleasant. In a sense, we can say that situational stress is also anticipatory stress, although the thought process that triggers it is somewhat more diffuse. Some people experience a great deal of situational stress in business meetings or conferences that involve conflict. Many people find conflict to be extremely disconcerting and personally threatening. When a "shouting match" begins, they may "clam up," physically withdraw into themselves, psychologically drop out of the group, and even try to leave the room. An alert observer can easily spot the individual who experiences great situational stress under these circumstances by observing nonverbal cues such as posture, facial expression, eye motion, and use of the hands.

All of us experience situational stress from time to time, and most of us can overcome it and do a good job of whatever we have undertaken. Whenever we find ourselves on the spot in a group situation, we probably experience a fairly marked stress reaction. The intensity of the reaction depends on individual factors such as the general reactivity, mood, and personal significance attached to the situation, as well as situational factors such as the behavior of others, social norms and controls, and available strategies for meeting one's own needs.

Chapter 7 offers some techniques for dealing with situational anxiety, such as re-engineering the situation and revising one's point of view about situational risks, especially the risk of ego damage. Although we don't yet know how to eliminate this or any other form of emotionally induced stress completely, nevertheless we can use a variety of strategies to reduce it to an acceptable minimum.

Encounter Stress

The stressor that induces encounter stress is simply another person, even a friendly one. Most of our encounters (the term as used here implies simply a transaction with another person, with no connotations of antagonism) proceed smoothly, with comparatively harmonious relations. Yet they all accumulate to give us a total dose of human contact within any one period of time. Probably everyone has felt from time to time a sense of overload in being around people. We all have need for the company of others, and we all have need for privacy and isolation, even if only for short periods. When one's comfort zone of human contact has been exceeded, he begins to feel the physical stress reaction as a manifestation of the need for aloneness.

Each individual has a characteristic level of need and preference for human contact, and this need plays a direct part in the kinds of work each person does best. A highly gregarious person, who enjoys being with others a large proportion of time, may actually become tense and anxious if deprived of contact for long periods. Conversely, a shy, introverted person who prefers to be alone for long periods and who prefers to associate with only a few close friends or well-known acquaintances may feel tense and anxious when thrust into a large group and forced to interact frequently and continuously with others. One experiences an underload of contact and the other experiences an overload.

Jobs vary widely in the amount of contact built into the tasks. A job such as research chemist or construction laborer has no essential encounter requirements. The person doing the job finds it necessary to transact with his supervisor occasionally and probably with fellow workers in isolated and specific instances. An observer in a forest fire lookout station experiences very few encounter requirements in carrying out the job tasks. On the other hand, being a waitress requires repeated human encounters as part of the task structure. Contact is built into the job. Indeed, the whole category of customer-contact employees includes jobs that require repeated encounters with other people to carry them out. Some jobs involve virtually nothing else but transactions with other people. And some jobs involve many encounters that are unpleasant and stressful for the employees who do them.

These facts open up the very important issues of *contact loading* as a basic feature of a job situation and the notion that contact overload can cause a great deal of stress for the individual worker. Three kinds of jobs involving very high levels of encounter stress are those of the physician, public welfare case worker, and psychotherapist. Workers in all three of these jobs spend a large proportion of their daily work time transacting with people who are in various states of personal distress. It seems that the factor of the distressed client plays a fundamental part in the stress reactions of the worker involved. It is as if some of the client's anxiety and bad feeling rubs off on the person who acts in the helping capacity.

For example, doctors mostly see people who do not feel well and who are usually anxious about their health. These people generally focus on their own difficulties and seldom think to make the encounter pleasant or emotionally rewarding for the physician. This fact, magnified by the effect of heavy patient schedules — caused either by the production mentality of hospital administrators or by the physician's own value system that emphasizes striving, hard work, and high income — tends to place the physician in a position of high stress and high psychological risk.

Physicians as a group seem to be tense, overextended, driven, and often in poor health themselves. *Doctors have the highest rate of alcoholism of any of the professions.* Each year in California alone, over 400 physicians are forced to give up their practices because of uncontrolled drinking problems (Lamott, 1975, p. 31).

Welfare workers form another interesting class of workers who experience alarming levels of job-induced encounter stress.

The typical eligibility worker, or EW in government parlance, interviews as many as 20 to 30 clients every working day, most of whom are poor, depressed, inarticulate, often frustrated and angry, and too absorbed in their own difficulties to pay much attention to the EW's needs for affirmation and positive human interaction. Many of them are at the edge of the social system, with histories of crime and antisocial behavior. Often the EW as a symbolic representative of "the establishment," bears the brunt of the anger and hostility carried around by poor and distressed members of minority segments of the population. Small wonder that stress presents a problem for workers doing this job every day.

In one large county government, a welfare supervisor reported, "My people have ulcers. They're feuding with each other within the unit. People break down and sob and sob, and have to go home. Two people left and committed themselves to rest homes. Six months ago a man shot himself. His supervisor thought the job was at least partially responsible." A female eligibility worker commented, "I've gone for a year without a period. My doctor said it was stress-related. I broke out in a red rash. My hands broke out in blisters and a couple of layers of skin peeled off. I lost twenty pounds, and I was weighing less than 100 pounds" (Fenly, 1977, p. A–18).

A closely related part of this situation is the insistence by county top management on a heavy, unrelenting schedule of "production," that is, the "processing" of a large number of incoming clients by the smallest possible staff of workers. This practice imposes an intense pressure on the EW's, who know that anything they can't get done today must be caught up tomorrow.

Add to this agonizing time stress the fact that most of the EWs tend to empathize with the poor people (very few of whom actually fit the common stereotype of welfare "swindlers") who come to them for help. However, they find that they must rush them through in order to maintain an industrial engineering type of time standard. The result is a powerful value conflict. Many EW's report a continuing feeling of frustration and powerlessness in this situation, in which there are all the ingredients for extreme, chronic, unrelieved anxiety. The results show very clearly. This particular county agency has instituted a pilot program in stress reduction along the lines of the approach described in Chapter 6. Initial results have been dramatic and encouraging.

Psychotherapists, of all people, also suffer extreme job-related stress resulting from contact overload. We might think that a therapist, specially trained in helping others to deal with their adjustment problems, would be especially adept at handling his own encounter stress. For the majority of therapists, however, this is simply not true. Most therapists seem to have substantial adjustment difficulties linked to the encounter stress of their daily activities. This fact makes more sense if we think through some of the kinds of encounters a therapist may have in a given week's work. Bear in mind that the therapist is usually dealing with distraught people.

How would you react if someone with whom you had been intimately involved for several months called you in the middle of the night, threatening to commit suicide, and insisting it was your obligation to dissuade him? Imagine spending a large proportion of your day with people who are chronically depressed. Add to this a very strong concern for professional reputation and the need for a sense of success in difficult therapeutic situations, and you have the ingredients for the therapist's debilitating type of job stress.

One of the most discouraging facts about job stress, and particularly about encounter stress, is that *psychiatrists have a higher suicide rate than any other profession* — and more than *five times higher* than the overall rate for American citizens (Lamott, 1975, p. 31). In the stress reduction workshops I've conducted at the University of California in San Diego, Riverside, Irvine, and Santa Cruz, I've had participants who were psychiatrists, as well as those who were welfare workers, physicians, nurses, and others in the helping professions. Attorneys also fall into the category of encounter-stressed workers.

As we have seen, encounter stress does not necessarily result only from hostile or threatening transactions or from transactions with people in states of distress. Simple contact overload seems to create encounter stress in some workers, even in situations where the transaction proceeds smoothly and without any particular disharmony. Bank tellers, for example, transact with a very large number of customers on Fridays and days preceding major holidays. Some of them tend to "robotize" their jobs, withdrawing psychologically from the customers and mechanically performing the motions. In a state of overload, a customer contact employee may become cold and impersonal, may brush aside a customer's attempts at socializing, may sidestep small favors or "extras," and may even resort to small, malicious acts such as walking up to a different counter window from the one the customer has come to and saying in an ice-cold, bored voice, "May I help you *over here?*"

I believe these are all ego defenses used by quite normal people when they experience the stress of contact overload. The same employee who would be friendly, helpful, and charming at the beginning of the shift might have withdrawn into this robotic mode by the end of the day. In addition, those employees who may not have a very strong self-image to begin with and who lack highly developed social skills may have had their fill of encounter activity earlier in the shift than others who are more mature and more skillful.

Managers have only recently begun to recognize these considerations and to speculate on possible ways to deal with them. In my opinion, what often passes for lack of communication skill among customer contact employees, or "bad attitude," may simply be the employee's normal manifestation of encounter stress and his attempts to escape the unpleasant but largely unrecognized gut feelings it causes. Chapter 5 offers a model for examining jobs in terms of stress-loading factors and for redesigning them to bring them within the comfort zones of the employees who perform them.

THE EXTRA HAZARDS OF BEING MALE

Being a man in the United States during the fourth quarter of the twentieth century apparently carries with it certain extra penalties that women do not — at least so far — experience. Men in this country die, on the average, almost eight years earlier than American women. Exhibit 3-1 shows the improvement in life expectancy at birth for males and females in the United States between 1900 and 1970. Clearly, females have benefited much more than males from the eradication of disease, reduction in accidents, and decrease in infant mortality. Whereas men have gained an average of about 21 additional years of life expectancy since the turn of the century, women have gained almost 27 years. Many sociologists and medical researchers have attributed this difference in life span to the enormous difference in the relative amounts of pressure experienced by men, on the average, as compared to that experienced by women.

Stress-linked diseases show a clear preference for males as victims over females. The facts that very few significant dietary differences exist between men and women, that a large proportion of women smoke, and that overweight and sedentary life patterns are just as common among women as among men tend

EXHIBIT 3-1.
Life Expectancy at Birth (Years)

	1900	1970	Increase
Males	46.3	67.1	20.8
Females	48.3	74.8	26.5
Difference	2.0	7.7	5.7

to isolate stress—especially job stress—as a key factor in male health.

Many more men than women commit violent crimes, steal, and damage property. Many more men than women are heavy drug users. Men contract ulcers and have heart attacks much more frequently than women. And men commit suicide at a rate well over twice the rate for women. Homosexuality among men far exceeds that among women.

Many social observers have noticed apparent differences between the physical appearances of women who have led protected, low-pressure lives and those who have had more difficult challenges to face, and especially men and women who, on the average, have faced higher levels of pressure more or less routinely. Writer Kenneth Lamott (1975) observes:

> A most striking illustration of the relationship of life stress and physical age was offered to me when I became involved with a group of ex-priests and ex-nuns. Although the priests' apparent age matched their real age, the nuns, women for the most part between thirty and forty, all looked five to ten years younger than their real ages. Their skin was clearer and less wrinkled, their eyes were brighter, their faces less mature [p. 54].

A social worker recently described to me her observations of a group of Vietnamese refugees with whom she had worked. "The women looked so innocent," she said, "almost child-like. Their husbands spoke for them, transferred my questions, and relayed their answers to me. The husbands made the decisions, took all responsibility, and did the worrying. The women were protected by the men in every way. The men tended to look tense and haggard, but the women had a beautiful, child-like look of innocence and softness."

Psychiatrist Herb Goldberg (1976) believes men pay an extremely high price for the "masculine privilege"—that is, for the dubious right to act out the role as the dominant figure, both in social settings and in their relationships with women. Goldberg observes:

> Men evaluate each other and are evaluated by many women largely by the degree to which they approximate the ideal masculine model. Our culture is saturated with successful male zombies, businessman zombies, golf zombies, sports car zombies, playboy zombies, etc. They are playing by the rules of the male game plan. They have lost touch with, or are running away from, their feelings and awareness of themselves as people. They have confused their social masks for their essence, and they are destroying themselves while fulfilling the traditional definitions of masculine-appropriate behavior. They set their life sails by these role definitions. They are the heroes, the studs, the providers, the warriors, the empire builders, the fearless ones. Their reality is always approached through the veils of gender expectations [p. 15].

The payment men must make for this role-locked life pattern is extremely high, in terms of both emotional well-being and happiness and in physical health. Ulcers are fairly common among middle-aged men, but they are rather rare among women. Heart attack is primarily a male disease — that is, those who live out imprisoning life patterns characteristic of the male stereotype tend to have heart attacks much more frequently than those who enjoy the role freedom that women have always had during this century — in the sense that women have always had a much greater "entitlement" to express emotion than males. Lamott (1975) observes that "a healthy American male runs a one-in-five chance of having a heart attack *before* he reaches the age sixty-five [italics supplied]." Men are breaking under the crushing load of stress at earlier and earlier ages.

Recently a California highway patrolman, while chasing a fleeing suspect across an open field, collapsed and died of a heart attack. He left a wife and three children behind. This man was 33 years old and "apparently" in good health. Many factors might have played a part in his death, but we do know one thing: *33 is too young to die.*

Lest we jump to the conclusion that cardiovascular disease is solely the genetic property of males, let's look at the results of studies of Type A women, conducted by Doctors Meyer Friedman and Ray Rosenman (1974). The intensive, overdriven Type A behavior pattern, according to Friedman and Rosenman, predisposes the person who has it to an extremely high probability of heart attack and related cardiovascular disease. A later section describes this pattern in some detail. Friedman and Rosenman observe, "The prevalence of coronary heart disease was also far more frequent in the Type A women than in the Type B women. Our Type A women, in fact, suffered as much coronary heart disease as their male counterparts [p. 78]."

In the first half of the twentieth century, American women mostly stayed in their homes and managed domestic affairs. Beginning in the 1960s and accelerating by the three-quarter-century mark, women have left their homes in unprecedented numbers and have joined the work force. There are more unmarried working women than ever before, in addition to more married working women, and the incidence of cardiovascular disease among these women has risen proportionately. Women in managerial positions experience heart disease at the same rates as men in similar positions. In Japan, the incidence of coronary heart disease among women has quadrupled since the time when General Douglas MacArthur's occupation policies liberated many women from the household and put them into the work force.

So we can say that a high rate of cardiovascular disease is primarily a male pattern because until only the last half of the century men have been primarily the ones who have lived and worked in the high-pressure business world, with its attendant deadlines, competition, conflict, and hostility. Friedman and Rosenman (1974) attribute the smaller number of Type A women to the fact that, traditionally, women have not lived within the business culture that tends to bring out the Type A pattern. However, as more and more women enter the work force and as more and more of them rise to challenging and high-pressure jobs, we can expect their rates of stress-linked diseases to rise to approximate those of their male counterparts.

STRESSFUL LIFE PATTERNS

Many people unknowingly subject themselves to unnecessary stress by adopting and maintaining patterns of behavior, habits, relationships, activities, and obligations that add to their stress scores day by day. During the business of living and working in American society, each of us accumulates a bank account of stress experiences, which in the aggregate help to determine our overall level of health and well-being. Too many stress points in too short a time, especially without relief and relaxation, will jeopardize our health.

A conscious review of your life pattern, from the point of view of stress accumulation, gives a clear and compelling picture of your stress patterns. Chapter 8 offers a method for making such an appraisal. The results of such a review, together with a new understanding of the physiology of stress and some techniques for stress reduction, can equip you to re-engineer your life style if necessary.

TYPE A BEHAVIOR — THE HEART ATTACK PATTERN

Since about 1970, researchers in the field of cardiology have become increasingly aware of important connections between the occurrence of heart attacks and the life patterns of the patients. Heart attacks, and the family of related cardiovascular diseases, are beginning to take their places alongside ulcers as stress-linked diseases.

Medical experts have traditionally considered diet a primary causative factor in heart attack. This, plus possible hereditary factors, overweight, smoking, and lack of exercise, all seemed linked with heart disease. Recently, however, researchers have uncovered some important links between heart disease and a highly stressful life pattern that has certain distinctive features. Researchers still argue heatedly about which factors may be the first-order causes of heart disease, but evidence is steadily piling up to incriminate the high-stress life pattern as an important linking factor, or catalyst, in precipitating heart attack.

For a number of years, Friedman and Rosenman (1974) have studied the connections between heart attack and life style and have succeeded in describing a distinctive pattern that they believe represents the hallmark of the typical heart attack victim. In their book, *Type A Behavior and Your Heart*, Friedman and Rosenman give this definition: "Type A Behavior Pattern is an action–emotion complex that can be observed in any person who is *aggressively* involved in a *chronic, incessant* struggle to achieve more and more in less and less time, and if required to do so, against the opposing efforts of other things or other persons. Persons possessing this pattern also are quite prone to exhibit a free-floating but extraordinarily well-rationalized hostility [p. 84]". Friedman and Rosenman summarize the Type A pattern as one of chronic *time urgency, achievement,* and *competitiveness.* They believe the pattern comes into play only when the Type A person faces challenges from his surroundings. Apparently, the pattern is a manifestation of the way the individual sees his relationship to things and events in the environment.

In a landmark study, Doctors Friedman and Rosenman (1974) enlisted over 3,500 men in a long-term study of life pattern and health. Beginning in 1960, they examined each of the men and developed fairly thorough profiles that described their styles of living and coping. After a period of 10 years, about 250 of the subjects had suffered coronary heart disease. The traditionally important variables of diet, exercise level, and cigarette smoking showed no strong correlation with the incidence of disease. On the other hand, Type A men were three times more likely to break down than Type B men were (Type B is the alternative to the intensive, overdriven Type A pattern). These findings led Friedman and Rosenman to study the Type A pattern in much greater depth and led them to the theory they propounded in their now-famous book.

In a scientific area such as this one, we must be careful not to jump to simple conclusions too soon, but this research does seem to offer a great deal of insight into the connections between life style and heart disease. Most researchers do not argue very much with the findings of Friedman and Rosenman, but some of them do offer alternative points of view about life style.

For example, nutritionists — who tend to see human health through an altogether different window — link much of the decline in American health to the gross overconsumption of animal fats and other forms of cholesterol-bearing foods. Many of them also cite the continuing degradation of the quality of the American food supply, especially the loss of natural vitamins such as E, the high concentration of refined sugars, and the unprecedented "doctoring" of processed foods with preservatives and cosmetic chemicals.

In another significant area, exercise physiologists advance the notion that if one achieves and maintains a very high level of physical conditioning, as represented by a *cardiopulmonary fitness level* sufficient for that person to complete a marathon run, he becomes virtually immune to cardiovascular disease until a very advanced age. Physicians such as Dr. Jack Scaff in Honolulu train many hundreds of people — including cardiac patients — every year to develop high levels of *aerobic fitness*, and to prove it by running in the Honolulu Marathon. Events such as the famous Boston Marathon have become much more numerous. Most people who participate in them run for reasons of personal health and achievement, not to compete with others.

Dr. Thaddeus Kostrubala (1976), a San Diego psychiatrist, uses slow long-distance runs of an hour's duration as an adjunct to group psychotherapy. Kostrubala believes that the physiological effects of this kind of extended activity, as well as the emotional components of personal achievement, can have profound effects on classical adjustment problems such as depression, and even possibly to some extent on more severe disorders such as schizophrenia.

Much more needs to be known about the connections between life style and stress effects. At the present, we can consider the work done by Friedman and Rosenman to offer very important and useful guidelines for personal stress reduction and stress management. By abandoning the distress-producing Type A pattern and by learning the more effective and rewarding pattern of achievement they call Type B, a person can reorganize his life and can gain protection from one of the most feared and most deadly diseases known to modern man.

LOW-STRESS LIFE PATTERNS

Just as we find certain life styles to be difficult and stressful, we can also specify life styles that allow one to operate within his individual comfort zone of challenge and stimulation. We refer to the low-stress life style as one in which the individual consciously makes choices, undertakes experiences, and manages his own time and energies in such a way as *consciously* to minimize or reduce the levels of stress and the accumulated point count of stress experiences.

The first key principle of the low-stress life style is *balance* — the proper proportion of work and play, of challenge and ease, of stress and relaxation, of striving and taking it easy, of companionship and solitude, of exercise and rest, of discipline and self-indulgence. To achieve this proportion means arranging one's life in such a way that one's needs are being fulfilled in a balanced way, that one is not overloaded with any of the experiences or events that produce intolerable stress, and also that one is not deprived of significant challenge and stimulation. Chapter 8 deals with this conscious approach to designing one's life for low-stress living and working.

The second key principle of the low-stress life style is *adaptation*, that is, the *psychological skill* of taking things in stride — of observing what is happening, of reacting strategically and maturely, and of letting provocations pass away and die out once they are over with. It includes the ability to relax physically and to unwind easily, the ability to monitor one's immediate reactions in stress situations and to consciously de-escalate one's internal arousal level at will. This is the basic skill imparted by stress reduction training, described more fully in Chapter 6.

A low-stress life style need not be boring or understimulating. Boredom and lack of challenge actually induce anxiety in and of themselves when they are prolonged and unrelieved. With a learned combination of adaptability and balance, one can continuously design and redesign his living pattern for the maximum in enjoyment, stimulation, and achievment, with the minimum in unrelieved stress. Exhibit 3-2 contrasts some of the features of the antistress life style with those of the stressful life style. You can add other factors to this list, based on your own experiences and views.

Notice that these descriptions of life style focus on behavior — *what the individual does* — that contributes to the continuing stress or lack of it that he experiences. One's life style is a matter of choice, and although quite a few people would rather believe that their lives have been designed and programmed by outside forces, the key to adopting the low-stress life style is in accepting responsibility for the way in which one lives.

Certainly, very few people would experience all the stressful factors identified in Exhibit 3-2, but many people live within patterns that have a number of these elements. In this respect, Exhibit 3-2 might serve as an assessment tool for reviewing one's life style and for deciding on constructive changes. Chapter 8 offers a variety of concepts and strategies for this purpose.

EXHIBIT 3-2.

Stressful Life Style	Low-Stress Life Style
Individual experiences chronic, unrelieved stress.	Individual accepts "creative" stress for distinct periods of challenging activity.
Becomes trapped in one or more continuing stressful situations.	Has "escape routes" allowing occasional detachment and relaxation.
Struggles with stressful interpersonal relationships (family, spouse, lover, boss, co-workers, etc.).	Asserts own rights and needs; negotiates low-stress relationships of mutual respect; selects friends carefully and establishes relationships that are nourishing and nontoxic.
Engages in distasteful, dull, toxic, or otherwise unpleasant and unrewarding work.	Engages in challenging, satisfying, worthwhile work that offers intrinsic rewards for accomplishment.
Experiences continual time stress; too much to be done in available time.	Maintains a well-balanced and challenging workload; overloads and crises are balanced by "breather" periods.
Worries about potentially unpleasant upcoming events.	Balances threatening events with worthwhile goals and positive events to look forward to.
Has poor health habits (e.g., eating, smoking, liquor, lack of exercise, poor level of physical fitness).	Maintains high level of physical fitness, eats well, uses alcohol and tobacco not at all or sparingly.
Life activities are "lopsided" or unbalanced (e.g., preoccupied with one activity such as work, social activities, making money, solitude, or physical activities).	Life activities are balanced; individual invests energies in a variety of activities, which in the aggregate bring feelings of satisfaction (e.g., work, social activities, recreation, solitude, cultural pursuits, family, and close relationships).
Finds it difficult to just "have a good time," relax, and enjoy momentary activities.	Finds pleasure in simple activities, without feeling a need to justify playful behavior.
Experiences sexual activities as unpleasant, unrewarding, or socially "programmed" (e.g., by manipulation, "one-upping.")	Enjoys a full and exuberant sex life, with honest expression of sexual appetite.
Sees life as a serious, difficult situation; little sense of humor.	Enjoys life on the whole; can laugh at himself; has a well-developed and well-exercised sense of humor.

(continued)

EXHIBIT 3-2 (continued).

Conforms to imprisoning, punishing social roles.	Lives a relatively role-free life; is able to express natural needs, desires, and feelings without apology.
Accepts high-pressure or stressful situations passively; suffers in silence.	Acts assertively to re-engineer pressure situations whenever possible; renegotiates impossible deadlines; avoids placing himself in unnecessary pressure situations; manages time effectively.

REFERENCES

Berne, Eric. *What Do You Say After You Say Hello?* New York: Grove, 1972.

Fenly, Leigh. "Welfare Workers' Stress Takes Toll." *San Diego Union*, August 28, 1977.

Friedman, Meyer and Ray Rosenman. *Type A Behavior and Your Heart.* Greenwich, CT: Fawcett Press, 1974.

Goldberg, Herb. *The Hazards of Being Male.* New York: Nash Publishing Corporation, 1976.

Kostrubala, Thaddeus. *The Joy of Running.* Philadelphia: J. B. Lippincott, 1976.

Korzybski, Alfred. *Science and Sanity: Introduction to Non-Aristotelian Systems and General Semantics.* Lancaster, PA: Science Press, 1933.

Lamott, Kenneth. *Escape From Stress.* New York: Berkeley Medallion, 1975.

Whorf, Benjamin. *Language, Thought and Reality.* Cambridge, MA: MIT Press, 1956.

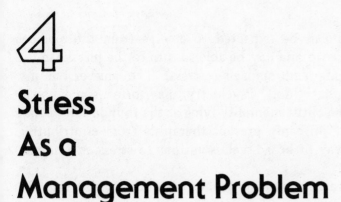

4

Stress
As a
Management Problem

ISN'T STRESS A MEDICAL PROBLEM?

The topic of stress, with its aspects of physiology and stress-linked disease, often brings to mind the medical profession. Our understanding of stress and its effects comes from the broad field known generally as *medical research*. Physiologists such as Harvard's Walter B. Cannon and biologists such as Hans Selye of the University of Montreal have laid the cornerstones of our understanding of stress as a human problem, and indeed, they have helped us to understand the effects of stress in the business world.

It seems quite natural to ask whether the solution to the

stress problem can be expected to emerge from the medical profession. Will we one day be able to turn to the physician for help in reducing and managing stress? The answer, in my opinion, is a flat "no." Psychiatry may offer some useful avenues, but the elitist mentality lying at the foundation of that profession will probably prevent therapists from contributing much in the way of broad-scale solutions to stress as a human problem.

Medical research will probably continue to add valuable pieces to the jigsaw puzzle of stress and health, and a growing number of practitioners such as Friedman and Rosenman, Kostrubala, Scaff, and others of a practical turn of mind will reach relatively large numbers of Americans. Nevertheless, I expect the rank and file of practicing physicians to remain relatively unaware of practical nonchemical avenues for stress reduction and even in many cases to resist their development and application.

To understand why the orthodox medical profession will probably offer inertial resistance to concepts such as stress reduction training and revision of patient life styles, we have to understand the current role of the physician and his economic roots in the practice of chemical medicine. Under the pull of a very powerful economic attraction, the majority of practicing physicians now constitute the marketing arm of the American pharmaceutical industry. What began as a modest industry, aimed at making available to physicians the fruits of medical research, has now mushroomed into a *$5 billion-a-year* business. Drug manufacturers now spend well over *$1 billion* a year in advertising and promotion of thousands of "ethical" drugs, virtually all of it directed not at the consumer but at physicians who are in a position to prescribe them.

By far the most popular drugs among physicians over the past 10 years have been the tranquilizers and other mood-leveling drugs. These drugs act to depress the functioning of the patient's central nervous system, chemically inhibiting the hormone reactions that constitute the stress response. The typical physician is bombarded with hundreds upon hundreds of drug advertisements in medical journals [such as the *Journal of the American Medical Association* (AMA)], direct mail pieces, and free samples. Drug companies employ more than 20,000 salesmen, known as detail men, who call on physicians, pharmacists, and hospital purchasing agents to push their products. There is an entire technical magazine, circulated free of charge to physicians, devoted to drug therapy.

Since the middle 1950s a very unhealthy metamorphosis has unfortunately taken place within the entire medical/pharmaceutical business. In an effort to keep incomes of physicians comfortably high, the American Medical Association has applied extreme pressure on medical schools to keep enrollments at comparatively low levels and has discouraged virtually all forms of paramedical practice that might make competent medical treatment available to Americans at lower costs. Because pharmaceutical companies provide a great deal of support, economic and otherwise, to the American Medical Association, practicing physicians have found themselves a party to a questionable marriage.

Economic temptations for physicians to raise the prices of their services have been virtually irresistible. In her provocative book, *American Medical Avarice*, Ruth Mulvey Harmer (1975) cites many instances in which physicians or groups of physicians have owned pharmacies or drug manufacturing companies and have increased the number of prescriptions of "their" drugs dramatically.

A conservative publication such as *Scientific American* (1973, p. 121) even remarked in one of its special publications about the huge number of prescriptions issued by physicians for ethical drugs. It cited a total of *1.5 billion prescriptions per year*, which equates to about 20 prescriptions per family per year. One of my colleagues, a psychologist, refers to her family doctor as "my pusher."

The AMA seems to approve of this practice. With the introduction of Medicare and Medicaid, costs of patient care suddenly increased, which suggests that competitive controls on prices do not exist in the medical profession as they do elsewhere.

The alarming incidence of fraud among physicians has now led many Americans to question their long-standing image of the doctor as a selfless, dedicated, overworked servant of mankind, gifted with an almost divine knowledge and skill, whose every word is self-evident truth, and who never taints his hands with anything so sordid as money. All the trappings of professionalism, such as the Hippocratic oath and the certificates on the wall, the white coat, the deferential nurses who serve him, and the remote cashier who takes the money, have served to delay this reappraisal. But the outrageous increases in healthcare costs in the United States and the conversion of substantial numbers of citizens into semiaddicts hooked on ethical drugs is now forcing a reappraisal. It will probably be a very harsh one.

The same drug merchandisers who have taught most of our physicians what chemicals to prescribe have also managed to develop a *$3 billion-dollar-a-year* market for nonprescription drugs such as aspirin and other headache remedies, laxatives, antacids, diet pills, sleeping potions, cough medicines, cold "remedies" (not one of which has ever been shown to work), and nonprescription tranquilizers. The sad state of affairs is that the pharmaceutical industry, with the passive cooperation of the great majority of practicing physicians, has succeeded in teaching the American public that the solutions to most of its personal and health problems are to be found in bottles of pills.

In my opinion, most physicians, having received the bulk of their practical medical education from the pharmaceutical industry and having an unavoidable economic stake in processing a large number of patients through their offices, will not be able or willing to revise their thinking about stress and stress-linked disorders. A number of doctors have remarked that perhaps as many as 80% of their patients suffer from nothing more than minor disorders caused by tension and anxiety.

What they don't say is that, if they cut down this steady flow of prescription buyers, they will slash their own personal incomes. In the present stituation, nonchemical forms of stress management simply do not make good economic sense to the ordinary physician. Stress has made medical care a seller's market.

Furthermore, the typical physician does not appear to understand the emotional and psychological roots of the American stress problem very well, judging by the fact that physicians themselves are among the most tense and anxious people in any of the professions. Nor do they enjoy especially good health themselves. Doctors, as mentioned previously, have the highest rate of alcoholism of any profession, a fact which may give you cause to wonder a bit the next time you visit your doctor. Caught up in the American upper-middle-class success ethic, wrapping their whole lives around making money and gaining feelings of significance by "curing" many people, many physicians apparently are the poorest equipped professionals for helping other people to deal with stress.

So, we can probably hope to gain some insight into stress from the efforts of medical researchers. However, those of us in the business world who are looking for ways to humanize American organizations and to help people reduce and manage job-related stress had better not hold our breaths waiting for doctors to provide the logistical avenues for making low-stress life styles available to large numbers of people. Clearly, stress in organizations is a *managerial problem*.

WHY WE MUST DEAL WITH STRESS
FROM THE MANAGEMENT POINT OF VIEW

From the point of view of the people who manage any organization, stress arises in two ways. First, they themselves as normal human beings experience pressure as a basic part of their own jobs. If they find themselves struggling with intolerable levels of stress, then they are paying too much in terms of their own health and well-being for the satisfactions they are getting. The quality of their own lives will not be what it should, and they will not be able to function as effectively as they should. They lose, and the organization loses. Second, if the workers of the organization experience intolerable levels of stress, then their lives will lack the quality to which they are entitled, and they too will not function as effectively as they should. Because managers have the special job of deciding and directing action, they — not the workers — have most of the opportunities to take the stress factor into account in daily business and to take constructive action toward stress reduction and stress management.

In this sense, every manager from top executive down to first-line supervisor finds himself faced with the need for a two-pronged approach to stress. He must first develop the necessary skills for reducing and managing the stress he himself feels in carrying out a challenging management job, and he must find ways to help the employees reduce and manage the stress they feel. This approach implies both a set of personal psychological skills on the part of managers and employees alike and an environment that they have jointly constructed and maintained to elicit human performance without the avoidable side effects of stress.

STRESS AND THE EXECUTIVE

Executive health and well-being are among the most critical resources available to an organization. A great portion of any organization's effectiveness derives directly from the personal effectiveness of the small number of people at the top. Those who set strategy, decide on major courses of action, allocate its major resources, and take the risks in guiding the organization invest themselves as human beings as well as merely their talents.

Some anecdotal evidence suggests that the "first tier" executives — that is, those who report directly to the chief executive officer — often experience stress more extensively than does the chief. According to Dr. Meyer Friedman (1974), those who make it to the very top have the opportunity to sit back and reflect on what's going on, more so than those who take direction from the top and try to carry out the chief's directions. Friedman also suggests that most chief executives tend toward the more benign Type B behavior pattern and have learned to deal with pressure situations without accumulating intolerable levels of stress.

In any case, it is a self-evident (but often overlooked) fact that the physical health and mental well-being of a small group of people — perhaps a dozen or two for a medium-sized organization — directly affect the quality of its overall operation. To the extent that they have learned to counteract the effects of the built-in pressures of executive life and to design their own life styles for low-stress living and working, they can function effectively. Those executives who have not learned these skills tend to function at lowered efficiency and to jeopardize their own health.

One of the ironies of American corporate life is in the timing of the executive health breakdown, which has become almost an expected stage of a senior executive's career. A grim anecdote has one middle-level executive saying to another, "Well, I just turned 45 and I just found out I have an ulcer. I wonder if I can make vice-president before I get my heart attack?" This type of gallows humor tends to surround the subject of executive health — when executives talk about it at all.

The age range of high probability for heart attacks among American executives is from about 45 to 65. How ironic it is that, just at the stage of such a man's career (they are generally men; fewer than 1% of American top executives are women) when he could be making his maximum contribution to the organization, a health breakdown takes him out of the action. The organization loses the value of his accumulated years of experience, his knowledge of the organization, his grasp of management practice, his maturity of judgment, and his strategic sense of leadership and direction just when they are at the peak of ripeness.

The postcardiac executive is usually a rather stereotyped figure in an organization. Some executives bounce back from a heart attack, but most of them never make it back into full stride. The dramatic change in personality and bearing often presents a touching, even pathetic picture. An executive previously known for his aggressive sense of drive and dedication may now move much more slowly, speak quietly, and carry himself with a kind of heavy-shouldered air of resignation. He may become cautious in his actions and decisions. He may seem less willing to go to bat for new ideas and unpopular causes. He portrays all the features of a marked man.

And indeed he is marked. The thing the cardiac survivor thinks about more than anything else is the possibility of having another attack. He will probably be under a doctor's care for a long period, with frequent checkups and possibly medication. He will probably have to cut out smoking, will watch his diet more carefully, and will spend a great deal of time re-evaluating his life and his priorities. During this period of readjustment, his colleagues will be careful not to overstress "Old George," lest they find themselves guilty of precipitating a recurrence. And George may begin to *act like* Old George, in unconscious fulfillment of the prophecy. During this period of adjustment, his contribution to the organization will be sharply curtailed, and little will be expected of him.

This kind of situation presents many costs to the executive who has suffered the health breakdown, to his colleagues, and to the organization. It makes a compelling case for a very "selfish," self-directed attitude on the part of an organization's executives, and it points to the need for all executives to learn the skills of personal stress reduction and stress management in order to continue to make their best contributions. Even if some executives may feel they cannot justify spending the company's money on executive stress reduction programs on the basis of their own health, they can certainly justify it from a dollars-and-cents point of view on behalf of the organization. The costs, in money and other forms of value, of a severe executive health breakdown make a compelling case for executive stress reduction. The executive should be a self-renewing resource for the organization and for himself, not one that is used up and discarded.

STRESS AND THE MANAGER

The operational manager, from the middle level on down to first-line supervisor, experiences stress physically the same way as does the executive, but the stressors vary somewhat. The manager may also respond to his stress differently and try to deal with it in some characteristic ways.

Many supervisors and middle managers feel pulled two ways during the day-to-day business of managing. They experience problems, pressures, and even demands from the employees they manage, and they also experience the pressure of demands imposed by the managers above them. In many ways, middle management can be one of the most frustrating areas of organizational life. Eager to succeed, anxious to perform well against the standards set for them, and feeling responsible for the malfunctions and failures that occur in their units, middle managers often find themselves on an emotional treadmill. Since a common management ethic is, "Keep your people on their toes," a manager may routinely put great pressure on his subordinates and may experience pressure from his boss in the same way.

Of course, many managers—perhaps most—have become so accustomed to tension and anxiety in their bodies that they no longer notice it. They feel just about the same each day, except for occasional levels of extremely high stress, during which they become conscious of their bodies' signals. Many managers apparently experience rather high stress levels routinely without being particularly aware of it.

One of the most dangerous features of managerial stress is its cumulative nature. If the manager has a high-stress life style and does little or nothing to counteract his chronic anxiety, then the stress score builds up over a period of years. When the bill comes due, the manager must pay off with a substantial health breakdown, with an escape into drinking, or even serious personal adjustment difficulties.

Most supervisors and middle managers tend to be comparatively young and therefore in comparatively good health. Whereas the 50-year-old executive may have serious concerns about health, especially as his colleagues and schoolmates begin dying off, the 35-year-old manager still enjoys the last remnants of that youthful feeling of immortality and indestructibility. He may joke about being hooked on cigarettes, about the extra 20 pounds of body weight, about the drinking habits, and about being out of shape, but his private feeling is, "I can always get back into shape and fix up my health when I get around to it." Unfortunately most 35-year-olds never get around to it. The transition from a youthful, energetic, active body at age 20 to a sedentary, anxious, probably overweight, and out-of-condition body at age 30 is usually never reversed for most Americans. Very few American men or women can say they are in better condition at age 30 than they were after graduating from high school or college.

For a manager leading the typical middle-class American sedentary life style and living with chronic job stress, the internal stress meter keeps clicking away. Just as the heavy smoker never expects to pay the bill for a self-inflicted affront to the body's chemical systems, so the young manager never expects to pay the bill for an unhealthy and dangerous life style. Yet this is precisely what happens. A heart attack, a kidney failure, or a liver degeneration at age 55 doesn't just arrive from outer space. One doesn't have *good* health one minute and a massive cardiovascular accident the next. The health breakdown is simply the logical conclusion of a self-induced disease development over a period of 10 to 20 years. One *develops* an ulcer over a long period of time, just as one plants a seed, waters, it, and cultivates the plant to maturity.

Unfortunately, the young manager, under the delusion of immortality, pushes the likelihood of health breakdown out of the range of consciousness and hopes for good luck. Each of us has a way of discounting the anticipated future, simply by keeping our attention on other things. One who considers a future event to be highly likely and extremely important will generally behave in the present in ways that account for the event.

The "discount rate" I apply to my eventual death, for example, is now quite high. When I pass age 60, I will probably begin to pay more attention to the possibility; it will affect my thinking in a variety of ways, most of which I hope will be constructive and creative. Apparently, most young and middle-aged people tend to apply a high discount rate to the possibility of health breakdown in their middle years. Yet cardiovascular disease in particular now strikes people at younger and younger ages. A 50-year-old executive whose health has given out was probably at one time a young manager who never thought it would happen.

This fact makes a very strong case for the young manager as well as the executive to assess carefully his life style and to adopt a comprehensive policy of stress reduction and stress management. It means that organizations can choose to *invest* in managerial stress reduction as a way to keeping their managerial people—one of their principal resources—healthy and functioning effectively.

STRESS AND THE WORKER

Most workers do not experience the same kinds of pressures that most managers experience. Nevertheless, many jobs entail stress levels that can create problems over the long term. For most workers, the most troublesome stressors are built into the structure of the job.

For example, a clerk behind the counter at my neighborhood post office finds that customers tend to become impatient, irritable, and less pleasant about midafternoon on most days. Standing in line, they become fidgety and anxious to finish their business. She finds their impatience and even impoliteness to be stressful. The heavy sigh she heaves as one customer leaves her counter and the next approaches is a signal of the stress she feels. Her glance at the clock doesn't signal laziness or lack of interest in doing a good job. It is her nonverbal expression of the desire to escape from the source of the unpleasant feelings in her stomach. She's experiencing contact overload and wanting some positive "strokes." ("Strokes" are simple messages from other people that acknowledge our existence as creatures.) She invariably brightens up a bit when I begin our transaction with a pleasant word or two.

A shy, sensitive worker may experience great anxiety for long periods when working for an aggressive, bullying supervisor. An individual who has significant personal adjustment difficulties, such as extreme lack of confidence or a highly reactive emotional nature, may even break down under the stress caused by job pressure and unrewarding interpersonal relationships.

As mentioned previously, workers who deal with distressed people as a basic part of their jobs tend to take on the bad feelings of the clients to some extent and often to empathize with the clients to the detriment of their own positive feelings. Furthermore, many of these kinds of clients — welfare recipients, for example — tend to be relatively unsophisticated and lacking in social skills. They often approach the workers with feelings of frustration and hostility, and they fail to recognize the workers' needs for positive contact. Consequently, these workers often suffer from an overload of relatively distasteful contacts and a deficit of positive strokes.

Some extreme job situations, which place the employee's life or physical well-being in jeopardy, can also cause continuing stress. Those persons who work with explosives, who work in high, precarious places, or who work with dangerous chemicals, dangerous animals, and so on, can all be expected to experience job stress. The long-term effects of these job factors will depend directly on the individual skills of the worker for handling stress.

Some jobs are so poorly designed that they place workers under constant, extreme levels of unrelieved stress. One of the best-known jobs in this category is the infamous job of air traffic controller at civilian airports. At a crowded airport, landings and takeoffs may occur at intervals of considerably less than 60 seconds. The typical controller is under enormous, unrelenting time stress because he must give instructions to several aircraft in quick succession and must stay alert for possible errors that may lead to serious accidents. Some large airports, such as Chicago's O'Hare Field, may average about one serious or "semi-serious" air traffic incident per day. Although the passengers seldom find out about them, the controllers are acutely aware of them.

Controllers report a constant, gnawing feeling of *fear* — an unshakable apprehension that the next one may be the unlucky one. They're afraid they may make a mistake, or that a pilot may misunderstand an instruction or make a wrong maneuver, and that a midair collision will lead to the horrible deaths of hundreds of people. The cumulative stress effects for these people are so extreme as to leave no doubt about the inappropriate design of the job. Controllers gulp antacid tablets like candy. They drink coffeee almost continuously throughout their shifts. Many of them report continuing nightmares about plane crashes or other catastrophes as well as episodic anxiety attacks triggered at random times. More than one controller has been carried off the job on a stretcher, with an acute anxiety attack, an emotional breakdown, or a severely bleeding ulcer. In the opinion of most observers, the Federal Aviation Administration has moved very slowly in trying to correct such an inhuman situation. Courts have held that employees who have emotionally induced health breakdowns connected with their jobs can qualify for workmen's compensation and paid psychiatric treatment. In some cases, courts have even awarded financial damages to cover the cost of rehabilitation and retraining for other, less stressful careers (Martindale, 1977, p. 71).

A new and alarming job stress phenomenon that we may be seeing to a much greater extent in the future has recently emerged. This is the incidence of "contagious" emotional breakdowns among groups of overstressed workers. Dr. Michael Smith, Director of Motivation and Stress Research at the National Institute of Occupational Safety and Health (NIOSH), described to me several incidents that he labels "mass psychogenic contagion." Others have referred to these outbreaks as "work hysteria." Dr. Smith says:

> What happens is that a worker — usually a sensitive, highly reactive one — will suddenly be seized with anxiety symptoms, which he or she interprets as symptoms of some form of physical illness. In the several cases we've investigated, the attack always followed the detection by employees of a physically noxious agent, such as a strong chemical odor in a factory setting.
>
> The first employee may feel dizzy, faint, or nauseated. When he or she tells neighboring workers about it, they immediately contract similar symptoms. Within minutes, there is an outbreak of actual illness, and a run on the health clinic.
>
> We investigated three such situations and found no physical stressors which could have caused the symptoms. In one case, the company physician stood next to me as a line of workers came in with various symptoms, demanding to be checked. In each case, he whispered to me "just hysteria, that's all." Then, one of the women vomited on him. It changed his impression of the seriousness of the situation.

Smith believes this phenomenon arises when a group of employees have been operating at high levels of chronic stress caused by certain "set-up" stressors. Chief among these, he believes, is the painful monotony and imprisonment of machine-paced jobs. Workers can continue just so long in this danger zone of chronic stress, and when some precipitating event or physical stressor arrives, they get pushed beyond their limits of tolerance (Colligan and Stockton, 1978, p. 93).

Mass psychogenic contagion, as Smith terms it, poses the frightening possibility of large numbers of workers simultaneously breaking down on the job. The disruption to operations and the attendant costs to the organization are nothing compared to the personal costs in emotional health and well-being payed by the workers themselves.

Although most employees don't have jobs quite so stressful as those discussed here, everyone experiences job stress to some extent. If the stress level is within the tolerance zone of the individual, then he can function effectively and can deal with the job as a constructive and satisfying part of his life. However, if the stress level is outside the limits *for a particular worker*, then it will inevitably create problems both in job performance and personal health and well-being. The price for intolerable stress must be paid, sooner or later.

This means that the managers of any organization actually have a fairly direct interest in the health and well-being of their workers; even if they aren't aware of it, managers have a stake in employee wellness. To the extent that an employee is overstressed, that person will generally not be able to function at full potential and effectiveness. Furthermore, the effects of job stress will add to the individual's total score of stress points and will have a direct impact on his health. Organizational programs in stress reduction and stress management make sense from the economic standpoint, from the broader standpoint of organizational effectiveness, and from the even broader humanitarian standpoint.

THE EFFECTS OF STRESS — HUMAN
AND ORGANIZATIONAL

By now, it should be apparent that I believe many people and many organizations pay an unnecessarily high price for chronic stress. I would venture a guess that as many as 25% of American workers — including managers — have substantial difficulties with their lives and jobs because of chronic, low-grade anxiety and insufficient avenues for escape and psychological recuperation. Perhaps another 25% are comparatively unhappy with their lives and jobs but manage to get along tolerably well. Probably 10% or less of American working people enjoy challenging, rewarding jobs and life styles that offer creative, manageable levels of stress.

It is helpful to identify some of the specific ways in which human beings pay the price of chronic, unrelieved stress. We need to look at concrete aspects of high-stress living in order to appreciate the specific penalties paid by the organization in which the overstressed person lives and works.

For the purposes of this discussion, let's lump job stress and the stress of private life together into a composite variable that we call *life stress*. By this we mean the total index of a person's emotional reactions to what's happening in all areas of his life. We do not include in the discussion physically induced forms of stress such as that caused by disease or injury.

When a person's life experiences impose frequent, unrelenting pressures and unhappiness on him and when he cannot or does not find avenues for significant periods of escape, rest, relaxation, and psychological detachment from the pressure situations, he begins to suffer — first in a general way and soon in specific self-damaging ways. His *stress-reactive behavior* will depend on his own particular personality pattern, his values and attitudes, and the particular variety of stressors he faces in the various areas of his life. For example, a high-pressure job with few real rewards, together with a deteriorating marriage and home life, may provide a powerful incentive for a middle-aged manager to increase his drinking to dangerous levels. On the other hand, if he never uses liquor, he may tend toward increased smoking, aggressive or hostile dealings with colleagues, or escapist activities such as absenteeism or extramarital affairs.

My general hypothesis about stress and behavior is this: *A person will act in ways that help to reduce the unpleasant and uncomfortable physical feelings caused by stress, within the constraints of his value system and his beliefs.* This is a key point in understanding stress-reactive behavior.

Stress feels physically unpleasant. After a long day's tension, one person may adjourn to a favorite cocktail lounge, another may go into isolation from family or others, another may put on jogging shoes and run a few miles, and another may go home to bully and intimidate spouse and children. Another may engage in a relaxing hobby; still another may slip into the fuzzy never-never land of Darvon or Valium.

These are all avenues that the individuals believe will help them feel better. Some are constructive avenues, whereas others may create extra problems that further diminish the quality of life for the individuals who choose them. Many people — perhaps most — choose avenues for stress relief quite unconsciously. Drinking a half liter of wine every evening at the local singles' bar may become "just my habit." Once a mode of stress escape becomes fully habituated, its user will probably not think of it as a reactive choice. It becomes simply something he "just does." Similarly, long-distance jogging or oil painting may become so enjoyable that the individual tends to view it as a pleasant experience in and of itself.

One of the key questions for examining one's life style in terms of stress-reactive behavior is: "What avenues have I chosen thus far for relieving the unpleasant feelings of stress?" The answer then leads the way to choosing more constructive avenues if one's current approach doesn't satisfy one's needs entirely, and for redesigning one's overall life style if necessary. Chapter 8 offers a thorough approach to such a personal review.

As a general proposition, we can say that the price a person pays for stress depends on how successfully he has designed his life style, the specific antistress modes of behavior he has adopted, and his personal level of neurological reactivity. All three of these factors offer possibilities for conscious improvement through deliberate antistress strategies.

Many people have learned to free themselves from chronic stress in various ways and to adopt low-stress life styles. However, an alarming number have not, and a large number find it very difficult because of a host of environmental influences, including their jobs. These people are the ones whose problems we need to study.

Specifically, then, what are the prices people pay for chronic stress? In general, chronic stress means a continuing deterioration in the quality of the individual's life. As mentioned before, we refer to life stress as the sum total of unrelieved stress the individual feels. This means that if the individual has significant avenues for escape, recuperation, and detachment, he will have a comparatively low life stress index, even if one area of his life tends to be strongly productive of stress. Life stress depends greatly on the *overall balance* of activities and experiences in one's life.

Of course, the index of chronic life stress and the index of quality of life are somewhat subjective, but we can apply some fairly specific criteria to both variables and develop a reasonably reliable yardstick for self-assessment. For example, a severe drinking problem almost always reduces one's job effectiveness, damages his interpersonal relationships, and jeopardizes his health. These outcomes certainly represent losses in the quality of life.

Similarly, drug addiction or heavy use of various "recreational chemicals," such as marijuana, interferes with a person's ability to carry out the normal business of a happy, challenging life. Both of these modes represent attempts to escape from the stressful reality the individual experiences. Unfortunately, they cause a vicious cycle that tends to make reality all the more unrewarding.

Escape into the foggy, detached, ultracomfortable world of tranquilizer dependency — also a counterproductive stress-reactive form of behavior — quickly deteriorates the quality of an individual's life. Life for these people is not enjoyable, merely bearable. They do not grow; they vegetate. They hang on grimly, with very little thought of adventure, change, experimentation, learning, or risk taking. They steadily drift out of contact with other people.

Some people escape from uncomfortable stress feelings by overeating. The "foodaholic" becomes preoccupied with pleasurable self-indulgence, substitutes eating for social interaction, gains weight, and jeopardizes his health. An overweight appearance makes fat people less attractive to others, makes them less inclined to exercise and enjoy physical activities, and causes them to tire easily. These effects certainly represent a loss in the quality of life for these people.

The organizational costs of stress derive directly from the collective individual costs. A person who works well below par because of a drinking problem costs the organization money. Other employees must take over parts of his work and often must do over work improperly done by the problem drinker. Drug abusers tend to be unreliable, subject to considerable absenteeism, and — if the habit has proceeded very far — marginally deficient in essential mental skills.

Many of the consequences of chronic stress are not so visible and easily recognizable as alcoholism or drug abuse. Much of it manifests itself in such general ways as habits, transactions with other people, and general coping styles. A worker who insults or affronts customers or who snaps at fellow workers has a negative impact on the organization's effectiveness, although it may be rather difficult to isolate and quantify that impact. Having two or three drinks over lunch does not qualify as alcoholism, but it does definitely impair the individual's mental faculties for most of the afternoon.

A person's relative level of *social adjustment* and maturity is a key element in the index of life stress that he experiences (especially in the level of job-stress). It seems that the person who has developed a high level of maturity, social skills, and adaptability to circumstance is much better equipped to ward off the stressful effects of a high-pressure job or situation. Therefore, learning stress-reduction skills amounts to learning a higher level of personal adjustment, that is, of maturity. We can conclude that to have the organization's managers pay specific attention to the nature of human growth and to create activities and conditions that promote it is a good idea. Human "capital" requires even more careful development and preservation than do the traditional forms of physical capital. This heretical point of view would have been considered laughable 10 to 15 years ago, but as we enter the last quarter of the century, it has a compelling attraction. It will not be easy to implement, by any means, but it is none the less necessary for being difficult.

STRESS AND THE BOTTOM LINE

Any attempt to estimate a dollar cost of chronic stress in a business organization or in American business in general, would of course involve gross guesswork and speculation. That's what I have done (brazenly) in this section. As an intellectual challenge, which may lend a measure of perspective to our thinking, let's make some crude assumptions about stress effects in a hypothetical business organization and see what the bottom line impact might be.

For our calculation, we'll consider an industrial firm of about 2,000 people, with gross sales of about $60 million per year. Here is a list of assumed parameters for our hypothetical organization:

Size:	2,000 people
Sales:	$60,000,000/year
Profit:	5% = $3,000,000/year

Average salary (gross average for all employees):	$6.00/hour
Personnel cost (salary + overhead costs):	$100/person-day
Absentee rate (excluding vacation):	4% = 10 days/person-year
Turnover rate (assume stable size of workforce)	5% = 100 people/year
Turnover cost (advertising, hiring, processing, etc.)	$1,000/person

The figures assumed here for absenteeism, turnover rate, and personnel costs are fairly conservative. Some organizations experience absentee rates as high as 15 to 20% and more, and some have turnover rates in the neighborhood of 20%. Some jobs in particular have especially high rates of absenteeism and turnover.

Now let's speculate about some of the costs of stress. We'll look at the three key human factors of absenteeism, turnover, and job performance. Without trying to defend any one assumption too strongly, we'll simply select some reasonable sounding numbers, run out the costs, and compare them to profits.

Personnel analysts have long recognized the direct connections between an employee's regularity of attendance on the job and his general level of health and well-being. Obviously, a person who never uses sick leave at all can be assumed to enjoy quite good health and to approach the job with reasonably positive attitudes. Although we cannot assume that the employee who uses every day of the allocated sick leave during the year is trying to get away from the job, this fact does invite our attention.

If we find that a large fraction of the work force is absent a large number of days, we must begin to wonder whether some factors in the organization's environment might be making the day's work psychologically threatening or otherwise unpleasant for them. We can assume that, of the total number of missed days each year, some days result directly from unavoidable illness or injury and some result from personal distress or aversive attitudes toward the job. Virtually everyone who ever worked for an organization has at some time called in sick when he felt only half-sick. And just about everyone has, at one time or another, had a negative and deteriorating relationship with a boss or co-workers that made him want to stay away from work.

So we will assume that, for this hypothetical company, half of the absenteeism rate (or 2%) comes from unavoidable disabilities, and half comes from the effects of stress. In this 2% figure we include any genuine illness that is stress-induced as well as effects of life stress that may originate outside the job. We're saying in this estimate that about half of the missed days relate to stress fairly directly, although we do not claim that we are able to eliminate all of that stress and get back all of the missed days. This is simply a "What if?" analysis.

Similarly, let's assume that 3% out of the overall 5% turnover comes from natural causes such as retirement, people quitting because of voluntary changes in their lives or careers, and the occasional dismissal of an employee for specific cause. The remaining 2% we assume to arise from stress-related causes, such as intolerable job conditions (the welfare worker syndrome, for example), unfair or bullying treatment by supervisors, toxic or otherwise intolerable physical working conditions, or life stress originating outside the job that interferes with the person's ability or inclination to remain on the job. Again, we don't know exactly how much of an impact we in the organization can have on these forms of stress-related turnover, but we can price them in this little analysis.

The third factor, job performance, presents a much more difficult estimating problem. How can we tell how much a person's stress level affects his job performance? Indeed, how can we even measure that performance in such cases as clerical or scientific work? One easy way to dodge this dilemma and to stay in the quantitative domain is the notion of "overstaffing."

We assume that, if a large proportion of people experience stress levels that degrade their performance capabilities, then we will need more people to get a given amount of work done — and to achieve a given level of sales and profits in our hypothetical company — than we otherwise would. This approach allows us to assume a percentage figure, called the "overstaffing ratio," and to compute total personnel costs. Let's assume that our hypothetical company has a 5% overstaffing ratio — that is, 5% of the work force, or 100 people, are on the payroll because of the reduced performance of the others.

Before proceeding to calculate the personnel costs of these assumed stress parameters, we should really add one more factor that seems to have a fairly strong connection to human stress — the cost of antisocial acts on the part of employees. Such acts are theft, sabotage, deliberate waste or breakage, "invisible" slow downs, and the like. This is also a very difficult figure to estimate, so let's take a very conservative level of $10 per employee. This means that the theft of a machine by one employee gets apportioned across all employees, as an equivalent cost. Similarly for a temper tantrum that results in a broken window or a damaged typewriter. And, of course, we have no way of knowing which of these costs are stress-linked and which are simply isolated events. However, we recognize that overstressed employees are more likely to carry out antisocial acts, either against fellow employees or against the abstract "company," which they may choose to see as guilty and deserving of punishment.

Running out these costs, then, we arrive at a set of figures for our hypothetical company that look like this:

Stress-linked absenteeism:	$1,000,000/year
Stress-linked turnover:	$40,000/year
Performance degradation (overstaffing cost):	$2,500,000/year
Antisocial acts:	$20,000/year
TOTAL	$3,560,000/year

This total may raise your eyebrows a bit. Three and one-half million dollars per year going into stress-linked personnel costs? When we stop to realize that this company pays $200,000 every day in total personnel costs, the number takes on a less unreal proportion.

These figures represent some fairly conservative assumptions, yet they tell an impressive story. For instance, the stress cost we came up with actually exceeds the profit figure for the company! Stress, in this assumed case, costs about 5.9% of sales, compared to a profit figure of about 5%. Even reducing our conservative estimates by a factor of two still produces a substantial figure.

We can do some more "What if?" thinking with these figures. For example, what if we were able to reduce stress-linked absenteeism by an average of two days per year per person? This reduction would result in a saving of $400,000! Even a one-day reduction would net a savings of $200,000. Or conversely, we would have an equivalent increase in personnel resources available for increased production and generation of additional sales. Reducing the overstaffing ratio (admittedly a subjective variable) from 5% to 4% would bring a cost saving of $500,000 to this firm.

Human resources effectiveness analysis—even as simple as in this example—is a largely overlooked approach to cost saving and profit maximization in most firms. In nonprofit organizations, precisely the same approach applies, with the exception of the profit figure. A county agency, for example, can serve its constituency better with a given staff level by improving its human resource utilization. Conversely, it can provide the same level of service with a smaller staff and smaller budget.

The person-by-person cost of stress in our hypothetical firm is $1,780 (total stress cost divided by the number of employees). If we are so bold as to use this figure (which is probably a conservative estimate) as a national average, we can multiply it by 80 million workers and come up with the mind-boggling figure $142,400,000,000! A national cost figure for stress-induced loss of effectiveness and efficiency approaching $150 billion no longer seems unbelievable. Other researchers have pegged the costs of alcoholism and drug abuse alone at a staggering $30 billion a year.

Of course, we cannot simply snap our fingers and change all this in a second. The causes of stress run to the very foundations of our culture and into the basic patterns of peoples' lives. However, we can make an accounting of the stressors in the organization and systematically eliminate those that do more harm than good. With a practical, reasonable organization development approach such as described in Chapters 9 and 10, we can make a substantial start in that direction. Clearly, a stress reduction approach to the organization's climate and operations promises substantial improvements in the figures on the bottom line.

REFERENCES

Colligan, Michael J. and William Stockton. "Assembly-Line Hysteria." *Psychology Today*, June 1978.

Friedman, Meyer and Ray Rosenman. *Type A Behavior and Your Heart.* Greenwich, CT: Fawcett Press, 1974.

Harmer, Ruth Mulvey. *American Medical Avarice.* New York: Abelard-Schuman, 1975.

Martindale, Davis. "Sweaty Palms in the Control Tower." *Psychology Today*, February 1977.

"Life and Death and Medicine." *Scientific American.* San Francisco: W. H. Freeman, 1973.

5

Stress
and the Quality
of
Working Life

ORGANIZATIONAL ECOLOGY

Every business organization constitutes a social system, peopled by real human beings with real attitudes, values, feelings and behaviors, as well as a technical system with capital, materials, and the associated factors of production. Scientists who study organizational behavior are tending increasingly toward the integration of these two points of view into the study of *sociotechnical systems*. Fundamental to every sociotechnical system is a well-defined *social climate* within which its people live, work, and relate to one another.

Every organization, therefore, has its own distinctive

human ecology (or qualitative psychological environment) which strongly affects the overall emotional-cognitive processes of the people who work there. Although most top managers tend to think of their organizations as being economic enterprises, most of their rank-and-file employees think of their organizations as being primarily social organizations. One company president may ask another, "How are you doing?" which actually means, "What's the overall economic performance of the system under your guidance?" But a typical employee may ask a friend who works for another company, "How do you like your job?" which usually means two things: "Are you satisfied with the money you're making?" and "How do you feel about your work?"

The company with a beautiful record of economic performance may be seen by a majority of its workers as an unpleasant, dehumanizing, toxic place in which to work. Yet its top managers may well think they're doing a good job of managing.

Unfortunately, most American top managers of all kinds, not merely those who manage industrial firms, seem to consider the topic of employee attitudes, morale, and emotional responses to the organization's ecology as a relatively unimportant one. The unspoken principle is: "Unless it gets really bad, so as to jeopardize the production of the organization, don't worry about it." For most executives, employee attitude is simply not a variable of primary importance.

Beginning about 1970, the concept of *quality of working life* has slowly and steadily been gaining notice as a matter of top management responsibility. Largely as a result of governmental influence and the activities of organizations such as the National Center for Productivity and Quality of Working Life, as well as various academic centers, experimental approaches to humanizing the workplace are being evaluated. Efforts to improve labor–management relationships, to account for the needs and values of employees in operating organizations, to create developmental opportunities for women and minorities, and to make human resources development a part of management responsibility are proceeding at modest rates. Organizations such as the American Society for Training and Development have adopted a *human resources development* approach, in place of the outmoded cut-and-dried "training" methods of the past.

Programs in stress reduction and stress management in organizations fit in effectively with these other approaches to improving the quality of working life. As of this writing, I know of only a few organizations whose executives have experimented with stress reduction programs, but the training techniques are steadily gaining interest and support, especially in certain kinds of organizations in which pressure is a basic part of the working situation. We have begun to understand the enormous magnitude of the effects of unresolved stress on human health and well-being and to appreciate the effects of occupational stress on the quality of working life.

It appears that a two-pronged approach will be necessary to achieve a substantial reduction of human stress and to keep it down to levels that are compatible with human health and fulfillment. One approach is educational; the other is technical. First, Americans in all kinds of pursuits, not merely managers or full-time workers, must learn and apply some advanced human skills for reducing their individual levels of reactivity and for divesting themselves of the cumulative physical and emotional effects of stress. Stress reduction training techniques, described in Chapter 6, seem to offer a great deal of promise for this solution.

Second, those who direct and control American organizations of all kinds must begin to apply the knowledge we have in order to redesign organizational environments to make them human environments. Organization development methods such as the organizational climate survey, job analysis, and job redesign have much to offer for re-engineering the environments in which people live and work.

We can achieve significant advances in the quality of American working life only when the top managers of American organizations understand and apply current knowledge to human needs; when they decide to put the psychological health and well-being of the members of the organization in the same category with the economic well-being of the organization as an abstract entity; when they perceive and strive to improve the human "bottom line" simultaneously with the financial bottom line.

AN ECOLOGICAL MODEL OF OCCUPATIONAL HEALTH AND WELL-BEING

In keeping with the previously mentioned ecological view of organizations as being sociotechnical systems, let's look at the problems of stress, job satisfaction, productivity, and quality of working life from the point of view of a single individual in the organization.

From the point of view of organizational objectives, a person is working productively when he is working at high capacity, at tasks worth doing, and with acceptable competence. From the point of view of the person's own objectives, we can say he is working productively when he is doing the aforementioned things and receiving a reasonable level of compensation while staying within his own personally defined comfort zone of pressure, stress, and challenge.

To have an appropriate match between the person and the organization, *both of these conditions must be met.* Organizational needs must be served, or the individual will not have a job. Personal needs must be served, or the organization will not have a person to do the work. These two demands modulate each other in the day-to-day flow of activities in the productive organization. Because so much of top management theory is necessarily organization-centered, we need to add a person-centered model to enable us to look at the way the individual

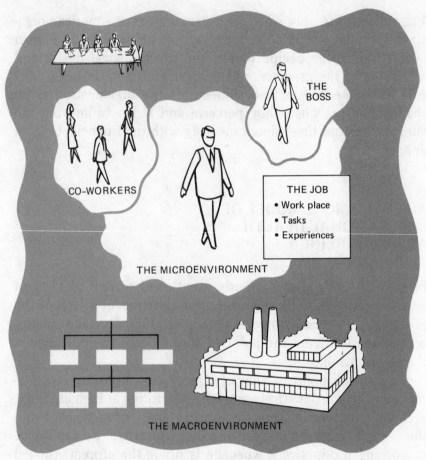

THE BOSS

CO-WORKERS

THE JOB
• Work place
• Tasks
• Experiences

THE MICROENVIRONMENT

THE MACROENVIRONMENT

EXHIBIT 5-1. The worker functions within a total ecological system.

interacts with the physical and abstract environment that constitutes his daily work life. Exhibit 5-1 shows an ecological view of work and the worker that we can use as a checklist of key factors in assessing the relative levels of pressure, stress, and productivity for the individual.

Assuming for the time being that we can specify fairly satisfactorily the elements of task productivity, competence, and compensation for some given job (an assumption that, unfortunately, is not always true), let's zero in on the comfort zone feature of the worker's interaction with the job and the job environment. Each person's comfort zone consists of a variety of variables, each of which must be within certain tolerance limits if he is to function effectively and to find satisfaction in any given activity. In the job and the job environment, we can single out some key variables that play an important part in defining the comfort zone in a general way for the vast majority of workers. Other factors may come into play for each individual, but there do tend to be certain relatively universal factors. The principal variables in overall job satisfaction and, consequently, in an effective balance between stress and reward for any one individual are:

1. Workload.
2. Physical variables.
3. Job status.
4. Accountability.
5. Task variety.
6. Human contact.
7. Physical challenge.
8. Mental challenge.

Each of these load factors plays a part in the worker's overall reaction to the job situation. Any individual worker can experience an overload or an underload on a given factor, depending on his appetite for that particular variable and the actual level of the variable at the time. Operating within one's comfort zone for some variable means experiencing an optimal loading of that particular variable over the long term.

The term *comfort zone* is not intended to imply that managers should make the employees' jobs as easy as possible or that they should try to remove all pressure from the employees. A coddling approach that sacrifices performance actually underloads the employees and forces them outside their comfort zones in other areas. The idea of the comfort zone is to find that level of loading for each of the factors that will optimize worker performance without producing undesirable side effects.

Let's examine each of these eight factors in more depth to see how we can use them to analyze various jobs and evaluate them for stress, productivity, and reward.

Workload

Workload makes itself readily known to the employee and his boss as a principal element of the job. An overload means that the worker simply has been assigned an unreasonable number of tasks or an unreasonable level of production to accomplish in a given period. This practice usually causes anxiety, frustration, and a sense of hopelessness and loss of reward. But an underload can cause exactly the same feelings. A worker without adequate work to do usually begins to feel frustrated, anxious about his worth and position in the social order of the organization, and distinctly unrewarded. Despite the views of many managers, very few workers will turn down *satisfying work* in favor of loafing. Curiously, as we have said earlier, work underloading can cause stress just as much as overloading can.

Physical Variables

Physical variables defining the comfort zone include temperature, humidity, sunlight exposure, weather, noise, air pollution, chemicals or processes harmful to the skin, vibration, and fatiguing tasks or positions for performing the work. The comfort zone for human beings in temperature is rather narrow — from about 65° F. to about 80° at most. Similarly, absolute silence can cause discomfort, just as high noise levels can. For most of these physical variables, some middle range defines the individual's general level of optimal functioning.

Job Status

Job status, interestingly, has a middle-range comfort zone instead of being open-ended. We know that jobs with low or negative social status cause some psychological discomfort in the individuals who perform them. Garbage collectors who want their job to be relabeled "sanitation specialist" are often laughed at, usually by people whose own jobs rate much higher on the social scale. In a few cases — not enough to be significant as a management problem — people have occupations that gain them so much social status that their entire lives are thrown into turmoil. Being a celebrity can be just as stressful as being an outcast. The number of movie stars and other famous people whose lives have been punctuated by tragedy, upheaval, suicide, alcoholism, and continuing misery attests to the possibility of status overload. As a management problem, however, status underload certainly constitutes the more interesting case.

Accountability

Accountability means the extent to which important outcomes depend on the individual's task performance in relation to the amount of control he has over results. Some jobs, such as those of psychotherapist, emergency room nurse or physician, or air traffic controller, have such a high risk element in performance and such a limited degree of control that the people doing them operate in an accountability overload condition much of the time. Without frequent relief and the variety provided by lower-accountability tasks mixed in with the main job tasks, these people invariably build up high cumulative stress scores. Accountability underload comes when the worker believes the work he is doing is meaningless, that nothing whatsoever will come of it. Or the worker may simply get no useful feedback about task effectiveness. In such cases, the worker begins to feel frustrated, alienated, and anxious about the quality of his contribution. To assign "busy work" to employees just to keep them moving is one of the surest ways a manager can lose their respect and induce eventual anxiety.

Task Variety

Task variety ranges all the way from deadly dull, monotonous, repetitive job tasks to confused, unpredictable, completely unprogrammed job situations in which the worker has very little idea about what to do next. Both create frustration, anxiety, and feelings of lack of real accomplishment. *Most of the dull, robotic jobs in American business have been designed by people who themselves have interesting jobs with high variety.* Despite reports that some workers actually seem to like monotonous jobs, I believe that many of them have merely made psychological adaptations to the jobs and feel they can handle them. I believe every human being has a basic neurological need for a moderate level of variety in physical experience in order to meet the needs of his brain and nervous system for stimulation. Very few people would deliberately apply for a monotonous job for its own sake. Most workers rate having an interesting job as being fairly high on their scale of priorities.

Human Contact

Human contact means nothing more than occasional satisfying transactions or even perfunctory encounters with other people at a rate and intensity that meet the individual's own needs. The need for "strokes," — as stated earlier, simple messages from other people that acknowledge our existence as creatures — is one of the most fundamental human needs. A job with too few contacts (such as forest-fire lookout observer, night watchman, or lighthouse keeper) needs to be enriched by occasional contact with other people to keep it within the job holder's own comfort zone. Conversely, contact overload (such as the kind experienced by busy personnel interviewers, welfare case workers, or counselors) can cause feelings of restlessness, anxiety, and desire for escape in those who perform them. Workers who deal routinely with such distressed people as welfare clients, therapy patients, people in personal crisis situations, or injured people often experience much greater accumulated stress than those who deal primarily with people whose lives are in good working order.

Physical Challenge

Physical challenge includes needs for dexterity, physical skill or strength, endurance, physical mobility, risk of personal danger, and opportunities to handle various physical artifacts or tools associated with the job. Some jobs are highly physical in their make-up whereas others require little more than the ability to talk and operate a ball-point pen. Physical underloading does not usually produce much anxiety or frustration unless the individual has a high appetite for activity. It does, however, force the worker to spend a great deal of his time in a sedentary mode, with no exercise or physical stimulation, which can lead to an overall inactive life style and consequent health problems. Physical overloading can lead to injury or illness if the demands of the task are beyond the capabilities of the individual assigned to perform it. A special category includes jobs in which the element of personal danger and risk of life forms a basic part of the task. Explosives experts, police officers, and construction workers among others can experience considerable stress induced by the risk features of their jobs.

Mental Challenge

Mental challenge includes brain activities which keep the individual psychologically involved with the job tasks. Processes such as observing, recognizing, memorizing, monitoring, comparing, evaluating, deciding, and reasoning all require a conscious thought process from the worker. It is a mistake to design a production job with the aim of eliminating all mental tasks from it. People perform more effectively and gain greater satisfaction when they must use their cognitive skills at least to some degree. They also perform much more effectively when they receive fairly immediate feedback about their performance, a fact that has been demonstrated repeatedly in industrial motivation studies. If the job itself contains built-in feedback mechanisms that allow the worker to evaluate his performance immediately, then he can zero in on those tasks and skills that get good results.

A mentally underloaded task actually prevents the worker from using his brain and often induces feelings of exasperation, frustration, detachment, and a desire to escape to something more stimulating. A mentally overloaded task, conversely, presents the worker with demands for mental activity beyond his level of competence and training, thus creating feelings of inadequacy and frustration. An optimally loaded task contains a level of mental challenge that is comfortable for the individual worker.

These eight job loading variables do not account for every single element of job satisfaction, but they suffice as an assessment scheme for examining various kinds of jobs. Exhibit 5-2 illustrates them pictorially with respect to the worker. Let's briefly review a few examples to see what we can learn about job design and worker satisfaction.

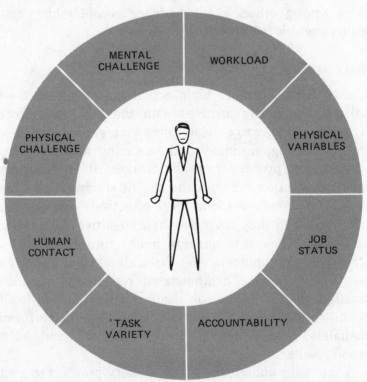

EXHIBIT 5-2. Each employee experiences a job stress total because of eight loading factors.

Interestingly, the job of *manager* is one of the most optimally loaded kinds of jobs in all of American business. For one thing, the manager usually has a great deal of discretion about how he can spend the day and so can choose to engage in activities that bring rewards. Managing involves a variable workload, and most managers who are overloaded for great periods of time inflict it on themselves. The technique of delegation is a built-in way for the manager to regulate his own workload to keep it in the comfort zone. Although most management jobs are not basically physical in nature, the manager can and should move freely about the physical facility, visiting others and tending to a variety of matters outside his own territory. And most managers, because of their status, enjoy fairly comfortable physical surroundings.

Job status, task variety, and human contact are also well represented in most management jobs. Accountability is usually fairly high, and the relative comfort associated with this variable depends as much on the individual doing the job as on the job itself. The management job also involves a challenging mental activity with the opportunity to learn and grow within the context of the job itself.

The job of *telephone operator* offers an interesting contrast. The workload virtually always stays within the individual's comfort zone, because she (most operators are women) receives calls on the basis of her availability to handle them. Except for some periods of heavy traffic, the operator can usually handle the workload without much discomfort. The physical surroundings are usually fairly comfortable, but the job is an extremely sedentary one. Very seldom does the operator have a chance to move about because the task requires her presence at the equipment. Overweight and lack of physical conditioning are common among full-time operators. Job status places the operator somewhere in the middle of the range of working people. For most individuals this is probably well within the comfort zone. Accountability usually presents few problems, because most operators have a clearly defined standard of performance. For some people, the job does not offer sufficient personal challenge — that is, it is not particularly achievement-oriented. For those people, the job may be somewhat underloaded in the accountability area. Task variety is usually underloaded for the job of telephone operator. In most situations, it requires only a few basic competencies, which can be quickly learned. It is an extremely repetitive job. Human contact varies with the situation. The operator gets a great deal of voice contact with the customers and may or may not experience this as being comfortable. In many situations, operators work side by side or within the same small facility. They can often chat among themselves during slow periods. On the other hand, privacy and seclusion are extremely rare. The job presents little in the way of physical challenge and little opportunity for the operator to diversify the tasks. Mental challenge ranges from low to moderate, depending on the other features of the job, how much the operator is supposed to know, whether she has other associated functions to perform, and the kinds of challenges that arise during the day-to-day performance of the job.

Notice how the eight-factor classification system focuses almost entirely on the worker as a person, rather than on organizational factors. Inasmuch as high productivity requires high involvement, commitment, and overall job satisfaction on the part of the producers, it behooves us to understand what workers get from their jobs.

You may find it interesting to assess some other kinds of jobs from this point of view. Take a pen and paper and run a quick review of the jobs of airline stewardess and highway construction worker. What major differences do you find? How might these affect the kinds of individuals who seek these jobs, how well they like them, and how long they stay? Which of the eight factors, along with pay and benefits, do you think might have the most impact on turnover? On absenteeism?

Now see how many jobs you can list that you consider optimally loaded in most or all of the eight factors. How does this evaluation compare to your subjective evaluation of the job as a satisfying thing to do? What job would be the least satisfying for you personally, on the basis of these factors?

To fully account for employee satisfaction and motivation, we must connect these eight factors with the obvious factor of pay and benefits and with the overall social climate in which the individual works. And we must give special emphasis to the quality of the supervision he experiences. These factors, taken as an integrated whole, define the level of employee satisfaction and reward in connection with job performance and point the way toward strategies for increasing productivity as well as reducing stress and improving the quality of working life.

STRESSORS IN THE EVERYDAY WORK ENVIRONMENT

By identifying the individual stressors in the work situation, we can assess more accurately the factors that bear on any one individual doing any one job. As before, we'll consider a stressor to be any element — tangible or intangible — of a person's interactions with his environment that leads the person to experience a significant level of stress. Stressors are in the environment; stress is in the person. For convenience in cataloguing some of these factors, we can subdivide them into three categories — physical factors, social factors, and emotional factors.

Physical factors are those aspects of the individual's immediate personal surroundings that cause him to become physically stressed or to become anxious about possible consequences. Social factors are those having to do with the individual's transactions with other people as part of living and working in the organization. The stressor in this case is another human being. Emotional factors are those abstractly conceived aspects of the worker's relationship to the environment that lead to anxiety, frustration, apprehension, anger, or other stress-derived emotions.

Physical factors include any of the following in excessive amounts:

Heat.
Cold.
Humidity.
Dryness.
Noise.
Vibration.
Air pollutants (dust, smoke, strong odors, chemical vapors, etc.).
Physical injury.
Radiation (x rays, gamma or beta rays, radio or microwave radiation).
Strong sunlight.
Ultraviolet or infrared radiation.
Dangerous machinery.
Dangerous animals.
Potentially explosive or toxic substances.

Social factors include the following:

The boss.
Co-workers.
Customers or clients.
Dangerous or potentially dangerous people.
Public scrutiny of one's activities.
Committee or "judicial" groups to which one must report.

Emotional factors include the following:

Deadlines.
Perceived risk of physical injury.
Personal financial risk.
Extreme accountability for high-risk tasks.

Ego risk (e.g., fear of loss of status or self-esteem).

Expectation of failure.

Expectation of disapproval from important others.

You can probably add other factors to these lists. Begin to develop your overall awareness of stressors around you as a means of improving your own stress tolerance and as a means of detecting the effects of stress in your employees.

Let me reinforce a critical point here about the physiology of stress. Each of the factors listed can generate the physiological stress reaction *within a human being's body*, when it exists in a sufficiently intensive form. For example, a high noise level is not only annoying; it also arouses an autonomic response in the bodies of those who must endure it. The classic fight-or-flight reaction sets in, and the individual becomes stressfully aroused. Similarly, a high radiation level, even though the individual may not be consciously aware of it, will trigger the physical stress reaction. A radiation level capable of this is, of course, extremely dangerous to survival.

We are dealing here with a variety of factors found to various degrees in the American business setting. Many of these factors can be controlled or minimized by concerned managers.

Unfortunately, most working Americans today rack up total stress scores that take them at least temporarily out of the comfort zone that affords a high quality of life. Furthermore, few of them so far have learned the skills of deep relaxation or even of quiet detachment necessary for them to counteract the accumulated stress successfully. The manager must account for the accumulated effects of the American social setting and the American life style in studying the effects of stress on his employees.

Such a study must involve an individualized approach because people differ widely in the amount of stressful experiences they have and in their abilities to counteract the effects of those experiences. For example, an office worker whose job tasks do not involve any unusual degree of pressure, who works with fairly congenial people, and who receives supportive supervision from the boss may suffer from an underdeveloped level of maturity and self-esteem and may have recently experienced a number of difficult problems in his private life. If so, he will be operating outside the comfort zone for much of the time, even though no specific feature of the work situation involves an unreasonable level of pressure. In such a case, the manager must still deal with the effects of the sum total of this person's stress experiences. To this extent, the person's private life does indeed affect job performance.

Conversely, another employee may have developed a high degree of maturity, self-esteem, and stress relief skills. This person may take on high-pressure jobs, may function well against fair but demanding deadlines, and may hold up better than many others in the occasional overload situations that arise. Most of the employees will, of course, fall in the middle of this range. Each person will have his own distinct combination of life stress, job stress, and stress relief skills, the summation of which will determine his overall stress score at any one time. Exhibit 5-3 illustrates this overall balance of forces.

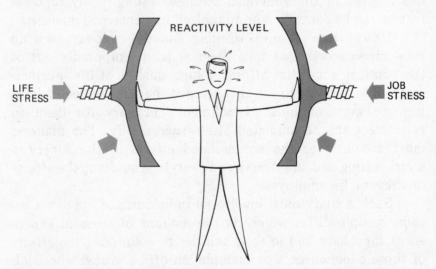

EXHIBIT 5-3. A person's total stress "score" depends on job stress, life stress, and his or her own reactivity level.

From the manager's point of view, the problem has now become one of matching people and job tasks in such a way as to help *the majority* of the employees to operate effectively and productively within their individual comfort zones of total life stress. The manager can try, to whatever extent seems practical, to help those who find themselves in overstressed modes, but he must establish some minimum level of performance that all workers must meet in the long run. This function of the manager has always been part of his job, of course. However, now that stress has emerged as the twentieth-century American disease, managers must face this problem more often, and they must solve it more creatively than was necessary in the past.

UNRELEASED HOSTILITY, FRUSTRATION, AND ANGER

One factor in business life that compounds the stress problem for the individual is the existence of powerful social norms that prohibit the overt expression of so-called negative emotional reactions. Although feelings of anger, frustration, and hostility are completely normal, and although every living human being has them from time to time, American social rules make the expression of these normal emotions something to be frowned on.

To lose one's temper in a problem situation is to expose one's self as being somehow less than mature, less than adequate. To show frustration with the behavior of others, especially in their presence, is to invite the judgment of onlookers as to one's skills in living and working. Direct conflict is one of the most feared and most carefully avoided aspects of human interaction in the business world. So many people live in unconscious (and sometimes conscious) fear of out-and-out conflict with another person, or of becoming drawn into a conflict between two other people, that manipulation and maneuvering have become the primary means for resolving strongly felt differences.

The result of this fear of dealing with human emotion directly is twofold. First, it leads to an enormous waste of human energy by inefficient political machinations, manipulation, factionalism, adversary behavior, attacks and counterattacks within the socially accepted processes of staff meetings and planning sessions, and downright dishonest dealings with others who should be colleagues and mutual protagonists in a common business endeavor.

Second, and perhaps more important in the long run, it leads to *buried emotion*. As psychiatrist Theodore Isaac Rubin (1969) observes, "Anger may be buried, but it's buried alive." It emerges again and again in various forms. It may emerge as passive resistance to cooperation with others. It may present itself as sugar-coated manipulation or as two-faced, hypocritical styles of dealing with others. The outwardly pliable and amenable person who lives in morbid fear of arousing the anger of others and of expressing his own anger overtly will often resort to the most despicable schemes for achieving occasional dominance over others. The pleasant, smiling, anxious-to-please Mr. Goodguy or Little Mary Sunshine can be the most deadly adversary in a hidden conflict. They attack from behind not because they mean to but because their inability to express normal, occasional angry feelings honestly forces them to actualize the feelings in whatever other ways they can find.

Clearly, one of the hallmarks of maturity and social competence is the ability to take things in stride and to avoid becoming upset or angry at small provocations. Unfortunately, many people can't tell the difference between not becoming angry in the first place and burying the anger they have experienced in order to give the impression of calmness.

Rubin (1969) claims that buried anger causes a great deal of psychosomatic disease and that many neurotic symptoms found in normal people arise from the internal turmoil between natural emotions and the superimposed controls used to keep behavior in unreasonable bounds — that is, boundaries that are difficult for the person to maintain. He cites symptoms such as headaches, depression, generalized anxiety feelings, sleepless-ness, overeating, excessive verbosity, overworking, loss of interest in sex, excessive alcohol consumption, drug abuse, and constant fatigue as consequences of frozen or bottled-up anger. These symptoms may also indicate other problems as well, of course.

Although I question Rubin's overly simplistic view of un-expressed anger as the root of nearly all human difficulty, it does seem that the physiological results of this kind of overcon-trol imposed on natural bodily processes can very seriously affect health and well-being. It is as if one were trying to oper-ate a machine in ways that counteract or disrupt many of its internal processes. The consequences for the machine are not likely to be beneficial or pleasant.

A far-reaching and as yet fairly idealistic view of humaniz-ing business organizations involves redefining the role of human emotion in everyday living and working and finding legitimate avenues for straightforward actualization of all normal emotions in *constructive activities* pertinent to the objectives of the organization.

Until our prevailing social norms have shifted far enough in that direction, the enlightened manager can at least develop a high level of awareness of these buried emotions in his em-ployees and co-workers. He can learn to detect the early signs that he may be causing unreasonable difficulties for his em-ployees or intensifying the stress levels they experience.

NEED FOR STRESS RELEASE ACTIVITIES IN THE WORK ENVIRONMENT

People should not have to escape from work in order to escape from stress. They should not have to experience work as *primar-ily* stressful or distasteful. But unfortunately, for most American workers, work is something you have to do to make ends meet. According to Dr. Frederick Herzberg (1965), a long-time student of motivation in American industry, most organizations compensate people for their work with symbolic rewards that they can "spend" only away from work. The annual vacation becomes a chance to get away from the job. The pension or retirement program offers something positive and pleasant only after one leaves the organization. Seldom, says Herzberg, do the managers of an organization design jobs and daily work activities in such a way that they provide intrinsic psychological rewards in and of themselves. Quite the contrary; most of the jobs in American business organizations, with the notable exception of management jobs, are relatively impoverished in one or more of the basic ingredients that lead to worker satisfaction.

Not only is it possible to design jobs that tend to maximize psychological involvement and sense of worker satisfaction, it is also possible to design work situations and activities that provide opportunities for stress relief and psychological refreshment. I believe this and other approaches to the quality of work life will gain considerable ground in the years to come. What seems preposterous or idealistic today will be accepted 10 years from now and will be considered essential 15 to 20 years hence. (Albrecht and Butteriss, 1979).

Counseling programs aimed at occupational health and mental hygiene can open up very important avenues for the very highly stressed employee who is having great difficulty in managing his life. More and more medium and large organizations are developing support services to help employees overcome personal problems such as drinking, drug abuse, and emotional disorders.

Top managers of these organizations consider these services to have benefits for the organization in terms of sustaining productivity, holding down costs due to absenteeism and turnover, and also in meeting the social obligations of the organization to the community from which it draws its work force. A large organization can maintain a full-time staff psychologist or counselor to help individuals with their personal difficulties, or it can maintain a contractual on-call relationship with one or more professionals of this type. A company physician or occupational health nurse can direct a troubled person to outside professional resources when necessary. The small company can, at the very least, direct the troubled employee to these kinds of services and to community resources that may not cost the individual anything.

Programs in stress reduction training, conducted in the organizational setting, can also provide significant avenues for stress relief. Stress reduction techniques enable the individual to live his life more effectively and consequently to function better on the job. In addition, a person who manages stress well in all aspects of his life can handle the pressures of the job much more effectively. Investing even a small amount of company time and organizational resources in stress reduction training shows the employee that top management considers the occupational health and well-being of all employees to be an important matter.

The increased flexibility provided by *autonomous time structuring* gives the employee another way to relieve stress in the work situation. The worker who is imprisoned by a piece of equipment for a full shift will experience boredom, frustration, and vague feelings of anxiety, whereas the worker who can move about from time to time can find psychological refreshment. Merely by rearranging a few elements of the job, managers can provide increased time flexibility with little or no sacrifice in manning efficiency and with an increase in alertness, mental acuity, and even motivation. More and more organizations have experimented with flexible working hours with generally pleasing results. Workers who can schedule their work day flexibily within pre-established limits find time for personal errands before and after work, and those with requirements for child care often find it easier to attend to them. The consequent feelings of freedom and the elimination of excessive rushing and time pressure contribute to greater job satisfaction and lower stress levels.

Employee activities during breaks at the work facility can

provide valuable avenues for psychological refreshment. Making Ping-Pong tables and other game equipment available for use during lunch and coffee breaks gives workers a means for mild exercise, recreation, and mental refreshment. Some organizations sponsor lunch-time and after-hours sports activities such as jogging, tennis, handball and swimming in the interests of a healthier work force.

An interesting break-time activity pioneered in Japan may well find its way into American organizations soon. This is the "aggressive exercise room," sometimes whimsically referred to as the "hostility room." It is merely a small room equipped with a few punching bags or a few inflatable figures that bounce back up when punched or struck with a small bat. Employees — and managers, too — can wander in on a break, take a few enthusiastic swings, and rid themselves of stored-up aggressive or hostile feelings. Although this may seem somewhat peculiar at first thought, any psychologist will testify to the value of this simple form of energy outlet as an aid to mental hygiene.

One university in Southern California, organized and managed along creative humanistic lines, gives its employees a few "goof-off days" each year, to be used as they see fit. The president of the university, an energetic and active man, believes that the time off is more than repaid in renewed enthusiasm and loyalty to the group. Furthermore, since a large number of the employees are knowledge workers, their productivity is not a strict function of hours worked. They get their jobs done in any case, and they use their goof-off days sparingly so as to manage their workloads effectively.

The emerging technology of *job engineering and job redesign* also offers significant avenues for directly reducing job-induced stress, as described in the next section. The extended application of these same concepts to the area of *environmental engineering*, described in the subsequent section, can have dramatic effects on the overall quality of working life in the organization as a social system.

At the level of the work group, the techniques of *team building* can help enormously to build morale, cooperation, and team spirit while reducing conflict and minimizing stress. Using the services of an outside consultant, the group members examine their relationships, modes of operating, and group norms, and they make new decisions as necessary about how to work together and live together in the organizational setting.

PRINCIPLES OF JOB ENGINEERING AND JOB REDESIGN

One of the most promising approaches available to managers for stress reduction and productivity improvement is in the new science of *job engineering,* which is a renewed application, updated by today's knowledge of the behavioral sciences, of Frederick Taylor's (1911) turn-of-the-century scientific approach to laying out the work. Taylor's methods, which were extremely effective in his time for improving the efficiency of purely tool-oriented work processes in the social setting of the hard-work ethic, are now so outmoded that their strict application to most job designs causes inevitable problems with employee motivation, job satisfaction, and even productivity itself. However, Taylor's basic idea is still valid: Analyze the work and the worker, and match the job and the person for greatest total effectiveness. In today's work world, total effectiveness must include the needs, values, and behavior patterns of the worker himself, in addition to the production objectives of the organization.

Job engineering calls for an integrated sociotechnical approach to deciding how the worker is to function on the job. No longer can we simply design the job in isolation from the human processes on the assumption that the person is merely an extension of the machine or the work station. We need a much more realistic merger of the behavioral and the technical views. Job engineering includes the methods of analysis, task design, redesign, and integration of human needs into the task structure. It can and should be applied at all levels of the organization, to every single job, including management jobs.

Exhibit 5-4 shows the basic steps in the cyclic process of job engineering. They are:

1. Define the job objectives.
2. Define the job conditions.
3. Define the job processes, equipment, and materials.

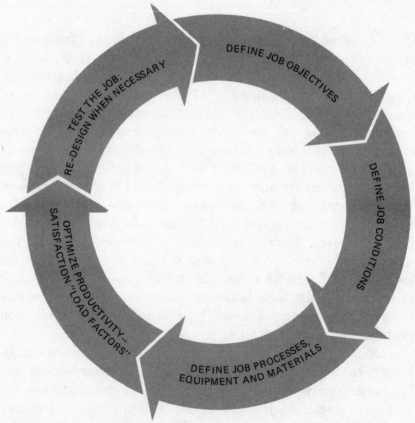

EXHIBIT 5-4. The job engineering cycle optimizes the relationship between production, stress, and job satisfaction.

4. Optimize the productivity–satisfaction "load factors."
5. Test the job design.
6. Re-evaluate and redesign the job whenever necessary.

This model applies to the design of brand-new jobs just as it applies to the evaluation and redesign of existing jobs. Indeed, most jobs have already been designed, and much of current management action in the area of *job enrichment* consists of making improvements in on-going work processes. Let's examine these steps one at a time to see what specific approaches a manager can take to develop a high-productivity, high-reward, low-stress job.

Define the Job Objectives

Every job, including the boss's job, should aim at accomplishing something of recognized value. Too many jobs in American business organizations are activity oriented rather than result oriented, especially white-collar jobs and so-called knowledge work jobs. Define the specific, tangible, payoff-oriented results you want from the job under consideration. If the job is part of an interlocked family of jobs, then you should also define the overall objective of the task family.

You can probably define the objectives of the job on two levels. One level is the *mundane objective*, such as "deliver the company mail," "answer the telephone switchboard," "write computer programs," "sell fabrics to wholesalers," or "supervise the accounts receivable section." Another level is the *creative objective*, defined along lines that invite the worker and the manager to think in terms of overall payoff, such as "help the members of the organization transfer information and ideas among themselves," "put people in touch with one another," "convert data into useful information," "match our products with the needs of our customers," or "keep our cash inflow healthy." Add any others that seem pertinent. Without a clear definition of the job objectives, you have no way to measure performance, no way to decide what the job is worth, and no way to decide who is qualified to perform it.

Define the Job Conditions

Decide what circumstances — physical, social, and psychological — will surround the performance of the work. Where will the person work? Under what physical influences or constraints? Who else will directly affect the performance of the job? Are customers or clients directly involved? How, and to what extent? Is handling money a part of the job? What physical risks are necessary? What time constraints, schedules, or specific locations are involved?

In this step, don't become imprisoned by tradition. Don't define a secretarial job solely in terms of those you've seen. Don't be afraid to add novel elements to the work situation or leave out those that don't seem to serve a useful purpose. Stick to those aspects of the job situation that can be tied directly to the achievement of the job objectives.

Ask "Why?" Why must the telephone operator sit down or stay in one spot? Why must the route salesman drive a car? Why should one person operate only one machine? And ask "Why not?" Why not have a male secretary? Why not have a female executive assistant? Why not require that each person be capable of operating a variety of machines? Why not have the employee figure out the best way of doing the job?

Define the Job Processes, Equipment, and Materials

Determine in general terms how the employee is to merge the elements of the job activity and what operations he needs to perform in order to achieve the job objectives. Make a flow diagram showing the major steps in the job process, and show how the employee must proceed. Also show how this job interacts with others, if it does in any significant way. *Do not overdefine the actual tasks.* Leave the final design of the details of the task to the employee's ingenuity whenever possible, so that the employee can "buy into" the job by adding something of himself. Leave room for the employee and the supervisor as a team to test and refine the job design during day-to-day operation. And allow a certain amount of discretion for changing some aspects of the job again for the same reasons.

Optimize the Productivity–Satisfaction Load Factors

Next, analyze the proposed job design from the point of view of the combined variables of productivity and worker satisfaction. How much work can the employee get done and how well? What are the rewards, both psychological and physical, the employee can derive from doing the job, and what is the relative degree of pressure and stress he will experience? Evaluate the relative loading of the job design in each of the eight categories of Workload, Physical Variables, Job Status, Accountability, Task Variety, Human Contact, Physical Challenge, and Mental Challenge (see pages 139–144). Identify any factors that might present a typical employee with a pronounced underload or overload. Enrich the job in those respects by adding, deleting, or modifying design elements to bring those factors back within the comfort zone.

Test the Job Design

Don't assume that the job is well designed once it comes off the drawing board. Many industrial engineers and other job designers have been embarrassed to find that the jobs they designed simply couldn't be performed by the employees — or that the employees *wouldn't* perform them. The equipment or the work station might be unworkable for reasons the designer could not anticipate. The employees might consider the job demeaning and insignificant and might sabotage it by working slowly and uncooperatively or by refusing to follow the procedures. A lack of sufficient mental challenge may produce boredom and detachment. Highly technical work processes might lead to high error rates that the worker would find discouraging. You must test the total combination of person, equipment, materials, processes, and surroundings as an integrated whole, and you must measure *both* productivity and employee satisfaction before you can say the job is well designed.

Re-evaluate and Redesign the Job When Necessary

Don't assume that a job, once designed, will continue to provide a good combination of productivity and satisfaction indefinitely. Every job needs to be retested and re-evaluated from time to time and redesigned when circumstances call for it. As social values shift, as technology provides new alternatives, and as demands for the organization's goods or services shift, some jobs must shift to enable the organization to adapt successfully. And as employee attitudes and values shift (which they seem to do from one generation to the next), jobs need to evolve in such a way as to provide the requisite rewards that will invite people to perform them well.

Obviously, designing a job from scratch presents a much greater challenge than evaluating an existing job and redesigning it. Except for the fact that tradition and the status quo can sometimes imprison our thinking about how jobs should be done, it is usually easier to start with something that exists rather than to dream up an entirely new design. On the other hand, since so many of the jobs in American business organizations seem to lack one or more of the important ingredients we've been studying, our first priority should be to evaluate existing jobs anyway. The potential for job enrichment as a means of improving American productivity and increasing the quality of working life is almost beyond comprehension.

Let's take a brief look at a few typical jobs and apply this assessment approach (Albrecht, 1978). The job of *manager*, for example, should not be exempt from the application of these principles. Every manager should have a set of clear, understandable, worthwhile, and important objectives for his approach to the problem of running the organizational unit. The mundane objective may be "supervise the blood dialysis unit." The creative objective may be a number of objectives, such as "provide important patient data to physicians," "help my employees develop and advance themselves in their professions," and "maintain good morale and job satisfaction under conditions of high pressure and fast pace." The big difference between the manager's job and the worker's job, in terms of objectives, is that the manager must set most of the objectives. This is part of his job.

Job conditions for the manager are usually highly diversified and to some extent subject to his own making. He can usually establish working patterns that get the job done and provide opportunities for job satisfaction. More than any other kind of worker in the organization, the manager can act to influence his own circumstances and to maximize job satisfaction.

Another job that is coming more and more under scrutiny is that of *secretary*. As more and more educated women move into the work force and as government and private pressures increase toward developing equal employment opportunities, the traditional job of secretary has less and less appeal. Fewer women are satisfied to be placed in dead-end jobs that offer only modest incomes and no avenues for advancement and that often involve demeaning, stereotyped tasks and relationships with managers based on sex role. The job role of office wife/ clerk typist/stewardess/sex symbol is now becoming obsolete. Not only do changes in social values operate to make the secretary's job role an outmoded one, but technological changes such as the development of word-processing equipment are reducing the need for mental skills and creative thinking. The traditional secretary job is gradually splitting into two distinct components, one of which can be filled by a worker of lower qualifications than the typical secretary and one that requires higher qualifications and improved social skills. The first component is the mechanistic job of generating, handling, and processing word information. The second component is executive support. The traditional secretary position may evolve into an administrative assistant role, with the outmoded "public utility" aspect of the role being taken over by word-processing specialists. In large organizations, managers must consciously review these roles, functions, and job definitions and redefine them in ways that maximize the use of human potential while maximizing the productivity of entire employee work units.

Other jobs will also probably evolve as a result of changing environmental factors. The traditional limited and narrow job of accounting clerk may evolve into a more sophisticated analytical job in addition to a data-handling job, especially with the coming advent of low-priced small computers. Fewer people with more training will do the accounting jobs.

Another job that must sooner or later shift into a more enriched task activity is that of the production line "robot" such as those employed by the large automobile manufacturers. Although the top managers and industrial engineers of the Big Three car manufacturers will probably resist to the last the humanization of these jobs, union pressure and the force of changing American values brought about by increasing numbers of women and young people in the work force will probably win eventually. The automobile industry may be forced to overhaul the entire process by which it applies human resources to the production of cars.

The job of physician may also change significantly over the next five to 10 years as more and more people begin to understand the holistic health concept and as stress reduction techniques cause the market for Valium, Darvon, Librium, and similar central nervous system depressants to dry up. Many of the less important jobs now being performed by physicians, such as routine checkups, minor surgical procedures, and treatment of minor injuries, may become the province of trained paraprofessionals such as nurse–practitioners and technicians. It is possible that the market for prescription treatment of anxiety-derived disorders will dry up, and doctors may then shift into the role of holistic health counselors. If so, they will have to learn a great deal about "normal" health, psychology, stress reduction, emotional influences on health, exercise physiology, and nutrition.

The job of teacher will almost certainly undergo radical changes, despite the dogged opposition of professional teachers' unions. With the coming boom in videotape recorders for home use, the wide use of audio cassettes, and the development of a cheap, small, general-purpose computer for consumer use, a great deal of learning can become self-directed and self-paced. The demand for these products, along with the increasing sense of frustration and failure associated with the American factory system of public education, may very well cause a shift toward consumer-oriented forms of learning, leaving the schools with the painful task of redefining their role in American life.

Similarly, the coming massive increase in the adult education market, caused preponderantly by the movement of the post-war "baby boom" population into the young adult years, will probably force a revolution in college and university systems. The almighty degree will probably become much less almighty, and the "contract" approach to criterion-based learning will probably come into its own. In this approach, the student sets his or her own learning goals according to competence criteria, and clears them ("contracts") with the teacher. The pursuit of the sheepskin will probably give way to the pursuit of lifelong learning, and new learning markets will probably open up to meet this demand. The adult teacher may well become something of a broker of learning resources rather than the traditional stand-up entertainer/controller/giver-of-knowledge.

In all these cases, both job satisfaction and productivity will depend on the extent to which the job is matched to the real world of demand and on the extent to which the elements of the job design are matched to the needs, capabilities, and values of the worker.

IMPROVING THE ORGANIZATIONAL CLIMATE

The psychological climate in an organization bears directly on the attitudes, well-being, and stress levels of each and every worker. High productivity and high levels of job satisfaction require a healthy, supportive organizational climate. It is the responsibility of top management to create and maintain a social setting in which people can work hard and well and in which they can gain satisfactions and rewards to keep them interested in working. Although the term *climate* is highly abstract and behavioral scientists have had great difficulty measuring it, we can identify some basic features, or clues, by which we can assess the climate of a typical organization and that we can use as guides for improving it.

First, the idea of the social climate applies primarily to the *individual worker*. Each human being uses himself as the reference point for the universe, and quite naturally so. Asking any one employee to evaluate the social climate in the organization amounts to asking, "How do *you* experience the social processes that make up the mainstream of life in this sociotechnical system?" Except for isolated situations, the worker will usually give his own perceptions of what's going on.

By surveying a large sample of employees and by drawing conclusions based on the frequency of their various comments and replies, you can describe the climate in terms of the prevailing view of the majority of workers. However, when it comes down to the effects on one individual worker, he is acutely aware of the circumstances that prevail in his own work life. To put it another way, if you are standing in the sunshine and I'm standing in the rain, then so far as I'm concerned the weather is rainy.

Still another way of stating the case, which is often so disconcerting to top managers, is that *the social climate of the organization is whatever most of the people think it is.* If top managers cannot set aside their needs to believe in themselves as benevolent dictators or father figures, they usually deceive themselves extremely about what's really happening among the workers. Walkouts and work stoppages usually come as huge surprises to the oppressive, myopic managers who control the organizations.

Top managers who regularly evaluate the social climate of their organizations, along with the other important variables such as productivity, financial performance, and progress on major projects, can and do¹ deal with the climate as an important element of their management responsibility. A psychological early warning system enables them to respond to potential human resource problems before they get out of hand and to account for the needs, values, and behavior of the people of the organization.

Let's consider some of the major aspects of organizational climate. Although the three factors discussed in the following paragraphs may not cover all situations completely, they do provide a very direct form of diagnosis. They express in relatively concrete terms how most employees feel about the social situation of their organization. The three factors are:

1. Degree of employee identification–alienation
2. Extent of labor–management polarization
3. Perceived social norms

Identification–Alienation

Identification–alienation refers to the extent to which employees personally identify themselves clearly and emphatically with the overall organization or the extent to which they separate themselves psychologically from it. Exhibit 5–5 illustrates this variable as operating along a continuum scale from

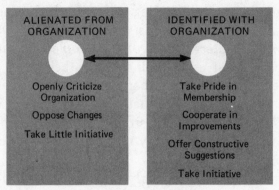

EXHIBIT 5-5. Employees feel relatively identified with, or alienated from, the organization at any one time.

"alienated" to "identified." There are ways to assess the degree of identification–alienation, and there are means for improvement. For example, attitude surveys usually give a fairly explicit measure of this factor. Questions such as, "Are you pleased when you tell friends and acquaintances you work for ABC organization?" with multiple-choice answers ranging from "Very Pleased," through "Moderately Pleased," "Neutral," "Not Pleased," to "I Usually Don't Tell Them," give employees a chance to state bluntly how they feel. Other questions that may be included are, "To what extent do you buy the company's products and encourage others to do so?", "To what extent do you take part in employee activities and social events?", and "How long do you see yourself staying with ABC?"

Managers who use questionnaire techniques to assess organizational climate must interpret the results carefully. Although results that seem to be highly favorable are less likely to be misinterpreted, unfavorable results can lead managers to go off on tangents with new projects, fads, or ill-advised changes. A disturbing result on an attitude survey usually calls for one specific action: *Take a closer look.* Interview a number of people, search for specific facts and factors they can name. Look into specific regions of the organization. Look at the performance of selected managers. Before putting all the managers in the organization through a training program, for example, make sure that training is the most promising intervention. The Appendix of this book offers a model Employee Attitude Survey Questionnaire with 25 basic questions designed to assess attitudes, stress levels, and job factors.

Many specific top management and middle management actions can foster a sense of identification on the part of the employees without the necessity for spending money. For example, when top management states to the employees, in clear and simple terms, the main goals and mission of the organization, the employees have a sense of being included in the operation. Recognizing individual achievements such as long years of service, attaining college degrees or advanced degrees, or personal achievements outside of work can also foster the conviction that the people of the organization are just as important as the top managers are.

Performance awards and awards for beneficial suggestions have the same effect if they are given sincerely and with appropriate dignity. An organizational newsletter provides an ideal instrument for this purpose. In my view, the main purpose of a newsletter is to focus attention on the people of the organization, not on the organizational structure or its top management. Workers enjoy reading about their friends and themselves and seeing their pictures in the company or agency newsletter. This, more than any top management pronouncements, creates the impression of the organization as a social entity as well as a business entity. Carefully selected social activities can also foster a sense of community spirit among the members of the organization.

Labor–Management Polarization

Labor-management polarization also forms a very basic element of the organizational climate. It is both a symptom of a problem and a problem in itself. Extreme polarization between the "ruling class" and the "working class" in the organization can virtually cripple human productivity, decrease job satisfaction, and lead to counterproductive clashes that tend to aggravate the situation. In a unionized organization, this factor usually stems directly from the quality (or lack of it) of the working relationship between the union leaders and the management group.

Top management usually must take the initiative in improving this factor because union leaders often seem to see themselves as simply reacting to the "atrocities" committed by the managers. One of the most effective approaches for reducing labor–management polarization is to make the top and middle managers more visible throughout the organization. When the chief executive never mingles with the employees, never makes public appearances among them, and never communicates directly with them from his high position, the employees develop an unconscious impression of the executive as a distant, unreal, impersonal entity. Many workers use the term "they" in referring to managers of the organization, most of whom the employees have never even seen. "They don't know what's going on around here;" "They don't give a damn about us;" and "They don't know how to run an organization."

By making themselves visible, the top managers also make themselves available. They become less mysterious and more real — more human. The workers begin to know them by face and name and to think of them as real, live, walking, talking, breathing persons. And curiously, most working people usually find it more difficult to depersonalize and criticize an executive whom they see once a week or so and with whom they exchange greetings as they pass in the parking lot or in the lobby of the office building.

Some executives occasionally have videotape recordings made of themselves, giving latest news or plans about the organization and explaining new programs. They send these around the organization or have them played over monitors in cafeterias and break areas. An occasional brief personal message from the chief executive in the newsletter can also help. Other executives make a habit of personally presenting awards for long service, special achievement, or beneficial suggestions. There are many natural opportunities for increasing executive visibility. Some of these can also increase the sense of labor–management solidarity by making union leaders and executives simultaneously visible to the members of the organization.

Perceived Social Norms

The third factor, perceived social norms, offers more difficulty in the assessment phase and is also somewhat more difficult to narrow down for specific corrective action. Social norms amount to relatively abstract organizational values — that is, the prevailing ideas about how people should act and how they should be treated. When a large number of the employees say, "You're nothing but a number around here," they are stating their perceptions of a prevailing norm. The top managers may not think of it that way, but in the end the perceptions of the employees form the source of the social climate to which they respond.

Workers may also frequently think in terms of "punishment" norms. Most of them know very clearly the circumstances under which one can lose his job, which infraction brings a reprimand, and especially the disciplinary style of the local manager or supervisor. Workers who consider a manager as heavy handed, critical, and punitive will not generally feel very enthusiastic about working for or supporting that person. Other terms in the vocabulary of the members of the organization that suggest their perceptions of prevailing social norms include "trust," "loyalty," "fair play," "speaking your mind," "getting ahead," "rules and regulations," and "playing favorites."

Managers at all levels can tune into employee attitudes by using questionnaires and informal interviews and by simply keeping their eyes and ears open. They can then isolate any specific organizational norms they have inadvertently created that lead to negative, alienated feelings on the part of many employees. Corrective measures include making managers aware at all levels of the results of attitude surveys, focusing on specific programs for constructive change, setting up management development programs, replacing certain managers if necessary, and publishing specific policies that are clear, fair, and evenhanded.

A comprehensive approach to improving the climate in any organization calls for carefully assessing the climate, prescribing corrective interventions from the management level, putting them into effect, and carefully assessing the results. A comprehensive program for improving the climate and, by association, the quality of working life for the members of the organization involves the three factors discussed in the foregoing paragraphs, together with job engineering to maximize productivity, job satisfaction, and sense of reward. When top managers take this humanistic approach to their organizations, they solve many of the associated problems at the same time. Improving the organizational climate automatically improves the quality of working life. It also automatically reduces the levels of stress felt by the employees. And it automatically moves toward optimal levels of productivity, because people who are committed to their organizations will work constructively to advance the goals of those organizations.

REFERENCES

Albrecht, Karl, and Margaret Butteriss. *New Management Tools: Ideas and Techniques to Help You as a Manager.* Englewood Cliffs, N.J.: Prentice-Hall, 1979.

Albrecht, Karl. *Successful Management by Objectives: An Action Manual.* Englewood Cliffs, N.J.: Prentice-Hall, 1978.

Herzberg, Frederick. *The Motivation to Work.* New York: John Wiley, 1965.

Rubin, Theodore Isaac. *The Angry Book.* New York: Macmillan, 1969.

Taylor, Frederick W. *The Principles of Scientific Management.* New York: W. W. Norton, 1911.

Stress-Reduction Training: A New Concept in Human Resources Development

WHAT STRESS REDUCTION TRAINING IS

Stress reduction training is a new application of some well-known techniques to the problems of living and working in the business world. As a human resources development approach in organizations, it is entirely new. One of the first job-focused stress reduction seminars to my knowledge was one I conducted at the University of California in Riverside, in early 1977. As early as 1975, I had experimented with stress reduction training in a workshop program called "Personal Effectiveness for Managers," at the University of California in San Diego.*

*I'd especially like to give credit to Mrs. Jean Bowie of the University of

Since that time, other consultants and trainers around the country have developed various programs as well, and the approach is becoming extremely popular in business organizations. Most of the techniques used in these training sessions have been known for a number of years. What is new is the systematic application of these techniques in an organized program of training for managers and workers that is focused on the job situation and its accompanying stress effects. I believe it is no overstatement to say that stress reduction training techniques have the potential of revolutionizing the lives and life styles of a vast number of people in the business world. Indeed, I expect this to happen. This chapter gives a brief overview of stress reduction training as an organization development modality. Chapters 7 and 8 explain the techniques and methods in much greater detail, with a focus on the individual's own patterns of living and working as a manager.

In a stress reduction training seminar, lasting usually one or two full days, a trainer helps the participants to acquire and apply three basic antistress skills:

1. *Physical relaxation* — the neurophysical skill of deep relaxation, acquired by any of a number of special training techniques. This skill enables the individual to deactivate the stress response deliberately, substituting the parasympathetic nervous system's so-called *relaxation response*. Practicing this technique in private carries over to enable a person to operate with a lower level of reactivity in social situations (Benson, 1975).
2. *Self-management* — the day-to-day, moment-to-moment skill of monitoring one's own internal arousal level and of responding to provocative situations with relative

California Extension, San Diego, and to Mr. Shelly Lisker of the University of California Extension, Riverside. Both of them have been willing to experiment with new and promising concepts like stress-reduction training, and they have provided a forum for bringing new knowledge and techniques to the business community.

calm and equanimity (*not*, of course, zombie-like withdrawal or detachment).

3. *Lifestyle Management* — the skill of continually assessing the relative balance of stresses and rewards in all areas of one's life and of making decisions about how to structure one's time and activities to optimize this balance and keep it optimal or near optimal.

The purpose of the training session is *to enable* — to provide an individual with techniques, concepts, and tools for taking command of his own life and for living that life according to his own values, with the objective of minimizing the stress penalty paid for living and working. The benefits of this increased capability for stress reduction and stress management for the individual are obvious. Just a little thought makes the benefits to the organization that sponsors the training for its people equally obvious.

BASIC TRAINING CONCEPTS

The foundation concept of stress reduction training is that *a great deal of today's stress is avoidable.* If an individual can learn the simple techniques of self-monitoring and self-regulation, he can live a rewarding, enjoyable life at work and elsewhere with no sacrifice in accomplishment.

A related principle is that *most stress is self-induced*, although certainly not deliberately so. By learning to maintain a high level of alertness for situations that might lead to stress and by reprogramming one's response patterns to these situations, one can develop a lower level of *reactivity*. This enables the individual to approach situations strategically, keeping his objectives in sight at all times, responding humanely to the needs and desires of others, and maintaining constructive levels of interpersonal harmony.

As the skill of deep relaxation improves, an individual becomes less reactive, less open to provocation, more tolerant of situations and events that would have been frustrating in the past, and more able to adapt to events as they unfold. Positive mental programming also enables the individual to substitute new, more productive reaction patterns in many provocative situations. This skill cannot be fully developed overnight, of course, but an individual can notice some significant improvements almost immediately. Often the mere discovery of a new idea or point of view for handling a certain problem situation is sufficient for an individual to switch to a new, less stressful strategy.

In addition to learning to reprogram his own reaction patterns, an individual can learn to reprogram problem situations to some extent. For example, one can analyze a problem situation, find the stress-producing elements, and systematically eliminate as many of them as possible, while still preserving the basic objectives. Some people who have difficulty compromising may find that this technique becomes a stress reduction strategy for them. One can analyze his specific communication behaviors and spot those that produce conflict, hard feelings, and the resulting stress for everyone involved. One can then experiment with new interpersonal strategies.

Of course, reprogramming problem situations and communicating in a low-stress manner do not mean avoiding all conflict. Some situations involve unavoidable conflict if one is to accomplish his objectives. Backing away from all forms of conflict — a style that many people in business unconsciously maintain — is not productive in the long run. It may not even reduce stress in the long run because buried conflicts often continue to intensify and may later erupt with even greater force. Low-stress communicating calls for *maintaining the lowest practical level of stress commensurate with getting the job done.*

The neurological skills of deep relaxation, de-escalation of one's internal arousal level, low-stress communicating, and other self-management techniques lead a person quite naturally to examine his entire life pattern and to move toward stress reduction and stress management in all areas of living. Once a person begins to recognize the physical symptoms of stress and to understand that various behaviors (such as excessive use of alcohol, smoking, drugs, tranquilizers, or escapist behaviors) are simply normal manifestations of the need to free one's self from stress, then he tends to re-examine basic values such as health, freedom from imprisoning habits, diet, exercise, personal relationships, and other variables that affect quality of life. It may seem like a long way from job stress to jogging, but the logical connections are quite natural, given the total-systems view of life, work, and stress.

Stress reduction training is one of the few forms of human resources development that focuses primarily on the individual's own *personal well-being* as an avenue to improved organizational operation. It will undoubtedly meet some resistance from old-school managers who adhere to the prewar Puritan ethic that demanded that people should not be "coddled" or helped to "grow" and that the organization should not get involved in its employees' personal lives, even if they want it to. However, I believe the majority of managers will immediately recognize the benefits to organizations and employees alike that are offered by stress reduction training. Indeed, I have found that the easiest way to sell a manager on the value of stress reduction is to induce him to take an hour to learn the deep relaxation skill. This usually produces a very dramatic change in his level of appreciation and interest.

I believe we've arrived at the point at which people and their organizations are intimately interdependent and that we're rapidly recognizing that the idea should no longer be, "What's good for the organization is good for everybody," but rather "What's good for everybody is good for the organization."

PERSONAL STRESS MANAGEMENT SKILLS

Let's look more closely at the skills and techniques imparted in stress reduction training. First, the individual learns to increase the basic attentional skill of *self-monitoring*, that is, the ability to "read" one's body from time to time and to assess one's relative internal arousal level. One soon learns exactly how his own body manifests the stress reaction, how the body tells of its internal arousal. For some people, prolonged stress may produce headaches. For others, it may produce stomach discomfort, digestive difficulties, constipation, or heartburn. For still others, the result may be overall body tension, muscle cramps, or menstrual irregularity. In many people, stress produces occasional feelings of wanting to break out of some invisible prison and to escape to some other more pleasant situation. In stress reduction training, each person studies his own stress signals.

Next, the student learns the all-important skill of *deep relaxation*, which is a much more extensive form of "letting go" than merely sitting quietly and relaxing. Deep relaxation is a physical and emotional act of profound surrender of the body to its own automatic processes. It is characterized by the physiological inverse of the fight-or-flight response described in Chapter 2, and it involves a full mobilization of the body's parasympathetic nervous system. Selected training procedures such as self-hypnosis, progressive relaxation, alternate tensing and relaxing of muscle groups, autogenic training, transcendental and other forms of meditation, biofeedback, and visualization techniques are used by a qualified trainer to impart the skill of deep relaxation. Some people learn the skill very quickly; others require some extra attention from the trainer. Nearly everyone can learn the deep relaxation skill in a one- or two-day seminar sufficiently to begin practicing it routinely. Many people have been disappointed in trying to learn these skills from reading books, but most find it fairly easy in a training seminar.

Having acquired the deep relaxation skill, the student then proceeds to develop "quickie" techniques such as mental trigger signals for *momentary relaxation* while engaged in the business of living. This amounts to unobtrusively de-escalating one's internal arousal level while actually engaged in a social situation. Using a simple technique of his own choosing, the student can at any time monitor his own stress level and achieve a measure of immediate relaxation. If properly carried out, the technique is virtually undetectable by others in normal social situations. This momentary relaxation technique has the additional benefit of helping the individual's logical faculties to come into play more fully in pressure situations.

These various skills, then, form the basis for self-management in all social and work situations. One begins to learn techniques for dealing with aggressive or abusive persons, for maintaining interpersonal harmony whenever possible, for communicating in ways that do not induce inappropriate stress in one's self or in others, for resolving conflict, and for managing one's own time in order to accomplish a great deal of high-priority work without experiencing unreasonable time stress.

The skills of deep relaxation and self-management lead naturally to the reassessment of one's *total pattern of living and behaving* and to the ability to identify sources of stress that the individual can remove or otherwise deal with. For most people, this involves a reassessment of their general level of health and physical condition, exercise habits, eating habits, and other health behaviors such as smoking, drinking, and consumption of various medications and chemicals. One then makes a plan for a steady and self-rewarding evolution of one's activity patterns into a new life style that optimizes *for him* the balance between stresses and rewards. Chapter 7 describes these various personal skills in greater depth.

STRESS REDUCTION TRAINING FOR EXECUTIVES

A variety of factors contribute to the total pressure load on an individual executive, and executives vary in the amount of pressure they can comfortably handle. These two factors are inseparable because pressure is largely a matter of perception.

Whereas some situations, such as a burning building or a threat of physical violence, would constitute pressure for almost everyone, other situations, such as an impending project deadline or a major problem in labor relations, might not present the same level of urgency to all people. One executive may feel extremely threatened by a certain situation because of his own personal make-up and personal history, but another might find it only mildly taxing.

Here again, stress reduction must center on the individual executive, his own situation, reaction patterns, and life style. The executive must learn the same fundamental skills as the middle manager or the worker, but the situations in which he applies them will be largely different.

Probably the greatest difficulty the executive faces, especially one who is very highly placed, is to become too immersed in work and consequently "lopsided" and unbalanced in his life's activities — the "workaholic" mode. Because of the many demands on the executive's time and also because of the very rich psychological rewards associated with wielding power and authority, a person in this position can be tempted to give over his entire life to running the company or the agency.

The feeling of "they need me" — which actually means "*I* need *them*" (in order to maintain my feelings of significance), leads many executives to spend 12 to 14 hours or more each day (even on weekends) on the job. Many executives actually seem to dread vacations with their families, possibly because they don't want their managers and workers to get used to getting along without them. In addition, the vacation offers very little chance to make large-scale decisions and to direct the activities of many people. Giving orders to his wife and children around the campsite does not offer the typical executive much in the way of feelings of significance. And many managers cannot surrender this ego-satisfying role in dealing with their families. Similarly, military officers are often accused by their wives of trying to run their families just as they run their units. Though such a practice is not emotionally healthy, it is understandable because giving orders and having them obeyed is fun.

Stress reduction training helps the executive to develop the personal skills of physical relaxation and day-to-day self-management. Equally important, it enables him to review his entire life style and to decide consciously what balance of activities he considers appropriate.

Especially because the executive is probably within the heart attack age range and may well have drifted into personal habits that vastly increase his chances of a major health breakdown, he needs to review his entire pattern of *health behavior.* Because of the lopsided "workaholic" pattern, the executive may be generally tense and unable to unwind, he may smoke heavily, he may drink too much, he may be considerably overweight, and he may be in very poor physical condition. For a man of age 45 or more, this pattern is one of virtual self-destruction. Such a person must consciously decide to rebalance his investment of energy in the various activity areas of his life and to escape from his addiction to the job. This rebalance amounts to finding a satisfying answer to the question, "What, really, is my best contribution to this organization, and how can I make it without sacrificing my health, well-being, or the pleasure available to me in the other areas of my life?"

The weekend retreat offers an ideal approach to an executive antistress program. The top executives of an organization, usually no more than about 10 to 15 people, spend a weekend together with a consultant/trainer. A Friday evening "unwinding" session — preferably with little or no alcohol — gives them a chance to make the transition from the day-to-day problems and to begin to think about themselves as people. The consultant makes a brief presentation of the basic concepts of stress, stress reduction, and stress management in organizations, and the executives have a chance to discuss their own organization.

After a good night's sleep, the participants spend a major portion of the next day learning the basic personal skills of deep relaxation and self-management. The day's schedule also allows time for private activities such as a country walk, recreational reading, or just "settin' and starin'." Mild sports and group activities can also help the executives unwind and recapture the feeling of relaxation and recreation without guilt. After a pleasant dinner, they can spend a few hours in an evening session analyzing the operation of their organization, thinking about improvements, and developing some agenda items for Monday morning problem solving. This program also provides an ideal atmosphere in which to develop team spirit.

The second day's session can focus on self-assessment and the planning of life styles. These activities should allow an element of privacy for each executive. Each should feel free to explore his values and activities and to make whatever private decisions he considers appropriate. The trainer/consultant can help the executives to clarify their ideas by offering assessment techniques and models and can facilitate an exchange of ideas and possibilities. Each executive should leave with a personal, private plan for rebalancing his life in order to optimize the relationship between stresses and rewards.

The executives can also spend part of the second day roughing out a plan for organizational improvements to be followed up when they return to work. With some additional practice in deep relaxation techniques and the rest of the day spent at whatever recreational activities they choose, they are ready to go back to their offices with more creative views of their roles in the organization, their most effective contributions, and their own health and well-being. Occasional follow-up workshops can reinforce these skills and attitudes. Continued reading and awareness of the entire subject of stress enable them to manage their respective organizations more effectively.

STRESS REDUCTION TRAINING FOR EMPLOYEES

Stress reduction training can enable the employee to approach his job with a greater sense of autonomy, self-control, and confidence in his ability to handle problems and provocations as they arise. For employees who have especially stressful jobs, this can mean the difference between longevity and turnover. The employee who learns to put the job into its proper perspective within the overall pattern of his life can learn not to overreact to daily events. Since many people in the last quarter of the twentieth century seem to have difficulties with their personal lives and since many of these difficulties spill over into job performance and attitudes, stress reduction training can enable these people to gain greater control over their lives in general and consequently to function better on the job.

Without intervening in the lives of the employees, the organization can help them to deal more effectively with emotional problems, difficulties with liquor or drugs (although serious addiction problems call for much more potent therapeutic interventions), problems with personal relationships, and living habits that endanger their health. The basic ideas of controlling one's reactivity level, de-escalating the internal arousal level, transacting with others in low-stress styles, and reorganizing one's activities and relationships all offer enormous possibilities for improvement of human effectiveness. Employees who have participated in one- or two-day stress reduction workshops report dramatic effects in their personal lives and in their ability to approach their jobs more effectively.

At the time of this writing, very few organizations have instituted antistress training programs. Therefore, the thesis of this chapter is largely still in the realm of conjecture. However, the few programs of which I am aware definitely confirm the notion that employee stress reduction training programs offer substantial improvements in morale, health, and personal well-being, which lead directly to improved job performance. One such organization worthy of note is the Department of Public Welfare in the County of San Diego. To counteract the increasing problems caused by job stress, especially among the welfare eligibility workers, this organization instituted a small pilot program in antistress training. The program consisted of a two-day session at conference facilities in San Diego's beautiful Balboa Park. The trainers helped the workers to learn the standard antistress skills of deep relaxation, self-management, and life style planning and the techniques for applying them to their jobs as well as to their private lives. Reported results of the pilot program have been excellent, and department management plans to expand the program substantially. The goal is eventually to provide every employee who desires it with this kind of training.

Workers who received the training spoke so enthusiastically about its practical usefulness that requests for attendance far exceeded the level of staff time allocated for the program. Workers returned to their offices refreshed and able to approach their jobs more enthusiastically and less anxiously. Their co-workers were influenced by these ideas and attitudes, and they also requested training. Some workers reported improvements in their health and personal habits as well. The County of Los Angeles has instituted a similar pilot program supported by a program of careful data-gathering in the areas of morale and stress-related disease among its employees.

I believe this is typical of what may be accomplished in employee morale, attitude, and job performance through stress reduction training programs. And I believe that more and more organizations will create similar programs as the benefits to organizational effectiveness become apparent.

REFERENCES

Benson, Herbert. *The Relaxation Response.* New York: Morrow, 1975.

7

How to Keep
Your Own
Stress Level Down

This chapter offers a personal "technology" for stress reduction and stress management that anyone can use as a beginning. The techniques apply equally well to the lives of managers and employees. Chapter 8 extends the stress reduction concept to include your entire life style, and Chapter 9 deals explicitly with management techniques that minimize organizational stress while getting work done effectively.

These techniques are all essentially *physical* techniques; they are things you do with your own body and your own nervous system. Learning each of them amounts to a *neurological retraining process* that you can undertake systematically. I suggest that you read over the following descriptions of the techniques and begin thinking about them. You'll probably find yourself using some of them from time to time, simply because they will come to mind often. As time goes on, you should also allocate some time every day to practice selected techniques that you find especially useful. Make the use of these techniques a matter of reward, rather than self-discipline or obligation. Find time for those that you consider especially worthwhile.

SELF-MONITORING

Begin to pay closer attention to the physical sensations of your body. Become intimately familiar with the signals that tell you the status of your arousal level. From these signals, you can infer a great deal about your overall reaction to various situations, which might not be at all obvious to you at the level of simple intellectual analysis. If your experience is like mine, you'll probably soon conclude that you've been assuming yourself to be much calmer and less moved by pressure situations than your body signals imply.

Most of us have a strong need to believe that we remain calm, cool, and collected in pressure situations. And most of us do indeed maintain our general composure and think on our feet fairly well. But this attitude can lead us to reject the facts of our natural stress response—literally to disown it—and to convince ourselves that we experience *no stress*, when in fact we experience a normal level of stress.

The more I studied the stress phenomenon, the more I found myself confronted with a pattern of my own body's feelings and reactions that correlated closely with upcoming events and situations in my life. It finally dawned on me how well I had rationalized as general "health problems" a number of normal feelings of stress reaction. For example, what I and my doctor referred to as a "nervous stomach"—that is, knotted feelings in my abdomen, irregular bowel movements, bloated feelings, and generally frequent feelings of discomfort—began to occur less frequently once I recognized that they *most often preceded upcoming situations* in which I expected to be "on the spot." The morning before I was to conduct a management seminar, make a major presentation to one of my consulting clients, or visit with a group of executives who were considering engaging my services, I usually experienced that familiar feeling. I had no choice but to conclude that I felt *normally anxious* about these situations, even though I felt competent and well prepared to handle them. My childlike "shadow self" chose to become worried and apprehensive, despite the logical assurances of my conscious, reasoning mind.

Similarly, I noted that my hands would become cold and clammy and that I would perspire mildly during the first hour or so of a management seminar with a group of managers I hadn't dealt with before. This sensation would come and go, depending on the relative sense of challenge I felt in dealing with the subject and my feelings about my general rapport with the group. I still experience this, and I have since found that other consultants and trainers notice these and other signals of stress.

I also found that the severe headaches I experienced from time to time virtually disappeared once I admitted that they resulted from unconscious worry about upcoming deadlines of major significance. I have learned to recognize and accept normal feelings of moderate anxiety as arising from my involvement in challenging situations. These are not bad, but understanding them is important to my overall understanding of my body's response mechanisms and to my planning and decision making about how to balance my life's activities.

In my own case, my automatic tendency to pretend to be "unhuman" presented the greatest barrier to developing the self-monitoring skill. Perhaps males, because of childhood conditioning to "keep a stiff upper lip" and to suppress hurts, fears, and disappointments, have a greater problem with denial of the stress response than do females. We seem to grant women the right to show injury or upsets but deny it to males. In any case, convince yourself that your stress response, as manifested by various body signals, is your *normal human reaction* to the situation and challenges that confront you. Your objective is not to eliminate it but to live with it constructively.

Right at this moment, pause to "read" your body. Close your eyes, and "listen" attentively to your insides. Find the pulse in your wrist and time it for about half a minute. Check each of the major muscle groups of your body, noting any differences in their relative tension or exertion. Try to induce a spreading feeling of relaxation — of de-escalation of your internal level — all over your body. Again, with your eyes closed, read the sensations in your forehead, facial muscles, and throughout your scalp. Release your jaw muscles for a few seconds, letting your jaw "float." Allow a feeling of relaxation and release to pass over all the muscles of your face, forehead, and back of the head.

Check the tension level in your *trapezius* muscles — the ones that descend from either side of your neck to the top of your shoulders. Shrug your shoulders a few times and then just let them hang freely. Wiggle your fingers and toes, letting them relax.

When next you have an opportunity, explore your nude body and renew your acquaintance with it. Begin to make a habit of tuning in to the sensations and signals that tell you of your functioning. After meals, note carefully how you feel. Do you feel pleasant and slightly euphoric or somewhat sleepy? Do your after-meal sensations feel different, depending on how big a meal you've eaten, how heavy the food, or how quickly you've eaten?

Now take a sheet of paper and make a list of as many of your unpleasant body sensations as you can remember. Recall the aches and pains, muscle tension, stomach sensations, headaches, and all the rest. Also identify any well-defined emotional "set," such as an occasional feeling of being trapped, or wanting to disappear from a situation, or a rising sense of anger, or a desire to strike out physically at whomever or whatever had contributed to your frustration. Add to this list from time to time. Get to know your own stress reaction patterns. And take full "ownership" of these patterns. Acknowledge and accept them as a normal part of your human make-up.

Make it a routine practice to monitor your *immediate feelings* in problem situations, especially in those involving possible interpersonal conflict. This may require some practice on your part, if—like most of us—you have learned to short-circuit your perceptions of your primary creature reactions because of childhood teachings that tell you they are not "nice."

For example, if an inconsiderate driver chases you back up onto the sidewalk as you try to walk across the street, what is your immediate reaction? Don't mistake your secondary, socialized, "rational" reaction for your immediate reaction. Your immediate reaction is probably one of split-second hostility and a general wish that you had some means to exterminate this reprehensible character. Your secondary reaction will probably be a very quick suppression of the primary response, substituting your learned social controls for the impulse to commit violence.

This normal and useful social conditioning enables us to live together in relative peace, but it need not mask our understanding of our primary creature responses. You have a right, as a functioning creature, to *want* to kill or physically conquer someone or to *want* to flee from some situation. You usually will not choose these behavioral strategies, but you need not deny the legitimacy of your primary response. Indeed, the supression beyond the level of normal awareness of natural feelings such as anger, hostility, and fear leads directly to emotional disturbance and adjustment difficulties. Learning the skill of self-monitoring means becoming acquainted with and accepting yourself in all your dimensions (Rubin, 1969).

As self-monitoring becomes a more familiar and natural routine for you, begin to monitor your health behaviors. Focus on smoking, on use of liquor, on use of consumer chemicals such as tranquilizers, aspirin, antacids, and sleeping pills, and on eating. If necessary, keep a smoking diary to find out for sure when and under what circumstances you use cigarettes. Begin to examine the situations themselves to isolate any elements that you might find stressful.

Find out exactly what your alcohol consumption patterns are over a period of two to three weeks. Where do you drink? Under what circumstances? What experiences usually precede your drinking activities? Who accompanies you when you drink? How much do you drink? What do you drink? What function do you think alcohol performs for you?

When you find yourself reaching for one of the pharmaceutical industry's miracle pills, note very carefully how you feel at that instant and review the events of the previous few hours. What's been happening that makes you want to dull your awareness of your body's signals? Without adopting an overly self-critical attitude, begin to study your eating behavior. What uses do you make of food in addition to sustaining your body? When and under what circumstances do you use sweets? What in your environment triggers your desire to eat something?

Remember to carry on this self-monitoring process in a self-supporting, constructive way, rather than as a guilt-inducing "detective" operation. Take your findings as they come. Don't hold a trial with yourself as defendant. Merely begin to use the findings of your self-observation process over an extended period of time as valuable information for shaping your life style as you see fit.

DEEP RELAXATION TECHNIQUES

This section gives a quick overview of some major training techniques that you can use to acquire the skill of *deep relaxation*. At the end of this chapter, you'll find a detailed description of one selected technique that is comparatively easy to learn and use.

Deep relaxation — or DR — is a highly specific neurological state of the body (Benson, 1974, p. 49; 1975). One cannot reach this state merely by sitting or lying down quietly. It requires a specific mental approach. Physiologically, the DR state amounts to the exact opposite of the fight-or-flight response. It involves the demobilization of the *sympathetic nervous system* and a complementary mobilization of the *parasympathetic nervous system.*

In the DR condition, one feels physically relaxed, somewhat detached from his immediate environment, and usually to some extent even detached from body sensations. It involves a feeling of voluntary and comfortable abandonment of one's conscious control and stewardship over major body functions. This abandonment requires a distinctly *passive attitude* in which one simply turns over control of his body to its own built-in "autopilot."

A few people find this feeling of surrender a bit disconcerting and tend to compulsively seize control again, interrupting the relaxation process. This happens mostly to those who tend to be fearful and overcontrolled, having never accepted their bodies as self-regulating automatic systems. With a little coaching from an instructor and a few mental techniques, they can usually overcome this apprehension fairly readily.

One's mental activity in the DR state can range from controlled concentration on positive programming messages or images, to drifting free association, to the "mental silence" characteristic of meditation. This aspect of relaxation depends on the technique one uses to produce it.

Deep relaxation is a profoundly *restful* condition. People who enter this state for 15 to 20 minutes open their eyes later feeling a pronounced sense of peacefulness and release from all former tension. Within a few moments of returning to an active condition, such as standing and stretching, they begin to feel buoyant, energetic, and even exuberant. Most people also report feelings of optimism, cheerfulness, kindliness toward and acceptance of others, and general good humor. Physiologists also report dramatic changes during the DR state in certain key body measurements such as heart rate, breathing rate, blood chemistry, skin temperature and electrical resistance, and blood pressure.

Repeated practice of a DR procedure—say, for 15 to 20 minutes a day with occasional one-minute "quickies"—has two important results. First, it feels good and it constitutes a very pleasant form of occasional detachment from your environment, during which your body can completely relinquish the stress reaction and enjoy the physiological and emotional benefits of demobilization. Some of those who are intimately familiar with various recreational chemicals describe the DR condition as a "natural high," in some aspects more pleasing than intoxication from drugs or liquor. As a substitute for the martini on arriving home from work, it has some obvious health advantages.

Second, repeated practice of deep relaxation gives you an increasing measure of control over your momentary reactions in problem situations and tends to reduce your overall reactivity level. It is as if the body, once having become familiar with the inverse of its stress response, can more easily go in that direction. With a little conscious help from your logical thinking processes, your body can maintain a greater level of calm and equanimity by having this relaxation response available. At the level of body physiology, the parasympathetic nervous system becomes revitalized, and its functions are rebalanced with those of the sympathetic nervous system. You can combine this lowered reactivity level with the self-monitoring skill to keep your internal stress meter clicking at a low enough level so that it will not cause trouble.

Many people are surprised when they discover that the DR state actually exists. They may report feeling pleasantly surprised at how relaxed they could actually become, having been so accustomed to a general level of unrecognized, chronic anxiety. Repeated practice of the DR technique enables these people to rid themselves of this burden, often for the first time in their lives. Having acquired the neurological skill of de-escalating their internal levels, they can then use a form of momentary relaxation—actually a small sample of the general DR skill—to keep themselves well adjusted to their daily experiences.

You can choose from at least five principal techniques for learning the deep relaxation condition. Each has its advocates who claim various special benefits and features. The following brief description simply catalogs them. I suggest that you study each of them to the extent practical and select one or a combination of techniques to suit your needs and interests.

Progressive Relaxation

Progressive relaxation is probably the simplest technique. Assume a comfortable position, sitting or lying, close your eyes and begin concentrating on the various muscles in your body, relaxing them one at a time. Use a systematic sequence, such as starting at the top of your head and progressing to your feet, releasing each of the muscle groups in turn. Concentrate fully on the sensations returning from the muscles and use them to guide your relaxation. You can also use mental imagery, such as imagining that your muscles are turning to jelly or that your arms and legs are made of iron or stone and are becoming extremely heavy. After the initial relaxation, make several mental "passes" through your body, inducing repeated waves of increasing relaxation. Aim for a feeling of utter inertness. Remain in this relaxed mode, occasionally deepening it, for about 15 or 20 minutes. Keep your mind on pleasant thoughts, especially pleasant visual images.

Hypnosis

Hypnosis is one of the easiest ways to learn the DR skill. Have a competent hypnotist guide you into the hypnotized state and give you suggestions for peaceful thoughts and for profound relaxation of your body. Ask to receive a posthypnotic suggestion that will enable you to reacquire the DR state any time you choose. Practice re-entering the DR state several times soon after the hypnotic training. *Self-hypnosis* has the same advantages, but many people find it difficult to enter the hypnotic state using only instructions from a book. By far the easiest way to learn the self-hypnosis skill is to have someone else hypnotize you. Thereafter you can reproduce the hypnotic condition by yourself. The posthypnotic instruction is useful but not essential.*

Meditation

Meditation can involve any of a number of techniques, all of which produce roughly the same DR state. The much-touted transcendental meditation amounts to the use of a mental device—a pleasant-sounding word, preferably one with no meaning—that you retain in your conscious field of thought. Try, for example, the word "one,"** or "alpha," or "stop," simply saying the word over and over in your mind as you sit and allow your body to relax (Benson, 1974). This is not an active mental process so much as a passive drifting along with the effects produced by keeping the selected word in your mind for a period of 15 to 20 minutes. If you tend to be unusually tense and restless, use the progressive relaxation technique a few times before trying the meditation approach. Then use it again as a first stage, following immediately with the meditation technique. If your mind wanders, simply bring it back to the key word and resume, almost in a disinterested way, your calm repetition. Other forms of meditation involve dwelling on colors, on abstract concepts, or close concentration on body sensations. All these, if properly employed, produce the same

*If you are interested in pursuing a training program in self-hypnosis, contact your local county medical society for a recommendation of a reputable clinic or training society. Some cities have societies for clinical hypnosis.

**The word "one" has been referred to whimsically as the "Harvard mantra." Dr. Herbert Benson suggested it in his article in the *Harvard Business Review* (1974).

desirable DR condition in the body. Differences between techniques are beyond the scope of our current interest.*

Autogenic Training

Autogenic training is a DR technique originated by a physician in Germany over 30 years ago, but it is little known in the United States (Lindemann, 1973). It involves the use of close concentration and mental images to produce specific body changes associated with relaxation. As with the other techniques, sit or lie quietly with your eyes closed. Begin to sense the state of your various muscles. Concentrate on your right arm and allow it to become very heavy. Keeping that feeling, do the same with your left arm. Focus on this heavy feeling and intensify it as much as possible. The muscles will relax profoundly as your imagination feeds back to the commands going from your brain to the muscles. Relax your legs in the same way. Next, return to the right arm and find a feeling of growing warmth there. Intensify it until it is pronounced and pleasant. Your arm will indeed become warm as a result of this mental process because the blood vessels dilate in your extremities as the relaxation response sets in. Tune in carefully for this subtle feeling of spreading warmth and use it to make it intensify itself. Make your other arm and your legs warm with the same technique. This method requires close and continuous concentration and careful "reading" of your body sensations. Autogenic training involves a total of six progressive exercises such as these. It is best learned with the help of a teacher, but if you can concentrate well and have a vivid imagination, you can master the technique in a few practice sessions. The autogenically derived DR state is also useful for positive mental programming and attitude development.

*Many cities have meditation study groups. You may be able to join such a group, or take a training course. If you have difficulty locating such a group, contact the psychology department of a local college or university and ask for information.

Biofeedback is the newest and most dramatic form of DR training (Brown, 1974, 1977). Some people have oversold biofeedback's current value, but it does have certain definite possibilities. With this approach, you usually work with a professional technician who connects certain kinds of sensors to selected points on your body. Then, by observing a visual display or listening to an auditory signal, you attempt to get the signal to change in some predetermined way by intuitively altering certain of your internal bodily processes. If the signal changes properly, then you are beginning to induce the DR state in your body. For example, a highly sophisticated instrument may measure the relative proportion of the alpha electrical activity of your brain and feed this measurement back to you in the form of a colored light or an audible tone. By observing the light or listening to the tone, you can discover certain subjective feelings or sensations in your body that are associated with the feedback. You can fairly quickly learn to alter those sensations with your mind and thereby produce the DR condition, causing the colored light to turn off or the audible tone to change or disappear. This direct and immediate feedback enables you to gain control of the key body variables of interest. Other variables used for biofeedback include your skin's electrical resistance, skin temperature, heart rate, blood pressure, and the electrical activity of various muscles. Devices available on the market for private, individual use generally measure skin resistance or muscle tension and are referred to as GSR devices (galvanic skin response) or EMG devices (electromyelograph, meaning muscle electricity). A GSR device simply involves attaching two electrodes to a cleaned area of your skin; the device applies a very tiny electrical voltage to your skin and measures the resistance to its flow. This measurement correlates fairly closely with the physiological conditions of the DR state. The EMG device uses a sensing electrode attached to the *frontalis* muscle of your forehead or to the *trapezius* muscle, which descends from the side of your neck to the top of your shoulder. Electrical activity in these two muscles gives a reliable measure of the overall level of arousal in the body. By learning to reduce the output signal, you learn to relax these muscles as well as the others in your body.

Many people have become interested in various forms of deep relaxation as a stress reduction skill. Meditation groups, biofeedback groups, and autogenic training classes are steadily proliferating. The value of these techniques in coping with normal tension and anxiety has been proven.

If you do not currently use some part of your day—half an hour at least—for privacy, detachment, and relaxation, perhaps you should re-evaluate your time priorities. And by relaxation, I don't mean retiring to a favorite club or cocktail lounge to lick the wounds of the day. It is my strong opinion that, in today's environment of business and living, the ability to retire to a private place and enter a state of deep relaxation for 15 to 20 minutes is a strategy for health and survival that no one should be without. And the greater the amount of pressure one experiences on the average, the more one needs this form of antistress protection.

Ironically, however, it seems that most of those who practice a daily deep relaxation procedure are those who need it less than many of those who don't engage in the practice. The ones who do already realize the importance of stress defense skills such as self-monitoring, self-management, and life style planning, and they often take excellent care of their health. Unfortunately, the high-speed Type A manager is often the one who says, "Deep relaxation? You mean meditation? I don't know what that is, but it isn't something I have the time for. I've got to bring this project in on schedule; I've got to go out of town for two weeks; I've got to get this deal closed; I've got to . . ." etc., etc. Many lopsided, overstressed people close themselves off from all new ideas they can't pick up and use in a split second. They think they can't take time away from their central life's pursuit—from which they may draw the only feelings of significance they know in their lives—long enough to explore and to learn.

If you're currently reassessing your life style and your personal health habits, I offer one recommendation. Learn a deep relaxation procedure and try it every day for one week. Use the technique given at the end of this chapter if you like. At the end of that time, see if you haven't made some significant changes in your attitude toward the overall pace of your life, your obligations, and the ways in which you want to live and work.

MOMENTARY RELAXATION

The skill of momentary relaxation comes automatically once you have learned the deep relaxation skill. Whereas deep relaxation is something you practice in private as a basic neurological skill for general well-being, momentary relaxation is a useful on-the-spot skill for dealing with situations that are likely to involve stress.

Imagine yourself about to enter a situation that will probably involve some sort of stress for you. It may be a conference that you expect will involve a great deal of conflict among the participants, or an interview with an important client or customer, or a presentation to a group of high-ranking executives, or a distasteful disciplinary interview with one of your employees. Picture the situation in detail and begin to feel the way you would feel in the actual situation. Now, while holding the mental picture, allow your whole body to relax as much as possible. The better you have learned the DR skill, the easier and quicker you will find this momentary relaxation to achieve. Now maintain the relaxed feeling as you mentally rehearse the problem situation through to the finish. See yourself completing the job successfully and staying relaxed.

The next time you find yourself about to deal with a challenging, stressful situation, simply pause for a few seconds, turn your attention to your body, and allow your whole body to relax as much as you can, keeping the situation in mind. You can easily learn to do this "quickie" relaxation technique in a few seconds and without the slightest outward sign of what you are doing. Anyone looking at you would notice, at most, that you had become silent and that you seemed to be thinking about something for a few seconds. You need not even close your eyes to do this.

If you happen to have a few moments alone before entering the challenge situation, you can relax yourself somewhat more thoroughly. Sit down, if possible, get comfortable, and close your eyes. Use your built-in muscle memory to bring back the feeling of deep relaxation and hold it for about a full minute. Then open your eyes and, as you go about the task at hand, try to retain the feeling of calmness that came with the relaxation.

After you try this technique a few times, I'm sure you'll agree that it has the added benefit of freeing your thought processes and enabling you to deal with the situation more flexibly than you might have if you were tense and if you overconcentrated on the problem at hand. As mentioned in Chapter 2, your stress reaction seems to interfere somewhat with the abstract processes of your brain, making it more difficult to observe carefully, to reason, to think of many alternatives, to compare alternatives, and to suspend action until you fully understand the situation. Relaxing, even a little bit, can help to bring these faculties back into play. You can also use the method to unwind again quickly after the situation is over.

This momentary relaxation technique will not, of course, prevent the stress reaction from coming into play within your body as you deal with the problem situation, but it will probably help to keep your stress level down to the point where it does not interfere with your successful functioning. In addition, frequent use of this technique throughout your daily experiences will prevent the development of the kind of chronic anxiety known as *stress buildup* — the bit-by-bit accumulation of a constant, unrelieved state of arousal from the many repeated stress episodes throughout a normal day. Think of momentary relaxation as a handy relief valve for pressure.

QUICK RECOVERY

A fairly reliable indication of a person's general level of emotional health and personal adjustment is the length of time it takes for him to recover from a strong emotional experience. We all know that people vary widely in this respect. One person will grieve for days after a disappointing experience, whereas another will get over it or at least come to terms with it before the day is out. Some people nurse personal tragedies for the rest of their lives; others pick up the pieces and proceed with the business of living. The person who takes a long time to recover from an upsetting experience is usually also the one who is easily upset. Both of these patterns derive from the individual's personal level of reactivity.

However, many people don't seem to realize that emotional reactivity is a *learned* response. By the use of deep relaxation training, self-management techniques, and a logical thought process, you can learn to recover quickly from upsetting experiences. Actually, the skill of quick recovery takes little more than a conscious awareness of the process of recovery. Once you begin to think about your emotional responses, you can recognize the process of returning to emotional equilibrium after a provocation has passed. For example, if you find yourself drawn into a very hostile exchange with another person or group of people, you may be angry and your stress reaction will be in full swing. Your higher level mental processes will probably not be functioning very well. However, at a certain point, your emotions will begin to subside and you will realize that you are angry. That is, you will experience your anger as an intellectual concept as well as a physical feeling.

At that point, you have the option to continue wallowing

in the bad feelings by rehashing the provocation, rejustifying your position, reopening a new attack on your adversaries, and becoming newly outraged by their unreasonable behavior. You also have the option to substitute your more rational thinking processes for the old ones and to refocus your attention on your objectives in the situation. You can change the subject, interrupt the conflict, depart, call into play some conflict resolution techniques, or offer a new approach to the problem at hand. Regardless of the technique you apply, the important thing is to return to the mode of rational thinking and decision making for your own benefit (Boshear & Albrecht, 1977, pp. 41–46).

For most people, developing this skill takes very little more than a careful attitude of alertness and self-monitoring. The skill of physical relaxation speeds the arrival of the point at which you emerge from the emotional fogbank and reacquire your higher level mental abilities. You can also use the momentary relaxation technique to de-escalate your arousal level further, improving your cognitive faculties all the more.

This concept of using relaxation skills to enhance the quick recovery skill implies that personal adjustment and emotional stability can be learned, at least to some extent. It means that developing the neurological skill to "stop, look, and listen" offers an important avenue to emotional freedom.

RETHINKING

The skill of *rethinking* involves recognizing dead-end thoughts when you fasten on to them and substituting more constructive thoughts for them. For example, all of us sometimes find ourselves in situations in which we are inconvenienced to the point of frustration. You may find that your airplane will not take off on schedule and that you must wait four hours for the next flight. In addition, the airline luggage crew has lost your suitcase. And, to make matters worse, you can't reach anyone at your destination by telephone to let them know about the dilemma.

In this situation, you may find yourself feeling frustrated, tense, and irritable. You may so preoccupy yourself with the frustration you feel that you are not ready to sit down, relax, and wait constructively for the next flight. In fact, that may not have even occurred to you yet. The monologue going on in your mind probably proceeds something like this:

"This is terrible."

"Why do these things always happen to me?!"

"I've got to get to Scranton."

"Isn't there some other way . . .?"

"No. Dammit, I'm stuck here."

"This is ridiculous. Those stupid people! Why can't they run an airline on time?"

"This is terrible."

Sound familiar? You may even say part of this monologue out loud. The problem here is that you're wasting mental energy by getting caught in a stressful, *anxiety-sustaining* mental loop. Since this negative, emotional dialogue cannot help you achieve your goal, then it makes sense to abandon it as soon as you can and to turn your mind to more constructive—and more relaxing—activities. If you cannot prevent your frustration reaction from setting in, then you need a little time to finish feeling justifiably angry in such a situation. Once the reaction arrives and the emotions come with it, it makes no sense to fight it or try to suppress it. It is best to accept the angry feelings *for a reasonable time*, but then it makes sense to get on with the business of living.

Rethinking consists of deliberately letting go of the dead-end thoughts and allowing your emotions to subside as the thoughts leave. A useful technique for rethinking is merely to substitute a new, more useful thought for the old one. When you hear yourself saying, "This is terrible," you can interrupt yourself and say (out loud, if it is practical), "No, this is merely what's happening at this time and in this place." *Focus your attention on the reality of the situation,* and if you have no real means for changing it, then acknowledge that it has happened and that the task at hand is to decide what to do next. The second statement you can make to yourself is, "Now that this has happened, what shall I do next?"

Don't accept the emotional retort from yourself, "Hah! What *can* I do? If those stupid idiots . . . ," etc. Demand — and get — from yourself a *rational* answer to the question. Change the focus of your attention from the past — the terrible thing that has happened — to the future. Put your mind into the problem-solving mode as soon as possible.

Other useful target thoughts for the rethinking technique are, "Since he's acting that way, how shall I deal with him?", "Those are the facts of the situation," "Let's see, what choices do I have at this point," and "Well, I suppose it's necessary to rethink my strategy on this." Rethinking does not require that you eliminate or suppress your normal emotional reactions, but it does mean that you *do nothing* that will unnecessarily prolong the bad feelings. This technique combines nicely with the previous one of quick recovery.

THOUGHT STOPPING

When you find yourself wrestling with troublesome thoughts and having difficulty getting them out of your mind, you can use the technique of *thought stopping* to clear your mental slate. You can also use it to improve your overall thinking processes, such as eliminating critical evaluations of other people when they are unnecessary.

Here is the technique. When you find yourself thinking about something you want to chase out of your mind, simply "hear" in your mind the shouted word, "Stop!" This will cause your mental machinery to come to a standstill for a second or so. Then you can immediately substitute a new and more productive train of thought for the old one. Change the subject in your mind to anything positive, useful, or constructive.

You can make this technique especially powerful by developing a vivid memory of the stop signal. Some time when you are completely alone, such as driving along in your car, simply yell "Stop!" loudly and authoritatively. Listen to the sound of your voice reverberate around you, and let it sink into your memory. Repeat this several times if you like. Later, when you call on this memory, it will come back with a very strong effect.

Learn to monitor your thoughts from time to time and spot those you consider to be negative, counterproductive, or otherwise deserving of elimination. If you tend to criticize other people in your mind as you look at them, or if you find yourself feeling sorry for yourself or criticizing yourself, bring in the stop signal and change the subject. Before long, you'll find that these thoughts come to mind less and less frequently.

MENTAL DIVERSION

Few people seem to realize that they can consciously choose to a great extent to focus their minds on positive thoughts and to spend less time on negative thoughts. For example, a manager who must make an important presentation to a group of high-ranking executives may spend all morning worrying about it, even though he has prepared thoroughly and will probably do an excellent job.

The technique of *mental diversion* merely requires that you have a few handy positive topics to devote your mind to and that you substitute one of them for the subject that is currently bothering you — provided, of course, that thinking about the old subject will not accomplish anything particularly useful.

I discovered some time ago that, if I allowed myself to, I

would spend the hour or two before conducting a large management seminar in worrying about whether I would do a good job. I'd go over my notes, check and recheck my materials, and keep asking myself whether I'd overlooked anything. After discovering the technique of mental diversion, I changed that pattern. Thereafter, I would prepare thoroughly for the seminar (or a meeting with executives, or an important presentation, or any other challenging task), get everything in order well in advance, and put it aside. I would then deliberately indulge in other mental activities that would bring me positive feelings, with the complete assurance that everything was taken care of. Driving to the location where I am to conduct a seminar, I frequently sing songs in the car—one of my favorite activities. This keeps my mind too busy to worry about the task ahead. I usually arrive at the location wishing I had more time to sing a half dozen other songs that have come to mind.

Don't mistake mental diversion for "putting something out of your mind." Very seldom can you merely force a negative or anxious thought out of your mind, *without having a suitable replacement for it*. Your mind doesn't tune things out; it only tunes things in. Unless you deliberately substitute a more constructive thought for the one that troubles you, your brain will have little choice but to focus on it. So, when you wish to use the mental diversion technique, make sure you give your brain a new task that is demanding and worthwhile. This technique combines especially well with the previously discussed method of thought stopping.

REHEARSAL

You can improve your effectiveness at handling challenging situations by *mental rehearsal* if you have some idea of what a given situation will involve. To make this technique most effective, take two or three minutes alone and put yourself into deep relaxation. Once relaxed, form a mental picture of the upcoming situation. Let the various people, things, possible happenings, and concepts ramble about in your mind for a little while, and then organize them into a vivid mental picture of the situation. See the actual place, the faces of the other people who will probably be there, and include as many details as necessary to create a feeling of actually being there.

Then, as if watching a high-speed movie sequence, see yourself carrying out your task, dealing with any problems or obstacles that arise, and successfully completing it. Repeat the rehearsal on any selected problem areas, developing alternative ways of handling them. Especially, develop a feeling of follow-through — a sense of completing the entire situation. This will reduce your sense of apprehension about the situation because that feeling is focused on what may go wrong rather than on successful completion.

For an especially big event or situation, you may want to use the rehearsal technique several times over a week or two beforehand. You can even jot down a brief "script" to help you guide your mental programming process. Work out alternative ways of handling the situation, test them in your imagination, and pick out the best one. Just be sure to keep a flexible attitude when the situation comes up, so that you can deal effectively with any turn of events you didn't predict during rehearsal.

Even if you don't have the time or privacy to use the DR preparation for rehearsal, you can still get good results. Even a few moments spent thinking through the upcoming situation will help you to account for snags or problems you might not have otherwise anticipated and to add creative touches to your approach.

DESENSITIZATION

The technique of desensitization will enable you to reduce the anxiety you feel about certain particularly troublesome situations. Therapists sometimes use a visualization technique to help people overcome such fears as the fear of flying, fear of animals, claustrophobia, or fear of certain impending situations. For example, a doctoral student may feel so apprehensive about the oral examination — a situation almost calculated to induce anxiety in one who is within an inch of receiving the long-sought degree — that he feels he will not be able to collect his thoughts and make a good showing. By carefully rehearsing the situation in his mind, he can gradually reduce the anxiety he feels about the whole matter and prepare himself to do a good job.

To use the desensitization technique, simply put yourself into deep relaxation for a few minutes and imagine yourself approaching the target situation in easy steps. For example, if the experience is to be a marketing presentation in a distant city, you can imagine yourself packing your briefcase and leaving your office. Maintain a calm, relaxed attitude as you visualize this easy step. Then see yourself driving to the airport, again keeping very relaxed. Next visualize the steps of boarding the plane, riding to your destination (presuming you have no intense fear of riding on airplanes), deplaning, riding to your hotel, checking in, having dinner, getting a good night's sleep, rising in the morning, going to the place of business, meeting the other people, engaging in the target situation, giving your presentation *and* completing it successfully, and gaining the respect of your colleagues.

If at any point in the sequence you feel yourself becoming even slightly anxious, *stop*. Back up to the previous step and rehearse it a few times. Then relax for another minute or so and come out of the DR state. Later on, repeat the process, quickly leading up to the last step you rehearsed, dwelling on it for a few seconds and then moving to the next step. Keep as calm as possible and make your mental images as detailed and realistic as possible. Take another step only when you can complete the preceding one feeling fully relaxed and calm.

It may take three or four desensitizations of three or four minutes each to reduce the anxious feelings to your satisfaction. You may find that you still feel somewhat anxious about the last step. Don't worry too much about this. Just make sure you have prepared yourself thoroughly to do a good job and that you've adopted a healthy attitude of "take it as it comes." Then you will find that you can keep your anxiety level to a reasonable minimum and handle the situation effectively.

A PROCEDURE FOR LEARNING DEEP RELAXATION

From virtually all the discussion in this book up to this point, you can see the fundamental importance of the deep relaxation skill in personal stress reduction and stress management. Routine practice of deep relaxation seems to offer several key benefits in this regard.

1. It reduces the level of long-term, chronic anxiety a person experiences; it enables him to drain off the accumulated physical tension caused by normal stress reactions.
2. It reduces his overall level of reactivity to problem situations, thereby diminishing the total stress score accumulated.
3. It enables the person to employ other constructive mental programming techniques such as momentary relaxation, quick recovery, rethinking, mental diversion, thought stopping, rehearsal, and desensitization.

To gain a full appreciation of these techniques, you must actually try them and physically experience the sensations they bring about in your body. Many people read about various DR methods, make a mental note to try them, and never follow through. I strongly recommend that you set aside a few hours over the next few weeks to teach yourself a simple DR technique and use it a few times. Then evaluate the skill in terms of your own life, your objectives, and the way in which you want to spend your time.

You can learn the deep relaxation skill merely by taking the time to do so. Here is a procedure that will work for probably 75% to 80% of the people who try it. It involves making a tape recording of your own voice and giving instructions to yourself for progressive relaxation of your body. This entire process will take about four hours of your time over a period of about a week. Appendix 2 gives the complete text for the instructions, which you can simply read as you speak into the microphone. The overall procedure is as follows:

1. Find a quiet, undisturbed place to work.

2. Get out your tape recorder, preferably a cassette machine of moderate-to-high quality, with 30 minutes of time on each side.

3. Set it up, plug in the microphone, and say a few test words to get accustomed to putting your voice on tape. Rewind the tape to the beginning.

4. Turn to the script in Appendix 2 and read through it out loud as a dry run, without the recorder running. Relax your body and overcome your consciousness of the microphone and recorder. Develop a natural, pleasing tone of voice.

5. Now start the recorder running, allow a 30-second "leader" of silence (to enable you later to turn on the machine, sit down, and start to relax before the instructions begin), and then begin to read the instructions.

6. Read the instructions in a soft, soothing, slightly authoritative voice, using a kind of easy "sing-song" pattern. Speak as if you are speaking *directly to* someone and helping them relax. If you like, impersonate a hypnotist in your style of talking. Speak slowly and distinctly, elongating the vowel sounds slightly. Talk directly into the microphone to produce a strong sound on the tape.

7. When you have finished, label the cassette carefully for future use and put it aside for a day or two.

8. Set aside a half-hour period when you can be completely alone and undisturbed. You may find it necessary to stay late or come in early to the office. Or you may choose to keep

the recorder and the cassette in your car for use at some opportune time (*not*, of course, while driving!).

9. Sit in a comfortable chair and adopt a position you can easily maintain for about 20 minutes. Make sure no muscle or muscle group will have to maintain any exertion to hold your body in position. A good position is one with your back straight, head upright and balanced, shoulders back and level, legs apart and feet flat on the floor, hands in your lap or palms down on your thighs. Don't lie down this first time because you'll probably fall asleep during the instructions.

10. Turn on the recorder, get comfortable in your chair, and adopt a kind of child-like, receptive attitude toward the voice coming from the tape.

11. After sitting through a complete session with the tape —about 20 or 30 minutes—switch off the recorder and remain quietly seated for a while longer. Let your thoughts drift about on pleasant subjects.

12. Repeat this relaxation session four more times on consecutive days. After five days in a row of deep relaxation, you will have mastered the skill and you will be able to use it as you choose.

REFERENCES

Benson, Herbert. "Your Innate Asset for Combating Stress." *Harvard Business Review*, July–August, 1974.

Benson, Herbert. *The Relaxation Response*. New York: Morrow, 1975.

Boshear, Walton and Karl Albrecht. *Understanding People: Models and Concepts*. La Jolla, CA: University Associates, 1977.

Brown, Barbara. *New Mind, New Body*. New York: Harper & Row, 1974.

Brown, Barbara. *Stress and the Art of Biofeedback*. New York: Harper & Row, 1977.

Lindemann, Hannes. *Relieve Tension the Autogenic Way*. New York: Wyden, 1973.

Rubin, Theodore Isaac. *The Angry Book*. New York: Macmillan, 1969.

Redesigning Your Life Style

This chapter deals with the third part of the stress reduction training approach, that of reorganizing your activities (and to some extent your viewpoints) to achieve a proper balance between stresses and rewards. This balance must be one of your own choosing. No one else can prescribe the kind of life you should live.

You may feel you already have an ideal balance in your life. You may feel happy, fulfilled, and fully in control of the decision processes that go into determining how you invest your time and energies. If so, fine. You'll probably find that the following suggestions confirm your views and that you've anticipated many of them.

However, if you're like most people, you probably feel the

need for greater control over these processes. The notion of re-designing your life style is certainly not new. What is new here is using the idea of your total stress score as a barometer for living—a guiding parameter for deciding what things you want more of and what you want less of. I believe this approach has been largely overlooked and consequently that many self-help systems have lacked a sense of focus.

By focusing on stress level as a rough measure of life adjustment and satisfaction, we can take an organized approach to the matter of personal well-being. As mentioned before, our basic premise is that *you as an individual have the right to balance the total amount of life stress you experience against the rewards you get from engaging in the various activities that lead you to experience that stress.*

Our goal is not to eliminate or avoid all stress. That is not possible. As Hans Selye has observed, "stress is the spice of life." We need not even try to reduce it to an absolute minimum. We merely want to keep it to a level at which we can cope effectively and at which we can enjoy the challenges of active living.

THE HOLMES–RAHE LIFE STRESS INVENTORY

The Holmes–Rahe list of stress-rated life changes has gained a great deal of attention as an assessment tool that seems to predict health breakdown as a consequence of stress overload. You may want to use it as part of your overall life style review. Doctors Thomas H. Holmes and Richard H. Rahe (1967) examined large numbers of medical case histories, looking for correlations between major health problems and the life experiences of the patients. They wanted to determine whether the relative amount of upheaval in a person's life—the extent to which his circumstances require him to change and adapt—could be used to predict the likelihood of serious illness.

Holmes and Rahe extended the work done by several other researchers in this area and integrated it into a statistical model. One of the first researchers to take an interest in the connections between change overload and health, Dr. Adolf Meyer (in Holmes & Holmes, 1974, p. 66) of Johns Hopkins University, began keeping "life charts" on his patients in the early 1900s. Meyer's biographies of the patients showed a clear and dramatic correlation between crisis and disease. Patients who experienced many major events in their lives within short periods very frequently became seriously ill.

In the 1940s and 1950s professor Harold G. Wolff (in Holmes & Holmes, 1974, p. 66) of Cornell University Medical College studied the emotional states that often accompany serious disease, as well as the environmental antecedents of health breakdowns. Dr. Holmes applied Meyer's charting technique to more than 5,000 case histories and discovered that certain life changes tended to appear over and over. Dr. Rahe studied case histories from 2,500 Navy men at sea on three cruisers. He found that the 30% of those who reported the highest life change scores became sick during the first month of a new cruise at vastly higher rates than did the 30% with the lowest scores. This unbalanced pattern of sickness continued throughout a typical six-month cruise (Holmes & Masuda, 1972).

Exhibit 8-1 gives the Holmes–Rahe inventory. The number assigned to each event is a statistical index of the relative severity of that change for a large sample of people. Notice that some of the life changes listed are positive events (at least for most people). Nevertheless, Holmes and Rahe found that these events create upheaval in one's life with a consequent need to readjust. Take a few moments to go over the list and add up your own score. Include only those changes that have occurred in the previous year.

Holmes and Rahe contend that a person who scores below 150 points on this inventory has a chance of a serious health problem of less than one in three in the next two years. A score

EXHIBIT 8-1.

The Holmes-Rahe Life Stress Inventory Gives an Index of the Level of Change and Readjustment in One's Life.

THE SOCIAL READJUSTMENT RATING SCALE*

Instructions: Check off each of these life events that has happened to you during the previous year. Total the associated points. A score of 150 or less means a relatively low amount of life change and a low susceptibility to stress-induced health breakdown. A score of 150 to 300 points implies about a 50% chance of a major health breakdown in the next two years. A score above 300 raises the odds to about 80%, according to the Holmes–Rahe statistical prediction model.

Life Event	Mean Value
1. Death of spouse	100
2. Divorce	73
3. Marital separation from mate	65
4. Detention in jail or other institution	63
5. Death of a close family member	63
6. Major personal injury or illness	53
7. Marriage	50
8. Being fired at work	47
9. Marital reconciliation with mate	45
10. Retirement from work	45
11. Major change in the health or behavior of a family member	44
12. Pregnancy	40
13. Sexual difficulties	39
14. Gaining a new family member (e.g., through birth, adoption, oldster moving in, etc.)	39
15. Major business readjustment (e.g., merger, reorganization, bankruptcy, etc.)	39
16. Major change in financial state (e.g., a lot worse off or a lot better off than usual)	38
17. Death of a close friend	37
18. Changing to a different line or work	36
19. Major change in the number of arguments with spouse (e.g., either a lot more or a lot less than usual regarding child-rearing, personal habits, etc.)	35
20. Taking on a mortgage greater than $10,000 (e.g., purchasing a home, business, etc.)	31
21. Foreclosure on a mortgage or loan	30
22. Major change in responsibilities at work (e.g., promotion, demotion, lateral transfer)	29
23. Son or daughter leaving home (e.g., marriage, attending college, etc.)	29
24. In-law troubles	29
25. Outstanding personal achievement	28
26. Wife beginning or ceasing work outside the home	26
27. Beginning or ceasing formal schooling	26

Life Event	Mean Value
28. Major change in living conditions (e.g., building a new home, remodeling, deterioration of home or neighborhood)	25
29. Revision of personal habits (dress, manners, associations, etc.)	24
30. Troubles with the boss	23
31. Major change in working hours or conditions	20
32. Change in residence	20
33. Changing to a new school	20
34. Major change in usual type and/or amount of recreation	19
35. Major change in church activities (e.g., a lot more or a lot less than usual)	19
36. Major change in social acitivities (e.g., clubs, dancing, movies, visiting, etc.)	18
37. Taking on a mortgage or loan less than $10,000 (e.g., purchasing a car, TV, freezer, etc.)	17
38. Major change in sleeping habits (a lot more or a lot less sleep, or change in part of day when asleep)	16
39. Major change in number of family get-togethers (e.g., a lot more or a lot less than usual)	15
40. Major change in eating habits (a lot more or a lot less food intake, or very different meal hours or surroundings)	15
41. Vacation	13
42. Christmas	12
43. Minor violations of the law (e.g., traffic tickets, jaywalking, disturbing the peace, etc.)	11

*Adapted and reprinted from *Journal of Psychosomatic Research*, Vol.11, Holmes/Rahe, "Holmes-Rahe Social Readjustment Rating Scale," © 1967 by Pergamon Press, Ltd. Reprinted with permission of Pergamon Press and the authors.

---

between 150 and 300 gives a likelihood of about 50%. A score of over 300, they believe, offers a risk of over 80% of a major health breakdown.

The notion of adaptive change as causing increased stress and general anxiety seems quite reasonable. Of course, the Holmes–Rahe inventory does not account for your own personal capability for meeting and dealing with stress. I consider this an all-important factor. For example, moving from one home to another may create tremendous turmoil and emotional upset for a family with already strained interpersonal relationships, but for a family whose members have learned to get along well and to take occasional upheavals in stride, the family setting may provide a sense of stability and emotional support to make the change less stressful.

Similarly, a self-employed, workaholic businessman with no forms of personal reward in his life pattern other than his career may experience a business loss or a bankruptcy as devastating. One with a more balanced reward system would probably also find the experience extremely stressful but would probably not become disabled by it.

Furthermore, a person who takes poor care of his health can be expected to succumb to the effects of stress much more readily than the person who has a well-balanced, healthful pattern of living. This is why a holistic approach to one's health and well-being is so important in dealing with stress and with the life changes that cause it.

A HOLISTIC MODEL OF MANAGERIAL LIFESTYLE

A feeble but steadily growing philosophy in the latter part of our century is that human happiness, health, and well-being are a *holistic* proposition. The holistic concept implies that you cannot be an unhealthy or ineffective person in private life and an effective person in your management job. If you have personal adjustment difficulties, health problems, or drinking problems in one functional area of your life, then you will experience the effects of these problems in other functional areas. Your style of living is a rather general pattern, characteristic of you as a whole person, and it transcends any one area or aspect of your life. It defines you as a *transactor* with your world. The holistic view of well-being looks at you as a whole person, in all your dimensions, with all your needs, desires, values, and habits. This is the basis for an organization development approach to stress, such as that described in Chapters 9 and 10.

To be a truly effective manager you must be *an effective person.* The overall pattern of human effectiveness arises again and again in psychological studies. The effective person is *gen-*

erally effective at most things. Being effective does not necessarily mean being famous or outstanding but, rather, effective and competent. The effective person is an effective manager, an effective spouse, an effective parent, an effective member of organizations, and an effective friend and companion.

The guiding principle of the holistic view of personal wellness is that *you* — no one else — *are responsible* for making yourself sick or well. By the things you do in your life and by the ways in which you deploy your mind and emotions, *you govern your own health and well-being.*

A second major principle of this view is that of *balance.* You have many needs as a human being, and to the extent that you act to fulfill those various needs, you tend toward wellness. If you pour all your energy into one area of your life, neglecting other needs, you become lopsided and less than whole.

This concept of balance deserves a bit more attention here, especially as it applies to managers. Many managers become workaholics, with shrivelled-up private lives and unbalanced reward systems. One reason a manager spends long hours at the job is that he gets psychic rewards from it. Managing a group of people means having a chance to give orders to others, to judge the efforts of others, to make decisions, and above all to feel important. Many management jobs entail counterbalancing negative factors, but if a manager spends a great deal of time at the job, it is likely that he gets strong rewards there *and few rewards anywhere else in life.*

Ironically, the "successful" executive or manager who works 60 to 70 hours a week, rises high in the organization, and makes a handsome salary while his marriage falls apart, his health declines, he smokes and drinks too heavily, and lives only for his work can be said to be a failure. He is a success at one narrow pursuit but a failure at life as a general matter. The term *workaholic* very aptly describes this addiction.

Such a person has discovered substantial rewards — mostly good feelings about himself and his own worth — in a single area and has become literally addicted to that pursuit. The manager, the small business owner, or the doctor who suffers through a vacation craving to get back into harness hasn't learned to find satisfactions in a variety of activities. He gets physically out of shape because he can't take the time away from his addiction to enjoy exercise. He smokes cigarettes and drinks coffee to keep himself going at this wonderful, rewarding activity. He eats a terrible diet because he hasn't got time to enjoy a relaxing meal.

Curiously, workaholism and alcoholism often go hand in hand. I believe the reason for this is that most high-performance, high-achievement jobs also involve high stress. The workaholic gets a mixture of good feelings from being important (how many typists or file clerks or janitors have you ever seen working 60 hours a week for no extra pay?) and uncomfortable stress feelings from facing the pressure and the threats to his heroic concept of himself. Not having learned how to step back from the job, with the assurance that he won't lose the source of his emotional "fix," he unconsciously begins to anesthetize the uncomfortable body feelings with alcohol. His doctor may help sustain his addiction by supplying him with tranquilizers, headache prescriptions, and blood pressure medication.

This view of the person as a reward-seeking transactor tells us that the workaholic pattern is simply an extreme imbalance in the person's life pattern that is caused by a lack of perceived rewards in other significant areas. To break the pattern — or any other pattern of imbalance and lopsidedness — one must review his life as an overall proposition and make some new decisions about how to invest time and energy.

Let's use this holistic approach to the rewards of life to construct an evaluation and planning model that you can use in making some basic decisions about your own life. The wheel diagram shown in Exhibit 8-2 gives a systems view of your life style in terms of a balance of six general areas of living. You might choose to include some other areas of special interest to you in adapting the model to your long-term use. For now, let's examine these six dimensions. They are as follows:

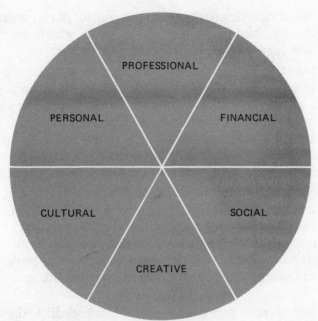

EXHIBIT 8-2. A holistic approach to managerial life style requires a balance of all dimensions of living and working.

1. *Professional* — whatever you do that constitutes your life's central activity; making your living; your relationship to the organization in which you work; your means of livelihood.

2. *Financial* — money, material goods and possessions, and the things that give you feelings of security and satisfaction; your salary, benefits, and other forms of compensation; investment income; your general financial position.

3. *Social* — Relationships and activities you share with others; family, friends, members of the opposite sex; organizations you belong to; colleagues with whom you associate; recreational activities involving other people.

4. *Cultural* — things you do for rewarding educational purposes; self-broadening activities such as traveling, reading, studying a foreign language, taking courses for the sake of learning, attending lectures, watching educa-

tional television programs, going to plays, worthwhile movies, and concerts; the ways in which you absorb new ideas and enjoy learning new things.

5. *Creative* — activities in which you express your personality, and through which you grow and enjoy being a person; hobbies, crafts, or artwork; playing a musical instrument; growing roses, houseplants, or a garden; building things; remodeling a home for the satisfaction it brings; singing, dancing; acting in a play; any avenues for enjoying yourself by expressing your uniqueness.

6. *Personal* — your physical health and well-being; recreation for the sake of relaxation and relief from tension; exercise; diet; privacy and self-understanding; spiritual pursuits of your own choosing; personal hygiene; emotional stability and personal adjustment; physical surroundings and your individual physical life space.

Take a pencil and paper and draw a wheel like the one in Exhibit 8-2. Now, think about each of the categories in turn for a moment or so and make a general, intuitive assessment of it. How do you feel at this moment about what's happening in that area of your life? What's the relative level of your satisfaction with that area? Take your pencil and shade in the segment of the wheel for that category, beginning from the center of the circle and moving outward. Let the size of the shaded area (i.e., the radius) indicate roughly how satisfied you are with it. This is equivalent to asking yourself whether you want to do anything to make some changes in a particular area. Once you've completed the rough diagram, you'll have a general assessment of the "shape" of your life, and you'll have some indication of your judgement as to the overall balance you've established.

A substantial "dent" in the shape of your wheel probably points to an area in which you would like to undertake some new and rewarding activities or to drop some unrewarding ones. A fairly round figure suggests that you feel your life provides rewards in roughly equal measure in each of the categories. Some people finish this exercise with a fairly round model but not a very big one. That is, they see themselves as receiving equally small rewards in all categories. Such a person may need to set some goals in each area and to begin a program of confidence building and improvement of his self-esteem.

THE WELLNESS TRIAD

Now, let's focus closely on one of the six categories of the holistic model that is of extreme importance to health and well-being and that is so often neglected. This is the *personal* area.

Personal activities include all those things you do that help you to live, thrive, enjoy living, and grow and develop as a total human being on a private, individual level. They include your personal, private activities, your thoughts, your self-development activities, your spiritual or religious pursuits, and your physical health behaviors.

Although space does not permit a detailed analysis of the personal area here, I would like to focus on three factors of fundamental importance to health and well-being. Each of these factors plays a part in your overall wellness, and we have known about them for a long time. However, I believe that most people — including medical people and health "experts" — have long overlooked the mutually supporting, synergistic relationship between the three factors of relaxation, exercise, and diet.

In stress reduction training programs, I present these factors not as three individual aspects of health but as an integrated triad of factors I refer to as the *wellness triad*. What you do in one area supports, enhances, and capitalizes on the other two areas. The "whole" result becomes more than the sum of the individual parts.

For some time, I have noted with some curiosity the tendency of various practitioners to specialize in certain approaches to good health. Some people tout meditation, hypnosis, autogenic training, or some other deep relaxation techniques as being the only true path to well-being. According to the Maharishi Mahesh Yogi, if we can get only 1% of the population of the United States to practice his transcendental meditation technique, we'll open the door to the new age of enlightenment and inner peace, but he has little to say about keeping one's body in good physical condition.

Conversely, many nutritionists dwell at great length on the inadequacies of the American diet and our needs for supplements and special approaches to eating. Extremists tout blackstrap molasses, sprouted wheat, brewer's yeast, dolomite pills, and a host of other chemicals—reminiscent of a counterrevolution against the physician's brand of chemical manipulation of the body—with little attention to the effects of stress or the benefits of exercise. Even Carlton Fredericks, a famous nutritionist, once commented in a lecture, "Whenever I feel the urge to exercise, or to engage in any other kind of physical activity, I simply lie down quietly until the feeling passes."

Exercise enthusiasts have their own approach to health, based principally on the proven value of *aerobic* exercises such as jogging.* They present very impressive evidence of the reduced incidence of cardiovascular disease among slow distance joggers. Yet very few of the writers in this field give more than passing mention to the problem of stress. It may be that a person who invests two to four hours per week running slowly and easily for long distances has a handy escape route from the pressures of working and living—at least during the time spent jogging.

I propose to unite these three factors and to deal with them as a synergistic whole—the wellness triad. Let's define

---

*An aerobic mode of exercise is one in which you exert yourself enough to breathe somewhat heavily, yet you do not consume oxygen faster than your heart and lungs can supply it to your muscles; that is, you don't get out of breath. For this reason, you can continue exercising aerobically for fairly extended periods without discomfort. This is the key to staying with a conditioning exercise such as jogging. (Cooper, 1968).

them more fully. The following description is inevitably distorted by my own particular biases and viewpoints. Feel free to modify it according to your own convictions. I'm sure you'll agree, however, on the synergistic potential of the three factors operating simultaneously in your life.

1. *Relaxation* — anything you do, including deep relaxation practice, to relieve the stress accumulated through your daily activities; recreational activities that enable you to relax (*not*, for example, fuming and cursing in front of a television set while your favorite team struggles with its opponents) and reduce the tension level in your body; refreshing sleep; sitting quietly and thinking pleasant thoughts; pleasant daydreams; listening to relaxing music; pursuing a hobby that absorbs your attention and gives you pleasant feelings; taking a stroll by yourself; taking a few minutes during the day to put your feet up and unwind; listening to a recorded deep relaxation cassette; meditating, or practicing any other DR technique.

2. *Exercise* — anything you do that causes you to breathe heavily more than three to five minutes (by this definition, many people don't get *any* exercise); jogging, handball, racquetball, tennis, energetic bicycle riding, *fast* and energetic walking, swimming, or similar activities requiring a high expenditure of energy (golf, by this definition, is not an exercise); activities that arouse your whole body, use your muscles vigorously, make you breathe heavily, and make your heart pump more rapidly and strongly.

3. *Diet* — the sum total of the substances you introduce into your body. A good diet consists of a balanced combination of foods that supply the basic ingredients of nutrition without an overbalance of fats, sugars, or calories; moderate quantities that do not cause an increase in body fat; vitamin supplements taken *in moderation* (such as a concentrated multivitamin and extra vitamin C); minimal use of "junk" foods and those heavily laced with additives, colorings, and preservatives; little or no alcohol (limited to celebrations and occasional social drinking); *no use of tobacco* (except possibly occasional pipe or cigar

smoking); *no use of hard drugs;* rare or occasional use of marijuana; rare use of aspirin or pain medication, unless required for medical management of a specific disorder; rare or no use of patent medicines such as antacids, cold remedies, laxatives, and so on; *no* use of tranquilizers, sleeping pills, or other central nervous system depressants; no use or moderate use of caffeine (coffee, tea, or cola drinks).

You can easily remember these three factors by uniting them in the acronym "RED". I frequently refer to this concept as the "RED triad." I feel compelled to defend my definitions of relaxation, exercise, and diet in order to give those who may disagree with me some basis for comparing this concept to their own.

First, many activities which people have defined as "relaxing" do not relax them at all. A man who rants, raves, cheers, and curses in front of the television set will become more aroused, not less. His stress response will be in full swing. The best that can be said for this experience is that it is episodic rather than prolonged, so his body can begin to recover after the experience is over, but it is not physical and neurological *relaxation,* according to my definition. Similarly, the woman who plays bridge with a group of very competitive companions or who finds the company of some of them distasteful does not relax very much according to this definition.

Watching a horror movie or a dramatic or violent episode on television does not constitute relaxation either. The next time you see a particularly violent, tense, or dramatic movie, tune in to your body afterward. Notice how you feel. See how long this feeling of arousal lasts. It may not be extreme arousal, but it is not relaxation. For some people, even reading the news in a typical paper produces more feelings of vague anxiety than of pleasant relaxation. Activities that many people label "relaxation" actually amount to less stressful escapes from other activities such as their jobs or troublesome relationships with their families. True relaxation comes from experiences that induce a feeling of mental and emotional peace and allow your body to reduce its internal arousal level.

Second, many people delude themselves — usually willingly — about the amount of real exercise they get. Taking an occasional stroll may be helpful, but it certainly will not suffice as exercise activity in promoting good conditioning. The image of the corpulent middle-aged man riding around the golf course on an electric cart makes a mockery of the game of golf as an exercise form. In addition, the counter-synergistic effect of his anger and frustration with his game may increase his stress level and detract from any constructive effects of his relaxation activities. A person who plays golf frequently and who walks the entire course at a very vigorous rate can get a moderate amount of exercise.

The unfortunate fact is that the more out of condition you are, the less you feel like exercise. And the better condition you've attained, the more you like to engage in vigorous physical activity — to you it's fun. Getting back into condition requires a carefully planned approach to avoid defeating yourself. A later section of this chapter offers some helpful suggestions for rebuilding your health by gradually and painlessly getting back into excellent condition.

Third, whether or not you like to accept it, the substances you put into your body are entirely your own responsibility. If your diet consists mostly of junk foods, sweets, liquor, cigarettes, and coffee, it is because you have chosen, probably only half consciously, to accept these things as fit for your consumption. Conversely, if you eat fairly carefully and you can use other substances rather than be used by them, it is because you have chosen to do so.

Granted, the typical American diet as found in most restaurants and in many homes is not particularly outstanding in balance and nutritional content. It is optimized for speed and convenience, and it emphasizes overstimulation of the taste buds. The typical restaurant meal contains too much food and too many calories, and the overweight person supplies the other half of the situation — the habit of eating more than his body needs. The "clean off your plate" habit is one of the factors that make most overweight people eat too much.

Let's now explore the benefits of integrating relaxation, exercise, and diet into a synergistic combination. Many people find dieting to be a form of self-imposed torture. Very few crash diets have ever resulted in permanent loss of weight. After the punishment is over, people usually go right back to their prior eating habits. Similarly, many people — perhaps most — experience the process of getting back into shape as a Spartan, punishing, lonely pursuit. They can usually be derailed at almost any point and for the flimsiest of "reasons." Actually, there is only one reason why a person doesn't continue with good eating behavior or good exercise behavior: *The process brings more punishments than rewards for them.*

If you want to get back into good condition and to revise your eating habits, you must carefully arrange the project in such a way that *the rewards you experience are stronger than the punishment you experience.* Generally, this means no crash diets. It also means that charging back into the gymnasium or out onto the running path and forcing yourself to exercise to the point of discomfort won't work either. You must adopt a gradual, planned, and patient approach if you are to have success in the long term. A later section of this chapter gives some suggestions for changing these patterns without defeating yourself.

The other element of the RED triad — relaxation — can help you to make progress in the other two areas. Indeed, learning the skill of deep relaxation may be a key step in many kinds of self-modification and self-improvement. For example, if you take a few seconds to relax just before you begin eating, you can overcome the excessive eating that results from unrelieved tension and stress.

In fact, each of these three factors will support and reinforce the others. For another example, when you begin jogging and start to feel physically better within about two weeks' time, you will also begin to look a bit better and have better feelings overall about yourself. This will probably lead you to pay more attention to diet and to start eating less if you are overweight. The physical improvement and a generally higher

EXHIBIT 8-3.

The Factors of Relaxation, Exercise, and Diet Form a Synergistic Wellness Triad.

This Factor:	Enhances This Factor:		
	Relaxation	Exercise	Diet
Relaxation	Calmer attitude makes living more enjoyable; relaxation and recreation get higher priority.	Changes time priority; makes it easier to make time for exercise.	Reduces anxiety-related eating; increased body awareness and relaxation reduce over-eating at meals.
Exercise	Improved physical condition enables the body to consume stress chemicals; makes relaxation skills easier to learn and maintain.	Improved physical condition raises energy level; makes more exercise easier and enjoyable.	Regular exercise burns calories, promotes gradual weight loss, increases metabolic level, reduces appetite.
Diet	Reducing consumption of alcohol, tobacco, and caffeine makes parasympathetic relaxation response easier.	High-quality diet increases energy level; exercise becomes easier as weight decreases.	Good eating habits become easier to maintain over time.

energy level due to aerobic exercise can also lead to a lessening of your appetite. Exhibit 8–3 shows some of the interrelationships that make the RED triad such a powerful combination of factors for improving your health and well-being.

THE WELLNESS BEHAVIOR TEST

Now let's use the wellness triad of factors as a checklist of your *wellness behaviors*. I prefer the term *behaviors* to habits because it strongly implies that they are voluntary. Here's a short quiz of a dozen items that will tell you how well you maintain the most important form of personal capital you will ever have — your own health.

Refer to the questions in Exhibit 8-4 and give yourself an A, B, C, D, or F, depending on your judgments. Be fair with yourself but be honest. After you've scored the test, you might want to compute the average grade. Assign four points to an A, three to a B, two to a C, and one to a D. If you flunk, you flunk —no points. Then add up all the points and divide by 12 to get your health grade-point average. Did you average at least a B-plus?

EXHIBIT 8-4.

The "Wellness Behavior" Test

This quiz will help you assess the behavior patterns that establish your own wellness. Use your judgment to give yourself a grade — A, B, C, D, or F, according to the following dozen questions.

Relaxation:

1. Do you take time to get completely away from work and other pressures, to unwind?

Frequently	A
Fairly often	B
Sometimes	C
Seldom	D
I "just can't"	F

2. Do you sleep well? Fall asleep easily? Sleep through the night?

Very well	A
Fairly well	B
Not so well	C
Have trouble	D
"Certified Insomniac"	F

3. Do you take, or feel you need, aspirin, tranquilizers, sleeping pills, stomach medicines, or laxatives?

Seldom or never	A
Occasionally	B
Fairly often	C
Quite often	D
I'm hooked	F

4. Do you practice a form of deep relaxation (e.g., meditation, progressive relaxation, autogenic training, etc.) daily?

Nearly every day	A
Often	B
Occasionally	C
Seldom	D
What's deep relaxation?	F

EXHIBIT 8-4 (continued).

Exercise:

1. Can you run a mile (at any speed) without becoming exhausted?

Easily	A
Fairly well	B
Can barely make it	C
Can't do it at all	D
Can't walk a mile	F

2. Can you play a fast game of tennis or other strenuous sport without becoming exhausted?

Easily	A
Fairly well	B
Get very tired	C
Get exhausted	D
Wouldn't try it	F

3. Do you jog or engage in some other very active exercise several times a week?

Usually	A
Fairly often	B
Occasionally	C
Seldom	D
Allergic to exercise	F

4. Are you fairly strong and physically able?

Very	A
Moderately	B
Adequate for my purposes	C
Quite weak	D
I can stand up in a strong wind	F

Diet:

1. Are you overweight? (Just check to see how much surface fat is visible on your body.)

Not at all	A
Mildly overweight	B
Moderate amount of flab	C
Quite a paunch	D
Butterball	F

2. Do you smoke?

Never	A
2 or 3 a day	B
Half-pack a day	C
Pack or more a day	D
Chain smoker	F

(continued)

EXHIBIT 8-4 (continued).

3. Do you drink liquor (including wine or beer)?	*Rarely or never*	A
	Socially and	
	seldom	B
	One a day	C
	Several a day	D
	I'm an alkie	F
4. Do you drink coffee, tea, cola drinks, or other sources of caffeine and sugar?	*Rarely or never*	A
	1 or 2 a day	B
	Several a day	C
	Regularly, including with meals	D
	Can't do without it	F

Putting these various models together — your grade-point average, your personal balance wheel, your life-stress score, and the present state of your health — will tell you most of what you need to know. In a sense, you are estimating your potential for handling stress and the amount of it you have developed in your overall patterns of living.

The purpose of this book is not to go deeply into techniques for building or rebuilding good health but merely to help you decide what you should do about it. Later sections give some useful pointers, but if you aren't satisfied with the results of your life style review, consider reading some of the books recommended there and making a plan for the personal category of your life.

REDEFINING YOUR LIFE STYLE

Thaddeus Kostrubala was an overweight, smoking, drinking, middle-aged professional man — a psychiatrist by trade. Let's hear what he has to say about his own personal process of revis-

230

ing his life style. The following excerpt comes from his candid and inspirational book *The Joy of Running* (1976):*

> I'm a physician. I didn't have to think very deeply or develop any insight to realize that I was a prime candidate for a heart attack. I weighed 230 pounds. I was 5 feet 11 inches tall. I drank heavily. I did not exercise; I didn't even take walks. I *never* ran. My blood cholesterol was quite high, and my blood pressure was beginning to rise. According to everything I knew about heart disease, I was in line to have a coronary. The number-one cause of death in men over thirty-five was stalking me.
>
> What does a "good chance" of having a coronary mean? Well, it meant to me that if I dared to look at myself without blinking, I could have one any day. I was embarrassed, depressed, and frightened; chagrined at my own inability to do even the simplest exercise without getting dizzy and out of breath. As I looked at [Dr.] John [Boyer] — ten years older than I — I was even more embarrassed. In spite of his graying hair he looked fifteen years younger than I. He said that he was beginning a [jogging] program within a few weeks for patients who had had coronary heart disease. If I had any doubt about the seriousness of my condition, it evaporated at that point. I was to be treated along with those men who had survived the dreaded killer. I wasn't a colleague any longer; I was a patient [p. 16].

Kostrubala enrolled in a gradual, medically managed program of slow, long-distance jogging, which helped him make a complete metamorphosis of his entire life style. He became so impressed with the potential of aerobic exercise — particularly slow running — that he eventually began to use it as an adjunct to his group therapy sessions. He would form a therapeutic group as a unit — a miniature society of people seeking their own growth

*From *The Joy of Running* by Thaddeus Kostrubala, M.D. Copyright © 1976 by Thaddeus Kostrubala. Reprinted by permission of J. B. Lippincott Company.

through group experience. He would train them in running over a period of weeks and months, and he found that the group running sessions of 30 minutes to an hour played a strong part in helping the patients reach their therapeutic objectives.

He also revised his own entire life style, reducing alcohol consumption, losing weight, eliminating cigarettes, and adopting a much more rewarding, less stressful pattern of living and working. Kostrubala now conducts Sunday morning training clinics in San Diego for people who want to learn the enjoyable exercise of slow distance running and to improve their overall health.

I offer this example to show what can be done with a person's life style, once he steps up to the responsibility for making it what it is. The growing popularity of jogging as a simple and effective way to improve cardiovascular and cardiopulmonary health attests to its value. In a later section of this chapter, I give a few valuable suggestions for getting back into *excellent* condition in a way that is rewarding and not self-defeating. Most of these I've discovered by blundering onto them and by talking to many people. This section does not preach to you about how you *should* remake your life style. It merely presents a way in which you *can* if you choose to do so. Since you must live it, you must also choose it. The following suggestions proceed from the assumption that you have reviewed your living pattern and have decided to evolve it into something somewhat different—something more to your liking. The suggestions focus on the personal area, because so many American professional people seem to have difficulty in making substantial changes there. Of course, it's always a good idea to strive for rewarding patterns of activity in all six of the assessment categories.

First, then, you can take a sheet of paper and state the results of your personal review process in terms of intentions. What changes will you now make in order to increase your feelings of reward in the areas you chose for improvement? Probably a simple one-page list will give you all you need in order to go ahead with the restyling process. Simply write down for each of the six areas those activities you will do more of and those you will do less of. To help you choose, you might jot down on a separate scratch pad as many enjoyable activities as you can think of for each area. Then choose a few — don't overdo it — that appeal to you most. Select one area as most deserving of priority attention, and let the others fall in line behind it. This way, you don't risk spreading yourself too thin and getting caught up in an exhausting self-improvement program that is demanding and unrewarding.

For the time being, don't include any activities in your plan that you do not consider rewarding. Don't undertake any new activity merely because it's "good for you." Do it because you will like doing it. Later on, after you've begun to enjoy the process of consciously shifting your life style into new areas, you can undertake low-risk improvements by using strategies that make them rewarding.

Once you've picked out a few activities that will help you rebalance your "balance wheel," begin to translate them into action. For example, if you decided to do more things along the creative line by way of self-expression, then enroll in an art class, sign up for piano lessons, join a woodcarving class, take singing lessons, or simply get out your stamp collection or your collection of miniature china cats and get involved with it again. Translate the thought into action *soon.* Decide how you will *make time* in your life's schedule for these new and important activities.

If you want to do more in the cultural category, look through the newspaper and find out what's going on that you might find enjoyable. Try something new or unfamiliar to you. Look around for some cultural events, such as ethnic dances, festivals, or displays. Visit the new museum you've heard about. Buy tickets for a concert or play and surprise your mate or best friend. Do something — however small — very soon. Indeed, you'll probably find it easier to pick something small. Try several small experiences rather than winding up for a massive dose of culture. Just begin to favor that area—or any other you've chosen—with specific actions.

You'll find that, after a first stage of inertia lasting a few weeks to a month, you'll be doing more things in more areas. If you happen to be a "certified workaholic," you'll probably find yourself feeling more inclined to stop when you've done a good day's work. With other rewarding activities to invite your attention, you'll find the job shrinking back to a more reasonable perspective. And you may also find yourself enjoying your work more, *simply because* it's no longer your only source of reward feelings.

Conversely, if you've found your work distasteful in the past, you may now have worked out some ways to change it— including leaving your job if necessary—to increase the rewards you feel. If so, your work may change from a form of punishment to a form of reward. Each person has a different set of life activities and a different mixture of rewards and dissatisfactions.

The purpose in setting such goals is not to begin a self-discipline approach to life. The purpose is to *add activities to your life that bring rewards outside of the lopsided areas.* Forcing yourself to pursue activities you don't really enjoy because they're supposed to be good for you will only lead to frustration and avoidance. Pick rewarding activities. Try something new that you've always wanted to try. Do something you used to enjoy but have gotten away from over the years. In short, *add value and reward to your life* across each of the six categories.

This holistic model of health and well-being is indeed a model for managerial effectiveness if you accept the notion that a well-rounded, highly fulfilled individual will make a better manager than a lopsided one who has narrowed down his life, interests, and thoughts to the routine of doing the job. Time after time, I've seen self-educating, well-rounded managers stumble across new ideas in one area of life and find applications for them on the job.

A manager who reads widely about changes taking place in American society, for example, may see some immediate implications for his organization and its products or services. One who takes a great interest in his own health and physical conditioning will tend to encourage employees to do the same. Such a manager will probably pay more attention to the overall well-being of his employees and will spot problems or difficulties earlier than the manager whose point of view is sharply narrowed to the routine functions of the job.

The well-rounded manager, according to this model, is a *learning and growing person.* This person can deal with each area of life as an opportunity to learn and develop, an opportunity to find challenges, and an opportunity to have rewarding experiences. Indeed, the whole notion of happiness may be looked at as a byproduct of a reward-getting style of living. A conscious approach to structuring one's life and activities to find ample rewards makes a person well-rounded and emotionally healthy and a more effective manager into the bargain.

This approach to redesigning your life style, let me repeat, differs from most forms of self-development in that it focuses on what you enjoy, not on what you "must" do. The idea is simply to gravitate naturally to a larger variety of experiences that you find rewarding and to undertake them by choice rather than as a form of medicine. Soul searching and self-examination, although often useful, are unnecessary with this approach. Feelings of increased happiness, self-worth, and personal effectiveness come automatically when you are *doing* the things that bring you rewards. And these feelings can pave the way for a highly constructive approach to changing yourself at deeper levels if you choose to do so.

REBUILDING YOUR HEALTH

Although the personal category can include many other facets, we can focus on the wellness triad of factors — relaxation, exercise, and diet — as a basis for building holistic health and well-being. A substantial level of wellness brought about by constructive action in each area forms a strong foundation for the others.

The following suggestions are based on the assumption that you didn't especially like your score on the previous wellness behavior test and that you would like to raise your grade-point average to at least a B-plus. Choose any or all of them for action. Just be sure you don't start off with a program that is too big or too ambitious. Stack the deck in favor of success, not defeat. Start small and get the taste of success before expanding your approach. Here are some suggestions for each of the three factors.

Relaxation

1. Record a deep relaxation cassette for yourself, following the instructions in Chapter 7 and using the script given in the Appendix.
2. Use the tape once a day in private in order to learn to relax completely.
3. Start using the momentary relaxation method from time to time during the day.
4. Take a course in meditation, autogenic training, or self-hypnosis that is oriented to relaxation training.
5. Program your thoughts with positive images of relaxation, tranquility, and pleasant human relations with others.
6. *Do not* change any of your medications without your doctor's concurrence.
7. Schedule specific times away from your work for real relaxation.
8. Find a certain amount of private time when you can be absolutely alone with yourself.
9. Develop the habit of self-monitoring. Pay attention to your body signals as you go about the day's activities, and frequently de-escalate your internal level and relax your muscles.
10. Watch less television and read interesting books more

often; watch fewer shows and movies with violent scenes or other anxiety-producing episodes; switch off radio news when it slings useless bad news.

11. Find a place that helps you to relax and detach yourself from the world for short periods. Visit a park, the beach, an untraveled back road, or a spot in the woods where you can feel remote from society and close to your own thoughts.

12. Start rethinking your time priorities and make time for regular periods of solitude and relaxation.

13. If you're heavily in the Type A pattern, read *Type A Behavior and Your Heart* (Friedman & Rosenman, 1974). Follow the authors' advice and begin to impersonate a Type B.

Exercise

1. *Do not* increase your exercise activities without making sure you are in reasonably good health.

2. If you are over 35, have a thorough medical examination and get your doctor's go-ahead before beginning any exercise program.

3. Find a healthy doctor who is in excellent physical condition himself (this may not be easy). Have him administer a heart-stress test (sometimes called an "exercise physical") and give you an idea of your cardiopulmonary fitness level and heart condition.

4. Read a book such as *The Joy of Running* (Kostrubala, 1976) or *Adult Fitness* (Kasch & Boyer, 1968). Begin to sell yourself on the importance of good exercise habits.

5. Join a class in slow long-distance jogging and begin to build up your stamina in easy stages.

6. Don't (ever) exercise so vigorously or for so long that you find it fatiguing and that you later are tempted to find many "reasons" to skip it "just this once." Make it so easy that you feel a sense of reward and accomplishment and want to do it again.

7. Take your time getting into shape. Don't become obsessed with the need to prove yourself or to get back into shape quickly. Again, *make exercise a pleasant growth experience for yourself.*

8. Give exercise the same priority as any other routine activity, such as grocery shopping, maintaining your car, cleaning or repairing the house, improving your education, tending to your investments, or even traveling to and from work.

9. Think about exercise as a long-term investment. Set an *easily attainable* goal for the next month and one for the next three months.

10. Exercise with other people if it helps you to find time for it. Associate with people who are trim and in good condition. Put yourself in situations in which you will be encouraged to engage in enjoyable physical activities.

Diet

1. If you are extremely overweight, get your doctor's concurrence before you undertake any weight-loss program. Find a trim, healthy doctor and ask him to help you work out a sensible diet program that is best for you.

2. Otherwise, if you need to lose a moderate amount of weight, *don't go on a crash diet — ever.* Think of losing weight as a long-term process of readjusting your eating habits so that you take in fewer calories while still enjoying eating fairly well.

3. Consider joining a weight reduction school or program — preferably one combined with an exercise program.

4. Make up your mind to be satisfied with a slow, steady loss of weight. A few pounds a month will soon add up to a respectable loss, and you won't feel as though you've tortured yourself to do it.

5. Resign your membership in the "Clean Off Your Plate Club." Learn to eat slowly until you feel your body's

hunger signal turn off; then leave the rest. Understand that the waste of food took place when it came out of the kitchen, not when you left it on your plate. Select a few morsels you plan to leave on the plate before you begin eating.

6. Read a book such as *How to Save Your Life* (Ubell, 1976) to find some extremely useful behavior modification strategies.

7. Read articles on diet, eating behavior, and losing weight to keep the subject in your attention from time to time.

8. Study your overall eating habits and decide for yourself what changes, if any, you should make. Begin to make them gradually and avoid the self-punishment syndrome of carrot sticks, skim milk and black coffee.

9. Read some of the literature on nutrition and form your own theory about vitamin supplements in your diet. Don't be intimidated by some physicians (most of whom know very little about nutrition — or wellness, for that matter) who smile indulgently on vitamin users. And don't be bamboozled by the "health freaks" who hop from one magical fad food or supplement to another, urging you to make eating a religious process of chemical manipulation of your body. Find your own middle road.

10. Make sure you have plenty of fiber (roughage) in your daily diet. You can easily and cheaply supplement it by taking a little bran with water now and then — a very effective and simple habit (Ruben, 1975).

11. Pay attention to your feelings after meals. Begin to favor fresh vegetables, salads, and fresh fruits, all of which contribute to your energy and are easy to digest. Don't worship the thick steak as the epitome of eating pleasure. Balance meat with a variety of vegetables and don't settle for tired, canned vegetables. Demand good-tasting, well-prepared dishes, preferably steamed. Eat lightly in the middle of the day to avoid the heavy, tired feeling of satiety and to function well in the afternoon.

12. Keep careful tabs on the amount of junk food you eat. This practice will lead you to reduce it over the long term if you feel you should.

13. Start letting go of supersweet snacks or desserts at a comfortable rate. Replace them, for example, with sweet fresh fruits or other tasty but less fattening substitutes (*not* carrot sticks, unless you especially like carrots!).

14. If you smoke, *give it up completely.* Read health articles, visit a healthy nonsmoking doctor, frighten yourself, associate with nonsmokers, take a no-smoking class or a clinical behavior conditioning program, or do whatever else you need to do to free yourself from this killer. You'll probably find that the physiological changes brought about by jogging will help enormously in letting go of the habit.

15. If you drink heavily, *cut back immediately.* If you flunked the wellness behavior test on this item, see your physician immediately. If you only feel you drink too much, change your activity patterns to find sources of relaxation that make drinking unnecessary. Break the habit of having a drink every day by making one day a week your "dry" day, and begin to cut down further from there. Use deep relaxation practice to help you overcome the tension you've been drowning with liquor.

16. If you take recreational drugs, tranquilizers, or patent medicines more often than rarely, see a healthy physician who understands stress reduction. Have him supervise your program of substituting deep relaxation for the use of these chemical controllers.

17. If you drink a great deal of coffee, tea, cola drinks, or other sources of caffeine, start tapering off at a comfortable rate. Take a month or two to get your use down to the "occasional" level. Use deep relaxation practice to get rid of the tension that leads you to overuse these stimulants.

These suggestions point up again the highly synergistic interplay between relaxation, exercise, and diet. Each plays its key part in enhancing the others. Here are some additional observations you may want to consider in planning your own wellness program.

First, there is absolutely no reason why the typical adult American who has no major disease or disability cannot be in excellent physical condition. Not only is good conditioning beneficial and poor conditioning dangerous, but getting in good shape and staying there take relatively little time. The time spent at a single bridge party, poker game, backyard barbecue, half an evening's television watching, or an after-work drinking session would, if spread out over three or four easy jogging sessions during the week, be sufficient to put a typical person in outstanding condition.

By outstanding condition, I mean a high average level of daily energy and staying power, the ability to engage in any strenuous sport or game and feel good after finishing, and the ability to do the polka or other vigorous dances all evening with nothing more than a generous amount of perspiration. And this level of conditioning, although not suitable for Olympic competition, will provide a vastly improved level of chemical functioning throughout the body that will make illness unlikely.

Although many kinds of exercise, if used sufficiently, will bring this high level of fitness, jogging has proven to be the most practical and easiest activity for most people. Well over 1,000,000 men and women now jog regularly, and the number is increasing rapidly. The sales of jogging shoes alone constitute a boom market for manufacturers. The phenomenal popularity of jogging, especially among a sedentary population such as that in the United States, attests to its effectiveness. Unless you have had a long history of athletic experience and feel you need only return to your former high level of conditioning, you will probably find jogging to be the easiest of all exercise forms to begin, to improve in, and to continue. It has the advantages of being an individual activity, it requires no special equipment except a good pair of shoes, and you can measure the exact amount of it you choose to do at any one time. Many books on running will give you tips on how to get started, how to overcome boredom, how to run at a safe heart-rate level, and so on. I'll just offer a single tip, which took me years to discover and which I believe is the key to starting and staying with jogging as a form of aerobic exercise.

The tip is simply this: When you go out to jog, on the street or the beach or a grassy surface, start jogging *at a very slow speed.* Men in particular may find this strange at first because of their years of achievement programming. But if you always run so slowly that you could actually hold a conversation with someone if that person were running beside you, then you can continue for some minutes without becoming overly fatigued. Simply run until you've had enough for the first session and check to see how many minutes you covered. Five minutes is plenty at first for someone in moderate condition. One minute may be enough for the first time if you're greatly out of condition. Just be sure to stop before the experience becomes unpleasant for you—even if it's only 100 yards. Your body will then immediately begin to make certain chemical adjustments and improvements to prepare to handle the task more easily next time. *Stay within the bounds of this physiological adjustment process.*

And don't pay any particular attention to the distance you cover. The important principle of jogging is to work your body only hard enough for your heart rate to increase to a safe and comfortable level (in the neighborhood of 130 to 140 beats per minute if you have no serious diseases or disabilities) and to keep it there for gradually increasing periods of time. This "time-running" approach is the basis of the widely known heart conditioning effect, wherein your resting heart rate will gradually decrease and your body's oxygen-handling capabilities will become much more efficient.

This approach reduces the exercise problem from one of self-punishment and forced agony to one of pleasant experience and time scheduling. Try to find three or four periods during the week to do some jogging, and within about two weeks you will notice that you have a bit more energy, you don't feel like quitting so soon when you jog, and you'll probably experience a curious desire from time to time to do something active and physical. This is your body's physiological adaptation process getting underway.

Running on streets and other hard surfaces poses no problems for your feet or ankles if you wear a pair of good quality athletic shoes with adequate shock absorption in the soles.

Incidentally, don't underestimate the value of jogging as a way to lose weight. Antiexercise people often enjoy reciting how many hours you would have to jog to lose a single pound. But if you follow through on the calculation, you'll see that's a feasible amount of exercise to do *over an extended time.* Certainly, if you want to lose 10 pounds in a week, no reasonable amount of exercise will help you. But when you consider that jogging burns about 12 to 15 calories per minute and that after a few months you can easily be running three or four 30-minute periods per week and enjoying it, you can see that 1,400 calories per week is not really such a small amount. It comes for free as a side effect of the energy consumption of jogging.

Since losing a pound of fat requires a deficit of about 3,500 calories (i.e., you must burn more calories than your body takes in and sustain this excess consumption for long enough to burn up stored fat), you can easily lose two to 2½ pounds per month *with no diet at all.* Many people would be delighted to lose 12 to 15 pounds in a six-month period without dieting. Combined with a reasonable modification of eating habits, exercise can make weight loss even more rapid.

Research into human physiology has shown that a wide variety of beneficial changes come about in the body of a person who engages in slow long-distance running over a period of several months. Some of the best known changes are, of course, a dramatic improvement in the efficiency of the heart-lung-bloodstream system, a decrease in resting heart rate (indicating that the heart has an easier time supplying the body with blood), an associated improvement in the oxygen-carrying capabilities of the blood itself, a marked drop in blood cholesterol level (usually associated with the risk of cardiovascular disease), and, of course, increased stamina and overall energy level.

Many people who jog regularly report a variety of other beneficial effects on their bodies. Running seems to cause the body to mobilize excess fat somehow, making it easier for the person to lose weight. Metabolism becomes more efficient and more regular. Many runners report feeling generally more cheerful and even-tempered, especially for a few hours after running. Some psychologists have even reported a general improvement in the self-image of patients who began running, which may relate fairly directly to feelings of confidence and efficacy due to improved leg strength and overall stamina. Thaddeus Kostrubala, author of *The Joy of Running* (1976) reports a kind of emotional transformation — a "runner's high" after about 40 minutes of continuous running at slow speed. Others have referred to this effect as the "third wind." The increased breathing and blood flow also help to purge the smoker's body of accumulated poisons.

Women who run long, slow distances often become more graceful and better coordinated, and they report improvements in overall body shape — probably due to selective reduction of fat deposits. Facial features of both men and women become better defined as fat deposits gradually dissipate.

Others report decreased tendencies to overeat and even a lessened interest in alcohol. Such tendencies may stem from a generally higher level of interest in overall health and a growing feeling that significant changes in one's overall physical condition are really feasible and easier to attain than previously thought.

Since the early work done by Dr. Kenneth Cooper, which resulted in his famous book *Aerobics*, (1968), many researchers and runners have added to the mountain of evidence that shows slow long-distance running to be a reliable, simple, and extremely effectual means of attaining a high level of overall fitness.

At the risk of being branded a zealot for this one particular aspect of holistic health, I'd like to add an excerpt from Kostrubala's *The Joy of Running*. Kostrubala, the previously overweight, smoking, drinking candidate for a heart attack, ran the Honolulu marathon and finished in a respectable time two years after he began to change his life habits. He completed the marathon at age 43. In his book, he describes a very moving sequence of events after the finish of the course, which testifies to the human potential for overcoming obstacles. The incidents he describes can, I think, offer food for thought to anyone thinking about his or her own health:*

I have finished: I have won.

Someone congratulates me. It is a blur. I get a can of Primo Beer in my hand. My legs hurt and I am stiff and even that pain and stiffness feels good. It helps keep the memory of that race alive. Everyone talks, congratulates everyone else. People drink beer and the award ceremonies begin.

Finally, there is a pause in the noise and action. A crowd is running in. Six hours have passed since we started and the last man is finishing. He is a sixty-eight-year-old native Hawaiian. Everyone smiles, cheers, takes his picture. This is his first marathon. Everyone is proud of him. We are all him. The award ceremonies continue. There are many trophies. For men of various ages, kids and women.

But at one time, twenty-two men get up on that stage. They are all dressed in black sweats with small white trim. Black, the color of death. They are from thirty to sixty years of age. They come from Canada, Hawaii and the other states. Those from Canada have an interesting insignia on their T-shirts. It is a red broken heart. We in the crowd know what that means, who they are. We stand up, tired as we are. Each one of these men finished this mara-

*From *The Joy of Running* by Thaddeus Kostrubala, M.D. Copyright © 1976 by Thaddeus Kostrubala. Reprinted by permission of J. B. Lippincott Company.

thon. And each one of these men had once had a heart attack.

We can only guess what this moment means to them. They had been there, at the edge of this life. They had been hit by the disease that kills more American men than any other disease. They had faced our number one killer. And now they are in a new category.

Many of us know an odd but strangely powerful fact. That fact is that *there has never been a proved death reported from coronary heart disease—a heart attack—in anyone who has finished a marathon within seven years after finishing* [Italics supplied, p. 169].

And most of us know, at least in general, what we must do to protect our health and to develop it to a high level of wellness. Probably the only thing we really need is a certain amount of inspiration to get started and a fairly methodical program for doing it.

OBLIGATING AND DEOBLIGATING

Much of our life stress arises from self-imposed obligations. We undertake crash projects, we accept deadlines, and we agree to do challenging tasks. And then we become our own slavedrivers, urging ourselves on and becoming anxious at the thought of not performing as well as we demand of ourselves.

For some people, a commitment once made takes on the form of a sword dangling over their heads, ready to fall on them if they should "fail." They unconsciously make the deadline or other desired result a sacred something that they must achieve at all costs. This unconscious attitude—a miniature compulsion, really—arises in all of us at one time or another, but by consciously studying the commitments we make, we can adopt a personal policy of making them realistic and readjusting them as necessary.

I find it intriguing that an employee will accept a task assignment from his boss and hesitate to negotiate a reasonable deadline. Or, the employee may encounter a snag in finishing the task and will hesitate to go back to the boss to get help or to get the task defined in a new and more realistic way. Since the boss usually has very little definite knowledge of the relative intensity of the employee's workload, he will usually assume — rightfully so — that if the employee accepts the task without comment, it can be done within the constraints offered.

Many managers fall into this trap as well. A junior executive or a middle manager may receive a mission from a top executive to carry out a challenging project, and the top executive may have only a vague notion of the resources required to carry it out. If the action person does not negotiate for a reasonable schedule, then he falls victim to the self-obligation habit.

Similarly, in other life situations, taking on more than you can handle can be the first step to creating highly stressful situations for yourself, many of which are completely avoidable. One way out of this trap is to revise your view of what constitutes an obligation. When you maintain a flexible attitude toward your commitments, keeping those that you can reasonably keep, renegotiating those that are no longer feasible, and declining to make those you don't consider reasonable, you can keep the sum total of your obligations within the rewarding range.

Examine a variety of situations you encounter and ask yourself, "What, realistically, is my obligation to this situation? What *must* I really accomplish? By when? For whom? Why? What is the payoff? What penalties will ensue if I don't?" This amounts to asking the question "What's in this situation (good and bad) for me?" What do you owe to others? To your husband, wife, mate, or lover? To your family? To your friends? To your boss? To the organization you work for? Or to anyone else?

For some people, a slightly rebellious attitude here might be a refreshing change from the habit of being pushed into unrewarding kinds of obligations. For others, an occasional review of their commitments might suffice. The key idea is to acknowledge that *you* obligate *yourself;* no one else obligates you. Other people may provide pressure, persuasion, and even occasional veiled threats, but in the end, only you can make something a "must," and only a must can induce stress in you.

TIME MANAGEMENT AS A STRESS REDUCTION TECHNIQUE

For many people, work life becomes a rat race of deadlines and time commitments. The skill of *time management* offers a great deal of potential for reducing stress while accomplishing even more.

Alan Lakein (1973), one of the pioneers of the time management technique, has developed a systematic method for deciding what things to do, in which priority order, and how to take less time to do them. The central notion of time management is simply using a *written list of things to do* that includes all significant demands on your time and all items you want to remember to get done. As new items crop up, either by your own choice or from your environment, you add them to the list. And you cross off the completed ones, making a fresh list once a week or so whenever it becomes filled up.

Lakein recommends that every single item on the list get a priority rating, such as high, medium, or low. His system uses A, B, and C as ratings. Only a few items on the list should get a priority A rating, and these should receive the most emphasis. Items with a B rating should generally come after A items are completed, although many times you will find it opportune to take care of an occasional lower priority item. Also, some items are best taken care of during your "prime time," when you can concentrate best and work efficiently. Others can be combined to reduce the total time required to get them done. But in general, the highest priority items deserve favored treatment in deciding how to use your time.

The great value of the time management approach in reducing stress is that when you come to the end of the day, the end of the week, or the end of your energy supply for the time being, you can feel fairly sure that you have spent your time well. You will have accomplished, on the average, more high-priority tasks, and consequently you will have contributed a higher value to yourself and your organization than would be the case if you simply attacked them as they came up. Most of us always have more things to do than we have time or energy for. This means there will always be things that simply won't get done. However, if you make a habit of getting most of the valuable, important things done, you need not worry very much about the lesser items. This change in attitude stemming from competence in managing time brings a real feeling of peace of mind. The end of a hard day's work brings feelings of achievement rather than desperation, and those positive feelings make for low-stress living and working.

AFFIRMATIONS, SLOGANS, AND ENVIRONMENTAL CUES

Because self-monitoring and awareness of stress situations play such an important part in low-stress living, any techniques that remind you from time to time of the need to relax and unwind will help you develop this personal skill. The approach of using environmental cues simply involves engineering your environment in such a way that you will get occasional reminder signals during the normal course of living and working.

A useful technique is to place a small colored dot in the center of your watch crystal. Then, whenever you glance at your watch — possibly when you are beginning to feel time stress — it will remind you to pause for a second or two, take a deep breath, and relax your body momentarily. You can also practice flashing a pleasant, peaceful thought through your mind at these times. Try using a small piece of the brightly colored adhesive-backed plastic tape used in the popular label-making devices found in most offices.

You can also hang on your wall a poster or photo enlargement depicting a pleasant scene. Take a few moments to study the scene and to acquire the pleasant, peaceful feelings you want to remember. Then form a strong association in your memory between the picture and the feeling. In this way, when you glance at the picture, it is very likely that it will remind you of the need to slow down and unwind occasionally.

You can extend this idea to the decor of your entire office. Conduct a quick survey of your furnishings, the color scheme, and the decorations you've chosen. How many of them convey the idea of order, peace, and tranquility? How many of them convey the "hurry up" feeling? Does the arrangement of your furniture say to a visitor, "Don't get too comfortable. Don't stay long." Or does it say, "Make yourself comfortable. Human beings live and work here"?

A friend of mine who was an aerospace executive had a framed cartoon hanging on his wall that conveyed his compulsive philosophy of working all too well. It showed a duck floating peacefully on a pond, wearing a shirt, tie, and suit jacket, and smoking a cigar. The duck's tranquil expression was belied by the caption, which said "On the surface, appear calm; underneath, paddle like hell!"

Do you have any posters, cartoons, or little slogans around you that convey negative feelings? Desperation, exasperation, frustration, confusion, boredom, despair? Look around a novelty shop and see how hard it is to find very many positive messages. I noted one post card with a cartoon showing a person about to swing at a golf ball. The caption said, "Sometimes I make a number of false starts before I make my final deadly mistake." It's funny, but at the same time it's grim. It accentuates the negative. And I strongly believe that messages like that in our environment affect our thinking processes in subtle ways.

If you surround yourself with positive, uplifting ideas and positive, uplifting people, you can easily maintain a positive frame of mind. This is an important part of eliminating unnecessary anxiety and maintaining a low-stress style of living, working, and thinking.

RULES FOR LOW-STRESS LIVING

Now let's summarize some of the key points of this chapter in terms of a brief list of rules for low-stress living. Add any others you care to and review the list from time to time. Make them a part of your basic creed for managing your own life.

1. Make time your ally, not your master.
2. Associate mostly with gentle people who affirm your personhood.
3. Learn and practice the skill of deep relaxation.
4. Use an aerobic exercise such as jogging to build your health to a high level of conditioning.
5. Manage your life as a total enterprise, much as you would manage a corporation.
6. Don't become lopsided in any one area; seek rewarding experiences in all dimensions of living.
7. Engage in meaningful, satisfying work.
8. Don't let your work dominate your entire life.
9. Get your body weight down to a level you can be pleased with, and keep it there.
10. Form and keep sensible eating habits. Use sweets rarely, minimize junk foods, emphasize foods you like that are good for you.
11. If you smoke, stop completely.
12. Use liquor only for social or ceremonial purposes, if at all; don't let it use you.
13. Minimize or eliminate the use of recreational drugs.
14. Free yourself from the chemical tyranny of tran-

quilizers, sleeping pills, headache pills, and other central nervous system depressants.

15. Free yourself from dependency on patent medicines such as antacids, laxatives, and cold remedies by teaching your body to relax and normalize its functions.

16. Have an annual physical examination to provide extra peace of mind.

17. Jealously guard your personal freedoms — the freedom to choose your friends, the freedom to live with and/or love whom you choose, the freedom to think and believe as you choose, the freedom to structure your time as you see fit, the freedom to set your own life's goals.

18. Find some time every day — even if only 10 minutes — for complete privacy, aloneness with your thoughts, and freedom from the pressures of work. Preferably do this for a few minutes several times a day. Maintain "stability zones," personal rituals, and comfortable patterns that insulate you somewhat from Future Shock.

19. Don't drift along in troublesome and stressful situations. Rehabilitate a bad marriage or else end it. "Fire" those friends from your life who are not really your friends. Take action to settle those matters that are troubling you. Don't leave trouble situations unresolved for so long that they make you worry needlessly.

20. Have one or more pastimes that give you a chance to do something relaxing without having to have something to show for it.

21. Open yourself up to new experiences. Try doing things you've never done before, sample foods you've never eaten, go places you've never seen. Find self-renewing opportunities.

22. Read interesting books and articles to freshen your ideas and broaden your points of view. Listen to the ideas and opinions of others in order to learn from them. Avoid "psychosclerosis" (also known as "har-

dening of the categories"). Reduce or eliminate television watching.

23. Form at least one or two high-quality relationships with people you trust and can be yourself with.
24. Review your "obligations" from time to time and make sure they will also bring rewards for you. Divest yourself of those that are not good for you.
25. Surround yourself with cues that affirm positive thoughts and positive approaches to life and that remind you to relax and unwind occasionally.

RULES FOR LOW-STRESS WORKING

Now let's focus on work activities as a subset of life activities and develop a list of basic principles for working in a style that gets things accomplished with a minimum accumulation of stress points. Add to this list as you see fit and review it from time to time. Use it to review and assess the balance between what you give to your work and what you get.

1. In the course of doing business, build rewarding, pleasant, cooperative relationships with as many of your colleagues and employees as you can.
2. Rate your work by order of importance and manage your time effectively; don't bite off more than you can chew.
3. Manage by objectives, to capture the initiative on as many problem areas as you can (Albrecht, 1977, 1978).
4. Build an especially effective and supportive relationship with your boss. Understand his problems and help the boss to understand yours. Teach your boss to respect your priorities and your workload and to keep assignments reasonable.
5. Negotiate realistic deadlines on important projects

with your boss. Be prepared to propose deadlines yourself, rather than have them imposed.

6. Study the future. Learn as much as you can about likely coming events and get as much lead time as you can to anticipate them. Manage and plan actively, not reactively.

7. Find time every day for detachment and relaxation. Close your door for five minutes each morning and afternoon, put up your feet, relax deeply, and take your mind off the work. Use pleasant thoughts or images to refresh your mind.

8. Take a walk now and then to keep your body refreshed and alert. Find reasons to walk to other parts of your building or facility. Greet people you meet along the way.

9. Make a noise survey of your office area and find ways to reduce unnecessary racket. Help your employees reduce the noise level wherever possible.

10. Get away from your office from time to time for a change of scene and a change of mind. Don't eat lunch there or hang around long after you should have gone home or gone out to enjoy other activities.

11. Reduce the amount of minutia and trivia to which you give your attention. Sign only those things that really require your study, understanding and approval. Delegate routine paperwork to others whenever possible.

12. Limit interruptions. Try to schedule certain periods of "interruptability" each day and conserve other periods for your own purposes. Take phone messages from your secretary and return all calls at a certain time (except for emergencies, of course).

13. Make sure you know how to delegate effectively. Inventory a typical day's work and find out how many things you tended to that could have been assigned to someone else whose job it really should have been.

14. Don't put off dealing with distasteful problems such

as counseling a problem employee or solving a human relations problem in your staff. Accept short-term stress instead of long-term anxiety and discomfort.

15. Make a constructive "worry list." Write down the problems that concern you and beside each one write down what you're going to do about it. Get a complete catalog of current worries, so that none of them will be hovering around the edges of your consciousness. Get them out into the open where you can deal with them.

REFERENCES

Albrecht, Karl. "Are You Running a 'Fire Department'?" *Supervisory Management*, June 1977.

Albrecht, Karl. *Successful Management by Objectives: An Action Manual.* Englewood Cliffs, N.J.: Prentice-Hall, 1978.

Cooper, Kenneth. *Aerobics.* New York: Bantam Books, 1968.

Friedman, Meyer and Ray Rosenman. *Type A Behavior and Your Heart.* Greenwich, CT: Fawcett Publications, 1974.

Holmes, T. and M. Masuda "Psychosomatic Syndrome." *Psychology Today*, April 1972.

Holmes, Thomas and Richard Rahe. "The Social Readjustment Rating Scale." *Journal of Psychosomatic Research*, 11:212-18, 1967.

Holmes, Thomas H. and T. Stephenson Holmes. "How Change Can Make Us Ill." *Stress.* Woodland Hills, CA: Blue Cross of Southern California, 1974.

Kasch, Fred W. and John L. Boyer. *Adult Fitness.* Palo Alto, CA: National Press Books, 1968.

Kostrubala, Thaddeus. *The Joy of Running.* Philadelphia: J. B. Lippincott, 1976.

Lakein, Alan. *How to Get Control of Your Time and Your Life.* New York: Peter H. Wyden, 1973.

Ruben, David. *The Save Your Life Diet.* New York: Ballantine, 1975.

Ubell, Earl. *How to Save Your Life.* New York: Penguin Books, 1976.

How to Manage For High Performance and Low Stress

Just as you as a manager can carry on your own day's work according to an enlightened policy of stress management, keeping your own stress score as low as reasonably possible, so also can you deal with your employees in ways that will help them do their jobs well without experiencing undue stress. In this chapter, we review the relationships between pressure, stress, and performance.

Apparently, many managers feel that the way to get a lot of work out of their employees is to "keep the pressure on." Some managers even consciously induce a general atmosphere of fear, apprehension, criticism, and blaming in order to maintain the upper hand and assure themselves that they are really in control. A prevalent theme among supervisors, especially in organizations in which much of the work is routine and repetitive, is that people won't work if you don't keep after them. This kind of thinking leads to *coercive* styles of management rather than to *facilitative* styles. It is well known that people who are subjected to continuing levels of pressure that go beyond their "challenge" levels into their "discomfort" levels will sooner or later show the effects of the pressure in stress-reactive behavior.

PRESSURE YES – STRESS NO

We know that human beings in any organization need a certain level of pressure to function together in any way at all. Without some reason for action, some common purpose, sense of necessity, or sense of obligation, they do not really constitute an organization. We also know that groups tend to pull together and function effectively when confronted by a common external enemy. In business organizations, this external enemy may take the form of a competitor, another organization or person threatening legal action, a nosy newspaper writer, a government agency, an oppressive top management group, or a neighboring department with which relations have become strained. Sometimes a group of employees will coalesce into a strongly defined psychological entity to counteract a bullying, unfair supervisor —usually by covert techniques such as forming a grapevine, leaking critical information to others in the organization, and undermining the supervisor's actions and decisions.

Sometimes the members of an organization will become highly mobilized and committed to their production goals or project objectives when they see the possibility of a major improvement in their circumstances. As an example, the opportunity to land a large and profitable contract may cause all or most of them to work together enthusiastically. Some groups pull together best in economic hard times.

These are many forms of pressure. They all confront the

members of the organization — individually as well as collectively — with the necessity for action. One of the functions of an effective manager is to impose a carefully controlled amount of constructive pressure on the members of the organization so that they have a well-defined sense of necessity and mission. It is perfectly reasonable for a manager to make assignments, impose deadlines, and exert a moderate amount of interpersonal pressure to focus employees' attention on their tasks and objectives. Agreements made and lived up to constitute the basis of doing business in any organization, and very few people really resent being held accountable for reasonable performance within reasonable constraints of time and resources. The key word is *reasonable*.

This point of view suggests that we look at pressure as being a continuously variable function that is at least partially under the control of the unit manager and that can be regulated to foster human effectiveness and to minimize stress. It means that one of the manager's specific functions should be to monitor and adjust the pace of the unit. Exhibit 9-1 shows the continuum of organizational pace, ranging from the unproductive "country club" atmosphere to the killing, stressful "sweat shop" atmosphere.

Each person has a fairly definite comfort zone of pressure

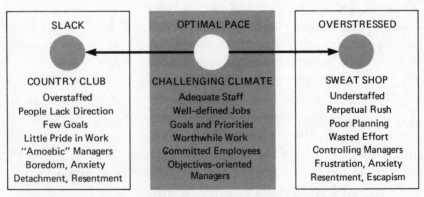

SLACK	OPTIMAL PACE	OVERSTRESSED
COUNTRY CLUB	CHALLENGING CLIMATE	SWEAT SHOP
Overstaffed	Adequate Staff	Understaffed
People Lack Direction	Well-defined Jobs	Perpetual Rush
Few Goals	Goals and Priorities	Poor Planning
Little Pride in Work	Worthwhile Work	Wasted Effort
"Amoebic" Managers	Committed Employees	Controlling Managers
Boredom, Anxiety	Objectives-oriented	Frustration, Anxiety
Detachment, Resentment	Managers	Resentment, Escapism

EXHIBIT 9-1. Each organization has a characteristic "pace" of activity.

and pace within which he works effectively. Below this zone, boredom and detachment set in. Above the comfort zone, anxiety and stress-reactive behavior appear. If either condition continues for an extended period, the reactions in the individual become more pronounced and the problem more chronic.

Boredom can induce stress just as overload can. A person who is bored with the job feels very little sense of reward. He may continue to carry out the repetitive, meaningless motions, but after a time a curious effect sets in. If the job is especially imprisoning (such as on a fixed-rate production line), the person will often experience a vague, slowly building sense of anger. He wants to escape but can't. Just as a weekend mechanic who has trouble disassembling the kitchen sink trap may become enraged and smash at it with a hammer (a decidedly irrational act), so the imprisoned employee may eventually strike out at the machine he sees as being synonymous with the bad feelings.

It is not unusual for a bored, frustrated employee suddenly and without warning to jam the spindle of a cutting machine through an expensive work piece, throw a hammer through a window, or jam the keys on an expensive typewriter or word-processing machine. When asked why he did this, such a worker will often offer a "rational" reason based on some specific provocation or other. The act has to be justified somehow.

However, more than likely the real cause of the explosion was a build-up of undifferentiated anxiety and an undefined form of anger that demanded release. I'm convinced that countless acts of employee sabotage, theft, personal violence, and even quality violations stem directly from the stress build-up experienced by bored workers. The pious attitude of the typical production supervisor —whose job is anything but boring—is to condemn such employees as being somehow inferior, unsocialized, and less than human. In fact, they are normal human beings reacting to stress build-up in normal human ways. Research has shown machine-paced jobs to be among the most stressful in all of industry.

The message for the enlightened manager is simply this:

Maintain a continuous awareness of organizational pace and pressure and act wherever possible to keep it within the comfort zones of the employees. In this way, the stress for the employees and its associated costs to the organization will be minimized, and human effectiveness on the job will be maximized.

AUTHORITY DYNAMICS

One way in which you as a manager can keep the pressure on your employees within a comfortable range is by deploying your authority gracefully and effectively. Probably every one of us has at some time been bullied, threatened, intimidated, or otherwise pushed around by an obnoxious supervisor who was somewhat lacking in social awareness and human relations skills. And we all know how anxious and uncomfortable this made us. It is a highly stressful experience to be accused, scolded, and threatened by a boss, especially in the company of others, and given no chance to explain your thoughts or problems. Some managers try to keep employees continually somewhat anxious by using exactly these tactics.

A more enlightened method of deploying managerial authority calls for using one's position as a manager to apply and maintain a comfortable level of pressure — a level that the employees find demanding and challenging but not threatening or overly stressful. Most of the specific interaction techniques for doing this are fairly straightforward and merely require an increased level of awareness of the anxiety factor on the part of the manager who is dealing with an employee. A few specific techniques and examples should serve to clarify the possibilities.

A school principal once mentioned to me a very simple and effective technique he used in communicating with teachers. He said:

Whenever I find it necessary to write a note to a teacher

asking him or her to see me about some matter, I always include a few words on the note telling what the matter is. I've found that they come into my office more relaxed and open to communication than they did when I just wrote "See me." I think it's because formerly they never knew whether they were being summoned into the office for something they screwed up on, or whether it was an item of normal business. Now they know, and they feel more at ease.

Remember that no matter how carefully you try to put the employee at ease, he seldom forgets one key fact: *You are the boss.* Most employees, however conscientious they may be, rightfully think of their own best interests in dealing with their bosses, and they keep alert for possible judgments their bosses might make about their competence, attitudes, and performance. This is quite normal, and every manager should keep it in mind in deciding how to deploy his authority in dealing with employees.

DELEGATING TASKS AND CLARIFYING RESPONSIBILITIES

One of the simplest and most reliable ways to help employees stay within their comfort zones of pressure, workload, and accountability is to define their jobs as clearly as possible. A worker who understands his job thoroughly, knows how to do it properly, and knows clearly what results constitute high performance becomes self-motivating and self-monitoring. Clarifying responsibility is one of the most basic responsibilities of the unit manager, yet many managers don't seem to follow through on it all the way.

When the manager takes a one-day-at-a-time approach to the affairs of the unit, the employee usually can't develop a clear picture of his job as a totality. When the manager parcels out work in bits and pieces, the employee feels dependent on the manager for every next move. Not only is this mode of operating very inefficient, but it tends to make the employee unsure of his contribution. He lacks the feeling of solid accomplishment necessary for job satisfaction. In the extreme case, where the manager runs a "fire department" with little or no direction, employees become anxious and disgruntled.

Effective delegation, on the other hand, gives the employee the sense of being an entrepreneur, enabling him to feel a sense of responsibility for a well-defined area of results and to work in a self-directed way to achieve results. One of the most important features of effective delegation is the concept of *closure*. An employee has a sense of closure when he receives a complete project or task to do, carries it through all of the important steps, and sees it completed. Closure experiences enable the worker to take full responsibility for the results and to take pride in completing the task. As a manager, you can foster this feeling of involvement and pride in the work by assigning just as much of the work as you possibly can in the form of whole tasks or whole projects. Simply include appropriate checkpoints in each assignment so that you can review intermediate results with the employee and make sure the activity is heading toward the preestablished objectives.

Speaking of objectives, we know that managing by objectives as an overall style also tends to increase feelings of autonomy and self-sufficiency on the part of the worker. If you as the unit manager have a clear idea of the future course of your operation and if you have set a few major objectives for the next six months to a year, then you have a consistent basis for planning the work of the group. With clear and specific objectives to shoot for, the employees can operate from day to day with a sense of meaning and accomplishment (Albrecht, 1978).

Most of these concepts and approaches are simply good sound management. Yet it is easy to overlook them in the rush of everyday business and the normal emergencies that arise.

However, if you can manage your own time effectively, you can spend a few minutes every day thinking about management itself. You can develop habits of managing that maximize your own performance and that of your employees while eliminating many of the stressors of uncertainty, confusion, and lack of direction.

REPLACING THREATS WITH REWARDS

Some managers seem to understand and apply almost by second nature the most basic principle of human nature, namely, that people have wants and that they do whatever they do only to fulfill those wants. These managers operate primarily by showing employees how they can fulfill their wants as part of the process of working effectively toward the objectives of the organization. These managers understand the concept of motivation, and they apply it. Not only do they realize that inducing high levels of stress in people is inhumane, but they also realize that it sooner or later impedes progress toward the organization's goals. They adopt the style of managing by reward because they know that it works better than management by threat of punishment.

Some other managers—too many, unfortunately—seem not to grasp this fundamental fact, preferring to manage by coercion. They make a habit of tripping up their employees, asking them questions intended to intimidate or belittle rather than to inform, checking up on them frequently, and generally implying to each of them that he is not to be trusted. The message is, "Be careful how you deal with me; remember that I have the means to punish you any time I want to." This intimidating mode of transacting amounts to a predominant *managerial style* with them (Boshear & Albrecht, 1977, pp. 178-182).

You may find it enlightening to review your own managerial style from this unusual viewpoint of stress induction. Ask yourself whether your employees and associates experience their dealings with you as being essentially positive, rewarding, and uplifting. Or do they find an encounter with you more or less "punishing"? Some managers pride themselves in terrorizing employees. The boss who says to me, "I don't get ulcers — I give 'em!" is telling me he doesn't manage. He bullies. The manager who understands what makes people do the things they do and capitalizes on this knowledge to enable them to meet their own personal and collective needs while achieving the goals of the organization really does understand the intellectual, social, and operational function of professional management.

LOW-STRESS COMMUNICATING

On the assumption that helping employees and colleagues to keep their own stress levels down will help you to keep yours down and that it will also help everyone to work more productively, let's look at some low-stress communication techniques.

A good rule of thumb is to try to make as many of your transactions as you can relatively rewarding and positive for the other person. Of course, you can't always do this because of the nature of some kinds of problems, because some other people may lack the social skills necessary to cooperate in making transactions positive, and because you occasionally need to take a strong position in opposition to others. However, over the course of your many transactions with your employees and your colleagues, you should be able to make the great majority of transactions go smoothly and comfortably.

This would seem such an obvious point as not to deserve mentioning if it were not for the fact that so many people who work together in organizations don't seem to grasp it at all. Many others can keep it in mind only under pleasant circumstances but lose their grip on it when the pressure is on. Relatively few managers seem to have developed the skill of putting others at ease and helping them stay there through the course of a business transaction, especially one that presents difficulties for them.

Think of your own personal communicating style as being either punishing or rewarding for others according to their individual reactions to the ways in which you treat them. You can assess this quite simply by studying their behavior toward you. In behavioral science terminology, a punishing experience is one an individual is not likely to repeat. A rewarding experience, on the other hand, is one he is likely to want to have again. This means that, if the people with whom you communicate usually experience their transactions with you as positive, affirming to their own self-esteem, and productive for them personally, *they will usually come back for more.* If they don't like the results, *they will tend to interact with you as little as possible.* This principle provides a very simple way to assess your comunicating skills and to inventory the specific managerial behaviors that cause stress in others as well as those that help them reduce stress.

Punishing behaviors include:

Monopolizing the conversation.

Interrupting.

Showing obvious disinterest.

Keeping a sour facial expression.

Withholding customary social cues such as greetings, nods, "uh-huh," and the like.

Throwing verbal barbs at others.

Using nonverbal put-downs.

Insulting or otherwise verbally abusing others.

Speaking dogmatically; not respecting others' opinions.

Complaining or whining excessively.

Criticizing excessively; fault finding.

Demanding one's own way; refusing to negotiate or compromise.

Ridiculing others.

Patronizing or talking down to others.

Making others feel guilty.

Soliciting approval from others excessively.

Losing one's temper frequently or easily.

Playing "games" with people; manipulating or competing in subtle ways.

Throwing "gotcha's" at others; embarrassing or belittling others.

Telling lies; evading honest questions; refusing to level with others.

Overusing "should" language; pushing others with words.

Displaying frustration frequently.

Making aggressive demands of others.

Diverting conversation capriciously; breaking others' train of thought.

Disagreeing routinely.

Restating others' ideas for them.

Asking loaded or accusing questions.

Overusing "why" questions.

Breaking confidences; failing to keep important promises.

Flattering others insincerely.

Joking at inappropriate times.

Bragging; showing off; talking only about self.

Rewarding behaviors include:

Giving others a chance to express views or share information.

Listening attentively; hearing other person out.

Sharing one's self with others; smiling; greeting others.

Giving positive nonverbal messages of acceptance and respect for others.

Praising and complimenting others sincerely.

Expressing respect for values and opinions of others.

Giving suggestions constructively.

Compromising; negotiating; helping others succeed.

Talking positively and constructively.

Affirming feelings and needs of others.

Treating others as equals whenever possible.

Stating one's needs and desires honestly.

Delaying automatic reactions; not flying off the handle easily.

Leveling with others; sharing information and opinions openly and honestly.

Confronting others constructively on difficult issues.

Staying on the conversational topic until others have been heard.

Stating agreement with others when possible.

Questioning others openly and honestly; asking straight-forward, nonloaded questions.

Keeping the confidences of others.

Giving one's word sparingly and keeping it.

Joking constructively and in good humor.

Expressing genuine interest in the other person.

Review these lists and add any other punishing or rewarding behaviors that come to your mind. Think about your own inter-personal style and see how many of these specific behaviors you can identify in your day-to-day patterns of working with others. These behaviors also apply in private life, of course, just as well as in work situations. Ask yourself the very blunt question: To what extent do people voluntarily seek me out; to what extent do they take the initiative in contacting me, communicating with me, sharing ideas and viewpoints with me, and including me in their personal and social activities?

The answer to those questions will give you the clearest possible indication of whether your management style is pri-marily that of a punisher or a rewarder. Over the long term, a rewarding style of dealing with others tends to keep your own stress score at a minimum; it helps others to do the same; and it makes work life a pleasant, enjoyable, achievement-oriented process.

MAINTAINING LOW-STRESS RELATIONSHIPS

You can extend the concept of a rewarding style of communicating to the process of developing and maintaining low-stress relationships with employers and colleagues. We can define a low-stress relationship as one in which the two people can deal with each other effectively in such a way that each meets his own needs — of whatever type — without jeopardizing the needs of the other and without causing undue tension or anxiety for either party.

For example, two managers at the same level may find it necessary to deal with each other from opposite sides of a particular issue, but if they take a long-term view of their relationship in the organization, they can deal with each other from positions of mutual respect, trust, and compromise. They will start by seeking a common solution, if possible, rather than start to do battle as a continuation of previous clashes. They will also find occasions in between the disagreements to focus on cooperation and constructive action in order to make sure their relationship does not shift into an adversary orientation.

You might find it interesting and productive to conduct a quick inventory of your principal relationships in the organization and assess them in terms of the relative degree of positive orientation between you and each of the other people. Not only does building constructive, congenial relationships with others help to minimize your overall stress score, but it plays a direct part in your career success and in your advancement in the organization.

THE SOCIAL CLIMATE OF THE WORK GROUP

At any given time, every work group has a well-defined social climate that is the sum of the relationships among the various members — including its leader. The members both establish this climate and are influenced strongly by it. The social climate of the unit can induce considerable stress within the individual member, or it can offer a supportive kind of assurance and sense of security.

In the first case, the group setting actually "turns off" the individual member, causing him to withdraw psychologically from its social processes in an attempt to minimize the stress it causes. This usually degrades job performance, especially when results depend on voluntary and constructive cooperation between workers. In the second case, the group setting draws the individual closer to his comrades in an attempt to maximize the good feelings that result. This almost always improves work relationships and results on cooperative tasks.

When all or most of the members of the work group experience their mutual relationships as being fairly cordial, cooperative, constructive, and emotionally satisfying, then they have created a low-stress working climate. In this situation, each person sees the others as predictably offering to transact — either socially or on task-related matters — in ways he will find satisfying overall. This does not mean that conflict is completely absent, or that the co-workers never have significant disagreements, or that they never have occasional unpleasant personal incidents. It simply means that these are the exception rather than the rule.

However, when the relationships in a work group degenerate to frequent interpersonal squabbles, habitual adversary arrangements, opposing factions within the group, or the everyman-for-himself mentality, we have a high-stress setting. In their transactions with one another, individuals come away feeling stressed, uncomfortable, and less likely to want to interact. One of the noticeable features of such an organizational climate is a relatively depressed level of general interaction. People stay away from one another unless their tasks require them to collaborate. When they finish their mutual tasks, they separate from one another. There is usually little social interaction, little use of "good mornings," little joking except in cliques, and little initiative taken to help one another.

Another ready clue to the high-stress environment is escapist behavior. Individuals usually absent themselves from the situation at the first legitimate opportunity. Absenteeism may increase, people may arrive a little late to begin work, and they may leave on the dot. Privately, they will often concede that they don't like their jobs. They may not even realize that they actually don't like their job *situations*.

Many factors often combine to create a high-stress work environment, but by far the most common factor is the personal influence of the manager who runs the group. As mentioned previously, managerial style has a direct and pronounced effect on employee attitudes and morale. The manager who lacks the personal confidence or the social skills to deal with employees constructively and supportively will routinely make them uncomfortable and anxious when they are in his presence. They will experience their transactions with the boss as being stressful and unrewarding. They may spread this punishing form of interpersonal style to one another in their unconscious (or conscious) attempts to stay on the good side of the boss. They may resort to shifting responsibility for mistakes, accusing and blaming one another, and trying to make one another look bad in the eyes of the boss. Factions and cliques may form around those members with the strongest personalities. Production goals and project objectives suffer.

Once you as a manager accept primary responsibility for the social climate you have created and fostered in the work unit, you can make a thorough evaluation of your own managerial style. You can identify the consequences—positive as well as negative—of your methods of dealing with subordinates and colleagues and decide whether you should make any significant changes. Extending this concept of low-stress social climate to the overall organization can lead to some remarkable improvements in organizational effectiveness, as discussed further in Chapter 10.

SMALL-GROUP COMMUNICATION PROCESSES

You as a manager, regardless of your level in the organization, probably conduct a large portion of your business in small-group, problem-solving situations. These groups probably range from three or four people to about a dozen. Group meetings much larger than that are comparatively unusual in most organizations. In each of the conferences you conduct or attend, you have an opportunity to foster communication processes that help the participants keep their stress levels down, cooperate more effectively, get more and better work done, and enjoy the process to a fair extent. Techniques of effective conference leading are fairly straightforward, but many managers haven't thought them through.

The effective conference leader first helps the participants settle down to the task at hand with minimum apprehension and with maximum intention to work cooperatively. He states clearly the objective of the meeting, gets agreement from the participants that this is indeed the objective, and then helps them keep their attention focused on it.

The effective conference leader facilitates the process of trading ideas, opinions, preferences, needs, values, and information. He does not stifle or steer clear of honest disagreement, but he does help the disagreeing parties to disagree around the important task issues without resorting to personal recriminations. He may prevent the group from rushing to consensus under the influence of one or two strong advocates, and he encourages alternative points of view when appropriate. This often requires coaxing the more quiet or shy group members to voice their opinions and ideas. Experience has shown again and again that the best ideas do not always come from the most vocal members of a problem-solving group. Many good ideas have gone unappreciated simply because the shy person who sat there thinking while the others were talking didn't have the courage to speak up and no one else had the presence of mind to invite him to do so.

For the individual participant, being involved in a well-conducted conference can be a constructive, rewarding, and even pleasing experience — especially when compared to the great number of run-of-the-mill meetings that take place in most business organizations. The person can have a chance to voice his ideas, to be included in the group's primary processes, and to feel a part of the solution once it is settled on. This experience is not only positive; it also builds commitment to the solution once it is time for action.

Begin to watch yourself in action as you conduct business meetings. Analyze the outcomes carefully. Are you making conferences constructive and rewarding for the participants, or are you making them unpleasant, stressful experiences? Do you make everyone a part of the problem-solving process or only the loudest and most forceful ones? And do you use a personal style of communicating that fosters understanding, constructive compromise, and cooperation? Since so much of the nation's business goes on in conference situations, it makes sense to develop and refine your skills for conference leadership (Albrecht, 1974, p. 17).

RESOLVING CONFLICT

Your skill in *conflict resolution* also determines to a great extent your capability for managing for high performance and low stress. Unnecessary and prolonged conflict is a primary cause of organizational ineffectiveness at all levels, and it is also a primary cause of personal stress for the protagonists. In your capacity as a manager, you may inadvertently encourage others to develop conflict situations by your applying unnecessary pressure, creating win-lose situations between pairs of employees, and by unbalancing the relative amounts of authority and responsibility of several people reporting to you at the same level. If you aren't sufficiently aware of conflict dynamics, you may become unknowingly drawn into the day-to-day social dramas that play out these conflicts.

By developing a keen awareness of the elements of conflict and the social conditions that foster it, you can maintain a low-stress, low-conflict social setting in the group of people who report to you. Some of the factors in the social setting that predispose individuals to engage in unnecessary conflict are as follows:

1. Poorly defined jobs, tasks, responsibilities, and ranges of authority.
2. Prior history of conflict between two or more people or groups.
3. Interdepartmental relationships that frequently place members at cross purposes; traditional adversary relationships such as sales versus engineering, production versus quality assurance, nursing versus administration, district office versus regional headquarters, and the like.
4. Unreasonable levels of pressure and pace in the organization.
5. Severe economic downturn that jeopardizes the job security of organization members.
6. Overly competitive climate fostered by top management and managers at various levels.
7. Favoritism shown by managers to one or two employees.
8. Punitive, accusative, or threatening style of treatment by a unit manager, leading to escapist behavior such as blaming others and shifting responsibility.
9. Unclear or arbitrary standards for advancement and promotion in the organization; inconsistent patterns

of rewarding accomplishment; overly secretive and competitive organizational politics.

10. Great confusion or uncertainty about upcoming major changes or upheavals in the organization; inability of employees to define their future roles and interactions.

Some of these factors, of course, may be far beyond your direct control, but most of them come under your influence to some extent and a positive influence can minimize the adverse impacts of the others. For example, simply by clarifying roles, relationships, responsibilities, and authority levels for the people who work for you, you can help them avoid doing battle with one another unnecessarily. This is an obvious principle of good management, but many, many managers fail to carry it through as far as they should.

A good general approach to minimizing conflict and resolving the conflicts that do occur consists of the following three basic steps:

1. Establish and maintain a low-conflict, low-stress climate, with cooperation being the general norm.
2. Isolate each significant conflict that does arise to a single, specific task issue or family of issues. Don't accept personality clashes but insist that the protagonists zero in on a concrete issue and its rational elements.
3. Help the protagonists to apply a rational problem-solving model or procedure to the issue; go for a workable compromise.

In this way, you eliminate the vague accusations and other forms of camouflage and enable the people involved in the problem situation to resolve it by cooperation and mature communication techniques. Your job as a manager is not to solve problems or to eliminate conflict but to help your employees solve the problems and to help them resolve their honest differences themselves without resorting to counterproductive interpersonal battles. The benefits of this approach in maintaining a low-stress, low-conflict style of operating on the group's productivity and overall effectiveness can be enormous.

ORGANIZATIONAL COMMUNICATIONS

Managers, as agents of authority and change operating inside an organization, are in excellent positions to foster a low-stress communication environment. However, very few managers seem to see this as their collective opportunity, to say nothing of their responsibility. Many managers seem to feel that it is the responsibility of the employees across the organization to communicate. Many do not realize how much of the day-to-day activity across the working level is affected by the activities of the managers themselves.

For example, it is very common for two department managers at the same level to have a continuing feud with each other and for this feud to polarize both their organizations into warring camps. This more or less forces their respective employees to take up the battle, simply in order to protect themselves from the supposed—and often real—onslaughts of "the enemy." Once this happens, the feud becomes a self-reinforcing situation. Adversary proceedings, accusations, and competitive behavior become the norm for the relationship. Sometimes an entire organization can split right down the middle simply because of a personal conflict between two executives.

Worse yet, some top executives seem to foster such "friendly competition" among junior executives in order to "keep the organization lean and mean." They usually succeed with the "mean" part, usually at the expense of employee morale, interunit cooperation, and overall levels of pressure and stress in the organization as a whole.

The truism, "It starts at the top," is quite true. An executive who cooperates with other executives in aiming toward organizational goals is telling his subordinates that cooperation is one of the organization's principal values. One who engages in infighting, personal feuds, and counterproductive politics is telling his subordinates that those are the accepted rules of the game. It is incumbent on every management team to review its collective communication behavior and to analyze the effects of that behavior on the organizational communication environment. Top managers, as well as managers at every other level of the organization, must accept responsibility and accountability for the communication environments they create and maintain.

REFERENCES

Albrecht, Karl. "How to Conduct a Conference." *Manage*, May–June 1974.

Albrecht, Karl. *Successful Management by Objectives: An Action Manual.* Englewood Cliffs, N.J.: Prentice-Hall, 1978.

Boshear, Walton and Karl Albrecht. *Understanding People: Models and Concepts.* La Jolla, CA: University Associates, 1977.

10

What Top Management Can Do About Stress

This chapter speaks directly to the person who is in the most important place of all for making the right things happen in the American business organization — the top manager. Chief executive officers, company presidents, directors of foundations, vice presidents, board chairmen, agency heads, military commanders, hospital administrators, and college presidents all occupy the one key position that enables them to see all parts of the organization *if they choose to* — the top. This chapter urges you, the top manager, and those who work directly with and for you to devote the necessary effort and resources to humanize the environment within which your people — your colleagues — live and work. This may well be the most challenging and significant thing you ever do in your business career.

THE VIEW FROM THE TOP

If there's one thing we've learned in a hundred and more years of business, it's that making a profit is possible, practical, and desirable. All but one of the 50 largest American corporations posted a profit in 1975. We've proven over and over again the basic principles of sound business management, and we've learned to apply most of them in the nonprofit sector as well. The Harvard Business School approach really does work. Some executives manage well, and their organizations do well. Others manage poorly, and their organizations do poorly. But the track record of most American executives has been quite good. Given a successful start-up and a going concern, most of them can keep it going rather well.

Now we must move a step further. Now that we have shown the corporation to be a fundamental basis for collective human endeavor and now we have shown that profit-making enterprises have the capability of advancing the human condition to virtually any conceivable level, it is time to build on this bedrock of economic and social strength a quality of human life to befit twentieth-century society. We have already come a long way from the attitude behind the famous statement attributed to Cornelius Vanderbilt, the millionaire capitalist of the late 1800s, "The public be damned! What do I care about the law? H'aint I got the power?" No longer are the livelihoods of many people concentrated in the hands of a few all-powerful financial giants. We now have a generation of professional managers — executives who look upon management as a service to the society in addition to a career involving the exercise of power and the allocation of resources.

Yet there is still much to do. Since the 1800s, when only about three out of 10 people made their livings by working in organizations, we have come to the last quarter of the twentieth century when nine out of 10 people are organizational workers. *The United States is now an organizational society.* And since a very large number of Americans spend about one-fourth of their waking time during their prime years living and working in their organizations, it behooves us to make those organizations places where people can live and function effectively for themselves, be healthy, and grow as self-fulfilling human beings.

It may help to conceive of the corporation—or any organization, for that matter—as having three equal dimensions. These are the *economic* dimension, the *social* dimension, and the *human* dimension. We understand the economic dimension fairly well. The social dimension includes all aspects of the organization's relationship with the society and its local community, including the environmental impacts of its operation. The human dimension includes all aspects of its own internal environment within which its people work each day. Exhibit 10-1 illustrates these three interrelated dimensions.

You as an executive will increasingly find over the next 10 years or so that the trends of social change in the United States are bringing specific forces to bear on your organization as a sociotechnical system. You will have to sense accurately what is happening in the country, in your workforce as a microcosm of the country, and in your managerial staff, which is your single most important asset for bringing about adaptive change. All executives will find it more and more necessary to focus on the human elements of organizational

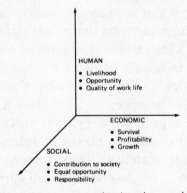

EXHIBIT 10-1. The modern corporation has three major dimensions of its activity.

management while maintaining an even keel on the traditional factors of operational performance and financial control.

Let me repeat a basic thesis: *Only our top executives and their immediate second-level executives have the visibility, sense of direction, and control of resources to make these changes happen.* You and your colleagues throughout the business world will be the principal agents for fostering constructive change, or for impeding it.

THE COMING SOCIAL (R)EVOLUTION IN BUSINESS ORGANIZATIONS

Major social changes will almost certainly take place in business organizations during the latter quarter of the twentieth century. Of that there can be very little doubt. The key questions are: What kinds of changes will come about? Who will change? How? What new processes and practices will we have? What old processes and practices will we still have? What old processes and practices will we have to abandon as being no longer effective? And, most important of all, will these changes be constructive or destructive? Will we have an evolution in the world of human organizations, or will it turn out to be an uncontrolled, destabilizing revolution?

We don't know the answers to these questions for certain, but we do know how to favor the constructive evolution if we choose to do so. This section summarizes some of the major forces building up in our society that will have direct bearing on you as an executive and on the sociotechnical system under your stewardship. The next section gives a prescription for adapting a major organization—either profit-making or non-profit—to these increasingly powerful forces without jeopardizing its economic stability. That prescription is largely a review and integration of the concepts and approaches discussed in this book so far.

At least *five major social forces*, or change processes, will hit the American industrial corporation during the latter part of our century, and they will present themselves in more or less the same form to the nonprofit organization as well. The only difference may be in the higher intensity felt by the corporation. Each of these changes, like a great sea wave, will slam into the corporation with a force that will reach to the very foundations of its structure. These changes will challenge the basic values of the corporation as a sociotechnical system and, indeed, may threaten its survival as an economic enterprise. I make no pretense to the melodramatic when I say that the responses of top managers to these coming changes may well spell the difference between the survival and the demise of the corporation as a basic part of American life and society.

The five most significant changes I believe will come, expressed in terms of the adaptational problems they will present to top managers, are:

1. The new worker problem.
2. The new manager problem.
3. The women and minorities problem.
4. The corporate accountability problem.
5. The stress problem.

Each of these processes will probably take place with great intensity and in fundamental and far-reaching ways. Top managers, unable to stop or reverse these changes, will have no choice but to come to terms with them. Those who fight delaying actions and try to ignore the changes to the last minute will probably lose the most, and their organizations will probably suffer most as economic entities. Those who anticipate the changes and who work out strategic adaptations to them will probably learn how to maintain the stability of their organizations while programming them into constructive paths of *planned change*.

The New Worker Problem

The new worker problem will stem from a fairly abrupt change in the make-up of the American labor force due to the coming of age of the well-known postwar baby boom. This population group strongly outnumbers every other equivalent segment of the population. The combination of the dramatic drop in birth rates during and after the Great Depression of the 1930s, the dramatic rise in birth rates during the 1950s following World War II and the Korean conflict, and the decline in birth rates beginning in the 1960s created a substantial bulge in the graph of age distributions, as shown in Exhibit 10-2.* The center of that population group reached the age range of 15 to 20 in 1975. At that point, they began to move with full force into the labor pool. That group outnumbered the age group 35 to 40 at that time by almost two to one. So in the latter part of this century, we will see the labor force statistically dominated by this large subgroup as it moves from its late teenage years into early middle age. No other single age group will have such a powerful influence, by virtue of sheer numbers, on American organizations, on work, on consumer spending patterns, and on social values in general.

These people were the rock-and-roll generation of the late 1960s and early 1970s. They were the spoiled, overindulged, television generation, many of whom were raised according to the principles of Doctor Spock. They were catered to, wooed, pampered, and lionized by Hollywood and by the fabulously profitable record industry (which, incidentally, will have to adapt to their changing tastes if it expects to follow this lucrative market through its maturing years). Collectively, they commanded more buying power — derivative, to be sure, but

*It is commonly believed that the postwar baby boom began precisely nine months after American troops returned from the war. Actually, it got under way much later, peaking in the mid-1950s. Demographers still debate the various underlying factors in this population expansion, which ran much the same course in other industrialized nations after World War II.

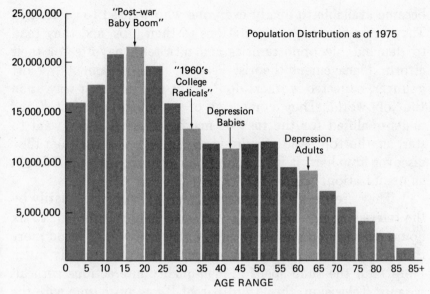

EXHIBIT 10-2. The American society has several distinct sub-populations.

buying power nonetheless — than most nations of the world enjoy as their total gross national products.

These young adults move into the work force and into the mainstream of American society with values and points of view very different from those of their parents and thóse of the managers of the organizations for whom they go to work. They have very high expectations of good jobs, good pay, and the American good life of consumption and middle-class materialism. They are indeed conspicuous consumers, despite their idealistic rejection of many parental values. They buy motorcycles, trucks, CB radios, records, tapes, liquor, and clothes with the same consumerist fervor their parents bring to automobiles, motor homes, household appliances, television sets, and vacation tours. Most of them have never known hunger or worried about how to survive in the depression or wartime environments their parents and grandparents knew.

They are, on the average, better schooled — although not necessarily better educated — than any other generation in history. They grew up in a time when a college education

283

became available to nearly everyone who wanted to go after it. They bring very high expectations to their jobs, and they tend to demand big opportunities and near-term payoffs for their efforts. Management theorist Peter F. Drucker laments, "Most younger, educated workers don't want to work their way up in the job world. They come out of college over-educated and under-qualified for the task of making a living. They want to start at the top. And they're very easily frustrated when they discover how hard it is to accomplish even the simplest thing in an organization."

They are the first American generation raised primarily by the television set. The average American child spends four to six hours per day in front of the television receiver, a period more than equal to the total time spent in school and usually much more than the time spent in high-quality interactions with his parents. Television, the "third parent," gets more time with the American child than the natural parents, many of whom have virtually abandoned the role of teaching and instilling social values and standards of behavior. They have come to see the world as a series of pat, simplified 30-minute episodes in which the good guys solve the problem and whip the bad guys, with eight minutes to spare for commercials and a preview of next week's episode. They tend to want simple solutions based on pushbutton American technological magic.

They are also very uncertain and confused about the United States and its future, perhaps more realistically so than their parents. They lack a sense of higher purpose, an organizing challenge for their life's activities, which their parents enjoyed a generation ago when the world was simpler and life was more highly structured and predefined. They face the awesome and frightening problem of deciding what the country should be and what their lives should be.

As part of this new perspective on life and work, the members of the new generation hold less respect than their parents did for traditions as traditions, they have less respect for authority and institutions, they tend to be much more critical of "business" (whether or not they understand what a career in "business" really means), and they tend to be much more cynical about government and statesmanship. As a group, they more or less "own" the so-called ecology issue, perhaps only because it provides a focus for the normal growing-up process of rejecting parental norms and challenging establishment values.

To a great extent, these will be the American workers of the late twentieth century. And many of their values will probably rub off on their neighboring age group, the young middle-aged workers. They will present you, the top manager, with unprecedented challenges and opportunities. One of the primary challenges will probably arise from the fact that they are not so easily governable as their parents were. They demand reasons, explanations, justifications from their leaders. They will probably present a strong form of counter-control to organizational managers, taking direction to the extent that it meets with their critical value systems.

I predict the development of employee activist groups among this segment of the working populace. Such groups may well emerge outside the boundaries of traditional union organizations, possibly because of dissatisfaction with the orthodox union structure, which after all resembles the corporation in many ways. They may well press for substantial social changes in their organizations, the magnitude and direction of which may be very difficult for traditional power-oriented executives to accept. Oppressive overcontrol on the part of top managers could well trigger widespread employee revolts among this group, again possibly outside the union structure. A young twentieth-century Karl Marx or Vladimir Lenin could well polarize large numbers of young, idealistic workers into disruptive movements in industry, much like those on college campuses in the 1960s.

All these possibilities are, of course, speculations. However, given the sharp differences in values, attitudes, viewpoints,

and wants between the new worker and the older, more traditional top manager, we can expect to see some interesting — and
possibly painful — adjustments taking place in organizational life.

The New Manager Problem

The new manager problem will probably face the tradition-
oriented top manager because of the moderate difference in
values between the well-defined prewar generation of executives
and the middle-aged transition generation. The transition
people, who were between the ages of 30 and 40 during 1975,
bring postwar values and views to the work situation, and many
of them have found their way into supervisory and management
jobs.

Just as the postwar baby boom (PWBB) generation has
buried the traditional work ethic as the center of life, these
young managers are buying the workaholic life style. Most of
them are willing to work hard and to strive for advancement in
organizations, but they no longer feel much of a sense of alle-
giance to the organization as an abstract concept. They change
jobs on the average of every three years or so, and they see
lateral mobility as being just as inviting as is upward mobility.
Dr. Louis Banks (1977) of MIT's Sloan School of Management
contends that a values gap has emerged between older,
tradition-oriented top executives and younger, more individualistic middle managers and supervisors [p. 24].

Some top managers say, "They just won't work long hours
any more. They don't want to give anything extra to the job.
They have outside activities and their family lives are much
more important than in the past. I just can't get the average
middle manager to work more than one night a week." Younger
executives say, "My career is just one part of my life. I want to
spend time with my family and to do the other things I find
enjoyable." Banks feels this separation signals a coming shift in
American values of significant proportions.

Many of these younger managers feel psychologically

closer to the PWBB workers than to the top executives, largely because they see themselves as being young and partly because their transitional stage in life gives them more in common with younger workers. You as a top executive can expect these managers of the new breed to bring individualistic approaches to the job of managing. The organization man of the late 1950s and early 1960s is dead, if indeed he ever really lived. The younger manager will probably not accept a strongly authoritarian treatment from top managers, nor will they apply it in dealing with the employees assigned to them. New, younger styles of management will almost certainly emerge based on fostering employee feelings of achievement and social reward. Your biggest challenge in this area will probably be to adapt your own managerial style to this changing work force and this changing managerial subculture.

The Women and Minorities Problem

The women and minorities problem will also hit most organizations hard. Although the issues of Equal Employment Opportunity (EEO) and Affirmative Action (AA) will continue to bear heavily on the matter of executive social responsibility, the changing roles of women in American organizations will probably bring about an upheaval the likes of which we've never seen before. Unfortunately, the EEO/AA issue has become more of a battlefield than an area for constructive action. It has also become a lawyer's playground, with great sums to be made in winning large punitive settlements. One attorney cracked, "With almost 40 million women in the work force, and with the average woman making almost $2.00 an hour less than the average man, that's an *$80-million-an-hour* claim building up. I'd sure like to have that one as a lawsuit!" Unfortunately, the adversary mentality existing between corporations and governmental compliance agencies, aggravated by the legal profession, has probably set back the cause of human rights rather than advanced it. Random hiring by quota of females with black, Latino, Asian, or other ethnic characteristics more often than not sets them up for failure and frustration and does little to change the basic social setting limiting the development of their potential.

We must also recognize that the women's movement is no longer a clumsy, self-conscious, undirected expression of anger and frustration, as it was during its formative years. The decline in the institution of marriage has dramatically increased the number of working women, career single women, and female heads of households. Large numbers of intelligent, well-qualified women are now moving into the work force, and they will demand jobs and opportunities commensurate with their qualifications. Some enlightened executives will realize that matching them with high-challenge jobs will be an extremely good business practice. Other executives will fight a long delaying action, gradually losing ground and losing organizational effectiveness because they cannot surrender or revise their traditional male values in a world in which they no longer work.

The two biggest issues you as a top manager will probably face as the women's movement matures and develops are *equal pay* and *equal power*. Not only will you have to ensure that a woman who does the same job as a man gets the same pay for equal performance, but you will also have to come to terms with the demands of women for a chance at high-level jobs leading to management positions. Currently, fewer than 1% of American top executives are women, although women represent about 40% of the work force. Probably the strongest single thrust of women's movements will be to open up the promotion paths in organizations so that women have truly equal opportunities to reach the top. Given the present male-dominated organizational structures throughout the American business world, this thrust will probably meet with an enormous monolithic resistance. The result of the collision of these two powerful forces is hard to predict, but it almost certainly spells upheaval in the current ways of doing work, of assigning responsibility, of apportioning power, and of carrying on the everyday politics basic to sociotechnical systems of all kinds.

The Social Accountability Problem

The social accountability problem is an emerging late-century issue that can also threaten the very foundations of corporate life and corporate operations. More and more, social activists are focusing public attention on the forms of interaction between the corporation and its environments—both physical and human. Whether justified or not, a large majority of young Americans believe major corporations make excessive profits, do little or nothing to protect the ecological balance, and do little or nothing consciously to make the society a better place to live. During the first stage of the energy crisis, when major oil companies quietly reported windfall profits, many Americans felt betrayed. They felt that big business—that is, the executives of the major energy companies—had taken economic advantage of their misfortune. The call to break up the large, vertically integrated oil firms stemmed largely from this sense of outrage.

The clumsy response of many of the oil companies was to mount a slick image-building campaign, using two-page color advertising spreads in major magazines, and to sponsor more "public interest" television programs. For many Americans, this obviously manipulative approach only deepened their cynical feelings.

The term *corporate social responsibility* has emerged as a key element of discussion about American business organizations. An American Management Association study conducted in 1976 by John Paluszek concluded that the issue of social responsibility will emerge as a number-one concern of our society during the last quarter of this century. The 644 corporate executives who responded to Paluszek's questionnaire agreed with the need to work out new ways of making the corporation answerable to the needs and values of society while maintaining its economic viability. More than 68% of them agreed strongly with the statement: "We have reason to be concerned whether the corporation as we know it . . . will survive into the next century . . . The corporation itself must change, consciously evolving into an institution adapted to the new environment." Most of them added strong views to extend the statement (Paluszek, 1976).

Issues and problems most often cited as part of the accountability problem include equal job opportunities for women and minorities, honesty and real fairness in advertising, consumer product safety, occupational health and safety, and reducing or preventing environmental damage caused by corporate operations of all kinds. Problems such as the pollution of streams and rivers, thermal pollution of water bodies, atmospheric pollution, landscape destruction, and possible extreme danger to population centers connected with nuclear power plants have caused intense feelings on all sides.

Many young Americans perceive major corporations as personalized entities in themselves, only vaguely conceiving that they are operated by relatively small handfuls of men. They seem to see many corporations as operating only in their own narrowly defined self-interests. Many believe that real, substantive, responsive changes in corporate operations, in the name of public accountability, will come about only by directly applied force. They seem to believe that very few corporate executives would willingly make significant changes in these key areas if the changes would reduce corporate profits. The prevailing view seems to be that the corporation, as a selfish, greedy, profit-directed enterprise, has little or no sense of responsibility or accountability to the country at large for the consequences of its operations.

And, sadly, they may be correct. For every chief executive officer who initiates responsive change, 10 others seem to content themselves with a modest investment in public relations advertising. Privately, many of them "support" the idea of socially responsible action with statements like, "I'm all for saving and protecting the environment, but . . . " The single most important word in that statement is "but."

You as a top manager will probably face this ever-increasing demand that the corporation make itself socially accountable for the sum total of its activities and operations and that social responsibility rank on a par with profit. This, very clearly, is the wave of the future. And you will probably see concrete evidence of it, not only from the direction of social activists and governmental influence but also from the ranks of the workers and managers in your own organization. More and more, they will probably insist that the total corporate enterprise fit within the overall need structure of American society. If they believe this way, they will tend to work this way and to manage this way. The most effective top management strategy on this score is not to *pretend* to be socially responsible but actually to *become socially responsible*.

Top management theorist Peter F. Drucker (1946/1972) focused heavily on the point of social responsiveness in the epilogue to the republished version of his landmark book *Concept of the Corporation*. This book, which Drucker wrote in 1946 after spending a number of years as a consultant at General Motors, described the phenomenal economic success of GM and traced the reasons for its growth in terms of management decisions, policies, and strategies. Yet, says Drucker, GM at the three-quarter point of the century was a failure as an institution. He observes:

> But, in retrospect, my critics within GM at that time have been proved right. Not to have changed anything has been the foundation for GM's success in terms of sales and profits.
>
> But it also clearly has been the source of GM's failure as an institution. For today GM is clearly in deep trouble — not because its cars do not sell or because it lacks efficiency. GM is in trouble because it is seen increasingly by more and more people as deeply at odds with basic needs and basic values of society and community [p. 247].

Just as Theodore Vail invited government regulation of the Bell Telephone Company around the beginning of the century as a strategic move to prevent a worse fate (such as nationalization), so the corporation can prevent some of the more unpleasant possible outcomes by making itself more accountable to the society at large. Not many people really want to see the corporation pass out of existence, but they do want to see it do business without doing damage.

The Stress Problem

The fifth problem area that will result from the coming social evolution (let's hope it's an evolution), the stress problem, is really the sum of all the others. Stated another way, it is the manifestation of our inability to solve the other problems completely. To the extent that we make progress in settling these social issues satisfactorily, to that extent will we develop an organizational ecology that promotes rather than stifles human growth and development.

Because stress has become the twentieth-century disease, you as an executive are seeing the consequences of the American style of living and working in the area of occupational health, or more correctly in occupational ill-health. Heart attacks and strokes now kill more people—including managers —than all other diseases combined. Cancer—a disease now thought to be stress-linked and certainly related to stress-reactive behaviors like smoking—hovers between second and third place. As a society, we have virtually conquered infectious diseases, but we have substituted diseases of degeneration— stress diseases—for them.

If you are like most top managers, you are finding and will find to a greater degree an alarming increase in the incidence of alcoholism, drug abuse, major health breakdown among workers and managers who should be in their prime, suicide, and missed time because of chronic health problems. Clearly, the excessive stress of American living and working are taking their toll of your colleagues and employees. And, as we've seen, you yourself are a candidate for an early health breakdown unless you take an active approach to maintaining a high level of personal wellness.

Top managers will increasingly face the problem of dealing with the effects of stress on the people of their organizations. Rather than view this as simply a problem, you can find ways to make it into an opportunity. Constructive approaches to occupational wellness certainly constitute important forms of the social responsibility so many people are demanding, and they can also have the effect of increasing the effectiveness of the members of the work force. Even an intensive organization-wide program of stress reduction and improvement of the social climate should pay for itself in the long run.

Because this book focuses on the topic of stress, it is appropriate to wind up this discussion of the coming evolution in American business from that point of view. Stress is both a problem and a symptom of a problem. On the one hand, long-term chronic stress damages human health and detracts from well-being. This in itself calls for solutions. On the other hand, the things you as a top manager can do to improve the quality of life in your organization will improve the organization's functioning in a number of ways and will reduce stress as a by-product. As we rush headlong into the last quarter of the twentieth century, we begin to realize it's time to reverse an old business adage. Instead of saying, "What's good for the company is good for everybody," we must now say, "What's good for everybody is good for the company."

ORGANIZATIONAL VALUES

One effective way to bring together all these complicated and sometimes confusing economic, social, and human issues is by means of the unifying concept of *organizational values*. An organizational value is a prevailing norm that guides, directs, or constrains the behavior of its people. Every group of people, large or small, has its standards of conduct and its system of rights, privileges, liberties, and obligations. For the corporation or any other large enterprise, many of the important norms arise from the attitudes and actions of the top managers. Taken as a group, these values dominate the day-to-day interactions between managers and workers.

The idea of an organizational value is rather abstract, of course, and we cannot simply define some set of all possible norms that can be inventoried like so many items of physical stock. The organization's norms exist primarily in the perceptions of its individual members, and many of them are unconsciously perceived and followed. Sometimes a norm or a prevailing value becomes clear to various members only when one or more of them act in ways to challenge it.

For example, a variety of standard norms seem to govern the behavior of most organizational members with respect to the chain of command. Most people "know" without ever having stopped to analyze the matter how they are supposed to deal with their bosses, the probable consequences of going over the boss's head, and how to behave in the presence of high-ranking officials. These values may vary from one organization to the next, but most of the people in a given organization understand and follow them almost by second nature. Unity of command is an old and revered value in most organizations.

Other key organizational values have to do with the basic mission of the business. What things will people — especially the top managers — do in order to turn a profit? Where do they draw the line in business ethics? When they discover that an important commercial product of the firm causes serious environmental problems or threatens human health, do they drop the product, or do they rationalize its continuation? Do they invest corporate resources in lobbying, buying influence, or downright bribery to prevent regulatory legislation? Do they try to justify to themselves and their employees the continuation of a questionable business practice?

The set of values that constitutes *business ethics* is coming more and more under public scrutiny in the last quarter of the twentieth century, and increasing numbers of people are demanding that corporate officers be required to abide by common standards of honesty and ethical practice. The infamous international Lockheed scandal in 1975 and 1976 brought to light many far-reaching issues and accusations and even forced Japanese Prime Minister Kakuei Tanaka out of office. Subsequent investigations of other corporate overseas dealings exposed a number of cases of bribery of foreign government officials for the purpose of gaining favorable treatment for American corporations operating in their countries. It is sometimes difficult for the employees of a company to hold to ethics of honesty and fair play on the job when their top managers seem to live by other rules.

Another area of corporate values lies in the relationship between profit requirements and the quality of working life for the corporation's people. When management ruthlessly cuts costs and refuses to spend any money at all on employee activities and reduces as many jobs as possible to low-cost, robotic functions, the employees perceive the socioeconomic value as, "You're just a number here." And if the same company's president expounds in the annual report about how important the people of the company are to its success and how "XYZ Company *is* people," he is communicating another significant organizational value — hypocrisy.

By their combined actions over the long term, the top managers of any organization communicate, mostly unconsciously — the values they hold about the organization, its people, its mission, and its relationship to the surrounding society. These organizational values are every bit as real and operational as the organization's basic charter, its plans, and its formal policies. The employees of the organization perceive these values — often consciously — and react to them accordingly.

The top manager who really does take human needs fully into account and who integrates concern for people and concern for society with concern for profit expresses these values in day-to-day actions. He teaches subordinate managers — again, primarily by action and example — to operate by these values. By encouraging certain kinds of behavior on the part of subordinate managers and discouraging other kinds, the top executive forms and communicates throughout the organization many of its most important prevailing values.

As a management consultant, I am often in the position of studying an organization from a variety of points of view. My interviews with executives, managers, and employees at a variety of levels and in many functions often give me a strikingly clear picture of the values which seem to prevail among them. By listening to what they are saying, what they are trying to say, and what they choose not to say, I can identify most of the important dynamics of their organization as a sociotechnical system. This review and appraisal of organizational values often provides an excellent foundation for executive planning, policy making, and programs of planned change.

Think about some other kinds of organizations you've known, such as military staff units, county or state government agencies, hospitals, school districts, and colleges. See if you don't agree that each has its distinctive set of organizational values. Some values that come to mind include "Don't fraternize with enlisted men," "Keep a record of everything to protect yourself later," "Don't be too familiar with the doctors," "Maintain control in the classroom," and "Publish or perish." Others include "Never disgrace your uniform" "Use the taxpayers' money effectively," "Patient care comes before anything else," "Help each child to develop in his own way," and "Contribute something of value and significance to the literature in your field."

In deciding how to adapt your organization to the demands of the future, you can make an excellent start by reviewing, or having reviewed, the apparent value system in it. Compare your own view of the value system with the perceptions of others. You can then decide which of these values you consciously accept and want to strengthen, which ones you consider damaging to the effectiveness of the organization or to the quality of working life among its people, and which others should be promoted in their places.

HUMANIZING THE BUSINESS ORGANIZATION

Probably the biggest, toughest, and most important challenge facing the future top managers of American corporations and their counterparts in nonprofit organizations of all kinds is that of humanizing these organizations. This will probably mean making major changes in the relationship between the typical corporation and the community in which it operates and making major changes in the local relationship between those who do the work and those who manage their efforts.

Humanizing the business organization is more than just a slogan or a nice generality. It means some very specific things. The humanistic organization will have some definite characteristics that pertain to the activities and feelings of its people. *Presupposing a necessary economic stability that underlies its functioning*, this organization will look something like the following:

1. A very large number of its members express overall satisfaction with their jobs and roles or feel themselves moving constructively toward greater satisfaction.

2. Its members, at many levels and in many functional areas, enjoy relatively high-quality relationships with one another during the course of getting their work done.

3. Its members work effectively and productively, according to definitions of job-related productivity that they and the organization's managers share.

4. Its members are in good health, with the incidence of stress diseases and occupational health problems at a practical minimum.

5. Its members enjoy relatively high-quality relationships with their various immediate supervisors; they feel respected, listened to, accounted for, and responsible to do their jobs well.

6. There is a standard of excellence throughout the organization and a sense that meeting it brings substantial rewards, both psychic and financial.

7. The top managers of the organization are well informed about the current attitudes of the members and understand their primary values and desires; they account for these factors in their decision making and planning.

8. The top managers make themselves visible and approachable by the members of the organization, and they respond sensitively to the feedback they get about their performance as managers.

9. Factionalism and interdepartmental rivalry are within "normal" ranges of human political interaction and do not seriously hamper the performance of the organization's basic mission.

10. A large majority of people in the organization see it as a place in which they can strive to better their conditions in terms of pay, position, or kinds of work they do. They believe that, on the whole, it is a pretty good place to live and work and that any alternative would have to be extremely attractive to win them away.

Humanizing an organization means bringing about these conditions. As a top manager you need not aim for perfection in all these things just as you cannot expect to achieve (or even define) perfection in economic or operational performance. In any organization, a certain number of people will be currently unhappy, misplaced, maladapted, or operating inefficiently. Some of them will bring immature or ineffective coping styles to the work situation, a factor over which their managers have little or no control. Others will have accumulated such high stress scores in the other areas of their lives that they will not be able to work effectively. However, when a large number of the members of your organization have these problems and fall far short of the factors described earlier, you can be sure your organization needs humanizing. Humanizing may not necessarily be the only thing it needs, but no other solutions can be fully effective without it.

As a top manager, you can bring about this humanization process by the same kind of problem-solving approach you apply to a production problem, a financial problem, a marketing problem, or a technological problem. You must assess the organization, define the desired changes you want to bring about, set objectives, and institute a program of planned change. A later section in this chapter provides a framework for such a program.

PRESERVING AND DEVELOPING HUMAN BEINGS

In the world of business organizations, the term *personnel administration* is steadily giving way to a new term —*human resources development*. The new term is unfortunately only a slogan to some personnel people who simply want to stay abreast of the new lingo of management theory, but for an increasing number of others it brings with it a new idea. It brings a new concept of the part people play in organizations and the part organizations play in the lives of people.

The term *human resources development* —shortened to HRD—implies that the function of the organization is *not to use people but to develop them.* It implies a subtle shift in emphasis from using people as a form of capital to providing opportunities for them to challenge themselves, to grow and develop, and to perform useful and productive work as a basic part of that process.

We are increasingly beginning to realize that most people work in order to work as well as to make money. They want to have a place to go, something useful and important to do, opportunities to prove themselves and to challenge themselves, to win the respect and approval of their peers, and to feel a part of a larger enterprise. The desire to work is one of the most ironic facts of the worker alienation phenomenon. Although many people want very much to feel a part of their organizations and many managers (at least presumably) want them to feel a part of the organizations, their managers nevertheless succeed so well in alienating them that the employees' services must be bought at high prices through power brokers called "labor unions."

In more and more organizations the old position of director of industrial relations — a euphemistic term for the member of the management camp who specialized in doing battle with the union — is giving way to the new position of director of human resources development. This position, usually fairly high in terms of executive "clout," has the function of pulling the attention of the executive staff frequently and energetically toward the possibilities for improving organizational performance by improving the human environment. The HRD function subsumes the traditional training function, employing it creatively as a mode of management problem solving. It approaches management development as an element of human resources development strategy wherein the managers can develop themselves as people and as career professionals, and the employees can benefit from the effects of more enlightened, humanistic management.

Rather than simply looking to the personnel director as a procurer of warm bodies from the labor market and a keeper of the books of account on human capital, more and more top executives are looking to the HRD executive as a colleague in solving the problems of the organization and as an advocate of a humanistic environment. This function will almost certainly become more popular and more realistically involved in the mainstream of top management action. It will probably expand to include all the traditional but neglected functions such as occupational health (now fast becoming occupational wellness), safety, employee development, compensation, managerial development, career counseling and career planning, equal employment opportunity (actual, not legalistic), and even (intriguingly) executive development. The HRD executive will frequently draw upon qualified consultants and special staff members for functions such as organizational climate assessment, prescriptive program development, job engineering and redesign, change agentry, and change processes such as team building and managerial development.

The HRD executive function will increasingly offer enlightened approaches to specifically perceived management problems. Rather than occasionally "call in the personnel man," top executives will work routinely with the HRD executive who represents a functional process as basic to organizational effectiveness as the functions of finance, marketing, engineering, research and development, and manufacturing. The HRD executive will insist that the process of preserving and developing the people of the organization receive just as much management attention, emphasis, and financial investment in proportion to its magnitude as the other basic functions. His guiding philosophy will be that the preservation and improvement of the holistic wellness of the employees, the creation and maintenance of a positive, reward-centered social climate, and the maintenance of opportunities for individual growth in the work situation form the bare necessities for organizational effectiveness. His job will be to win top management support for the HRD function, just as it is the function of the marketing executive to win top management's recognition and support of the market concept in the total process of planning and decision making.

Preserving and developing human beings will not only be the right thing to do from the standpoint of humanistic treatment of employees, but it will also make excellent sense economically and operationally.

PROMOTING THE WELLNESS OF MANAGERS AND EMPLOYEES

Because executives and managers of an organization constitute one of its most important and most expensive resources, their physical health and emotional well-being are extremely important to the effectiveness of the organization. Developing these people as professional managers has always made sense to top executives, but only recently has the matter of their physical health become important. With the steady increase in stress and stress disease and the compounding factor of the typical middle-aged manager's sedentary life style, managerial health breakdowns now pose a real threat to the organization as well as to the individuals themselves.

Top managers are also beginning to realize that an investment in employee wellness pays off, and indeed it may become a necessary routine cost of doing business effectively. By 1977 the President's Council on Physical Fitness counted some 300 larger companies offering physical fitness programs to employees. Others offer special executive health programs and special programs for overweight employees. Reasons cited for these programs include reducing the enormous cost of medical benefit plans, greater work output with less stress, less exhaustion at the end of the day, and more enthusiasm for work.

The Diamond Shamrock Corporation, a chemical manufacturing company, offers free periodic medical check-ups to its 700 employees in a specially outfitted trailer. Fifty other companies also use the service for their own employees, paying a fixed fee for each person examined. The top managers of Diamond Shamrock hope to identify patterns of occupational stress that can be reduced or eliminated.

The R. J. Reynolds Company has created a health care plan for its own employees. Its Health Maintenance Organization offers cheap medical services and stress prevention to its 10,000 employees. Reynolds executives have found that the approach reduces overall corporate expenditures for employee health. However, they stress that the important factor is the improved health and well-being of Reynolds employees. Ironically, though, Reynolds is one of the world's largest manufacturers of cigarettes.

General Motors has developed a computerized mobile health screening unit for use at the Saginaw Steering Gear Division that provides results at about one-fourth the cost of a conventional fixed facility. GM executives believe the use of the system has reduced the number of lost working hours and has possibly headed off many serious health problems. (Rosow, 1977).

Approaches such as these are not limited to applications in the managerial ranks, as the foregoing examples show. However, there are several advantages in focusing first on *executive wellness* in getting programs started in these areas. First, executives and managers down to the middle levels in the organization tend to be older than most of the other employees. This puts them in the danger zone of health breakdown, the age range of about 40 to 60. Second, since most of them enjoy their jobs, there is a greater temptation for them to become workaholics and consequently to unbalance their lives and drift into the extremely dangerous sedentary life style. Third, they work under pressure, and all the aforementioned factors tend to combine to give them higher stress levels than the other employees experience. The sum of all these influences means that your managerial staff, your most important organizational resource, runs the risk of constant attrition through health breakdown and chronic stress disease. A wellness program tailored to their needs makes a great deal of sense.

Of course, if you have not been keeping your own health up to a high standard, if you are significantly overweight, if you exercise too little, if you drink too much, if you live on coffee and cigarettes throughout the day, and if you don't take opportunities for detachment, relaxation, and stress relief, you may have already skipped over this discussion. Perhaps it makes you uncomfortable to have me remind you of your own mortality. But if you're like an increasing number of executives, you read widely and you're familiar with the problems the executive life style can cause. Increasingly, chief executives are improving their physical conditioning and building stress-relief modes into their lives. It seems that chief executives tend to maintain higher levels of personal wellness than do second-level executives and middle managers. They also seem to experience lower stress levels overall, possibly because they have more or less "made it" in their quests for significance and achievement.

Business writer Angela Fox Dunn (1977) interviewed 20 chief executives in California and found them remarkably fit, relaxed, and in charge of their lives. Virtually all of them made vigorous exercise a habit. All worked long hours, had very busy schedules, and reported a great deal of satisfaction with their work. They seldom visited doctors and had a very low incidence of sickness or even corrective surgery [p. 106].

The chief executive probably has the best position of all in the organization for minimizing his own stress. He enjoys exactly the opposite state of affairs from the overstressed machine-paced worker. Whereas the machine worker suffers from a sense of task obligation and lack of control, the chief executive enjoys the freedom to innovate, to guide, and to experiment, and he also has the greatest sense of control of anyone in the organization. This means that, barring highly unusual circumstances, he enjoys the highest ratio of personal reward to stress of anyone. No wonder the men interviewed by Dunn worked 12 hours a day and loved it!

One of the ironies of the top- or second-level executive position is the frequent temptation on the part of the executive to think, "I don't need this myself, but it will be good for the boys." If you have imprisoned yourself in the social role of executive-as-superbeing, you may find it difficult to re-evaluate your own health behaviors objectively and to decide to do whatever needs to be done about them. If so, it is unlikely that you will ever be able to persuade your subordinate managers to take serious action to achieve high levels of wellness themselves.

But if you have a more flexible, self-accepting attitude, you will probably think of yourself and your executive colleagues as a team whose individual and collective health and well-being are significant resources that warrant an investment in time and cost.

The fourth reason why I believe it will be most effective for you to start with a managerial staff in reducing stress and increasing wellness is that it will become much easier to sell the concept to employees in the next phase. Managers who begin to get back into good physical condition will feel physically better, and they will feel better about themselves as persons. They will automatically begin to sense the far-reaching effects of wellness in their personal lives, and they will soon see this concept as applying to the entire population of the organization. It is likely that you will find employees asking for or even demanding programs of their own. We all know that the most effective way to bring about a new program in an organization is for the employees to advocate it themselves. The task is then no longer one of selling change but simply one of facilitating change.

A PRACTICAL PLAN OF ACTION

Let's review in terms of the steps required the process of humanizing an organization and rebalancing stress with rewards. A general *organization development* approach to improving the quality of work life has four basic steps and forms a closed cycle as illustrated by Exhibit 10-3. These steps are:

1. Assessment.
2. Planning.
3. Action.
4. Follow-through.

Let's review them one at a time.

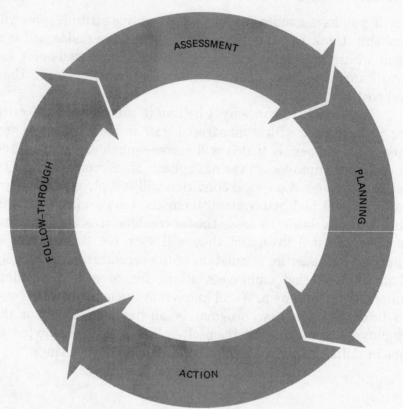

EXHIBIT 10-3. The organization development cycle offers an effective top management approach to stress reduction and stress management.

Assessment

Assessment includes all the diagnostic activities you can think of that will tell you what's going on in the organization. It involves a variety of techniques, but most of all it involves a *listening orientation* —one of curiosity, investigation, and sensitive awareness of what's happening with and to human beings at all levels and in all areas of the organization. Assessment methods include:

1. Conduct an employee attitude survey; include managers as well. Find out what people think of their jobs, their

peer relationships, their managers, their organization at large, and you (see Appendix 1 for a model survey questionnaire).

2. Conduct a health survey. Find out what kind of health problems prevail and what kinds might relate to occupational stress.

3. Conduct a stress survey. Find out by direct and indirect questions what stress levels the people of your organization are experiencing. Try to detect stress-reactive behaviors.

4. Assess the quality of the union–management relationship if your organization is a union shop.

5. Assess your total compensation program to detect any major areas of weakness or employee dissatisfaction. Are the benefits truly relevant to the needs of your particular work force?

6. Analyze jobs to identify areas of unreasonable stress and dissatisfaction.

Planning

Planning involves finding the key opportunities for substantial improvement in the overall quality of life by enriching the work experiences and by reducing stress. It means choosing a small number of improvements with high payoff and working out ways to put them into play. Planning includes the following steps:

1. Get the support of your managers in determining what needs to be done. Work by team operation and involvement, not by edict.

2. Get the support of employee groups, including the labor union if possible.

3. Correct any major problems first. Give some "pain relief" if it is needed in any significant area. Create an acceptable level of mental and social hygiene before trying to improve the overall climate.

4. Identify as many attractive improvements as you can. Analyze each in terms of value, costs, time to implement, and relative ease of implementation (refer to the discussion in Chapter 5 on improvement techniques).

5. Select only two or three high-priority, high-payoff improvements. Don't abandon the others, but give the most promising ones the most effort and the most resources.

6. Make a master plan for a one- to five-year program of planned change.

Action

Action defines itself. If you can put the results of the planning process into action, you can get what you want. Although this sounds very simple, it is usually anything but simple. Given the complexities of organizational life and the possible obstacles presented by the very same social climate you want to improve, you may find a great gap between your desires and your results. This practical view of reality favors a very simple program, one that everyone can understand and one that almost everyone can support. It should not be overly ambitious, and it should aim for the most desirable improvements first. Action steps include:

1. Begin immediately to act on the highest priority improvements. Don't wait for any big "kick-off." Get everybody working toward them and give them your personal attention. Consider solutions such as stress reduction training, job engineering and redesign, health screening, fitness programs, and improving the social climate.

2. Publicize the planned improvements. Don't use too much fanfare, but let people know what to expect. (Don't be discouraged by an initial reaction of cynicism; people in large organizations are not easily impressed by top management actions.)

3. Focus everyone's attention on the two or three high-priority projects; don't diffuse your resources over many areas of unequal payoff.
4. Make the changes voluntary and attractive. Don't try to force people into something that's "good for them." Let them take ownership of the new programs.

Follow-Through

Follow-through counts most of all. If we added up all the costs and all the hours spent in false starts and projects that never went anywhere in business organizations, simply because no one ever pushed them through to useful results, we'd probably have enough money to start 10 new countries. In the area of social change especially, lack of follow-through can produce negative results — worse than no program at all. This is because the initial enthusiasm phase creates high hopes and big expectations, and the "fizzle" phase dashes hopes and leads to disillusionment and cynicism. If you're not really going to follow through, *don't start the program.* And don't bite off more than you can follow through on. It is much better to start a small program with modest objectives that succeed than to start a grandiose program that falls flat. Follow-through activities include:

1. Keep the attention of all managers focused on the improvement program, and maintain a long attention span. Give each executive a part to play, and follow up on assignments.
2. Personally participate in the program. Set a good example of personal fitness, holistic wellness, and low-stress managing.
3. Review progress formally from time to time. Compare results with the plan in terms of specific milestones and accomplishments.
4. Assess all or part of the program frequently. See whether the human situation is improving and whether the problem is changing.

5. Get feedback from all levels of the organization on progress, problems, and snags.
6. Revise the program as the human situation improves and priorities shift.
7. Make this process of planned improvement in the human dimension of the organization a habit. Make it a way of life and build it into your everyday management processes.

Many people can help you in this process. Human resources consultants, personnel specialists, trainers, management specialists, your top executives, managers at all levels, and the employees themselves. But never forget that this process of planned change and humanization of the organization needs your guidance. It is your personal and professional obligation to the people of the community from which your organization draws its members. Although you can subdivide the tasks to be done and delegate them to various managers, you cannot delegate the obligation. Nor can you delegate your personal involvement and commitment, which are the two ingredients without which you and your organization cannot adapt to the changing times.

THE BOTTOM LINE REVISITED

Throughout all the discussion in this book we have seen that there are really *three bottom lines* — the financial one, the social one, and the human one. We also know that they are inseparably linked. In the organization, what detracts from the economic bottom line eventually detracts from the human bottom line. Without an economically viable organization, there can be no jobs, no managers, and no social climate. And what detracts from the human bottom line eventually detracts from the economic bottom line. Without the human payoff in money, job satisfaction, personal fulfillment, respect for human values and human rights, and opportunities for individual growth, the economic bottom line becomes harder and harder to maintain. The price for inhuman use of human beings must be paid sooner or later, and I believe *it is always paid in actual dollars and cents.*

As we enter the last quarter of this, the exponential century, we now realize that there need be no necessary conflict between the human bottom line and the economic bottom line. We need not opt for a mindless, robotic pursuit of profit to the extent that it makes a business enterprise empty, barren, and meaningless. And we need not swing the pendulum over toward anarchy, country-club management, corporate "welfarism," or a preoccupation with everyone "doing his own thing" at the expense of the higher purposes of the enterprises from which those "everyones" draw their livelihood and even part of their sense of purpose in life. We can indeed integrate the three bottom lines into a single, socioeconomic bottom line—one that satisfies a number of needs at a variety of levels.

I believe that most of the formidable problems facing the United States as a society—and there are many—and those that face all the developed and developing nations of the world can be substantially solved if we can learn to focus resources and human talents on them by means of that amazing twentieth-century socioeconomic phenomenon, the corporation. Time and again we have seen the goal-directed corporation outstrip the clumsy, diffused, drifting government agency in bringing about economic and social change rapidly and efficiently. We must learn how to focus the corporation as an action mechanism upon the new and emerging problems of our society. We must take the business resources now being squandered on useless products and incredibly wasteful advertising and focus them on producing products and services that can advance the quality of life for people in the United States and in poorer countries everywhere.

This may sound like a wild-eyed, utopian view of the remainder of our century, but I believe it is perfectly possible. And I believe the first step is for many of this country's top managers —people like you and those you will teach to do the same work you do —to evolve their organizations from primarily economic entities into socioeconomic entities. We must develop socioeconomic corporations that are fully accountable to the society and communities within which they thrive and that play an active and conscious part in changing that society and those communities for the best. And this socioeconomic evolution must begin with the humanization of the corporations themselves, by raising the quality of work life and by eliminating unnecessary stress.

We must deal with the fact of stress, the twentieth-century disease, as a problem in itself, as a symptom of needed changes in the fabric of our society, and as a guiding barometer in telling us whether we are doing the right things. Many of the available solutions to the problem of stress begin with you, the manager. You must create practical programs, and you must bring them to reality. I'm convinced this is the number-one management challenge for the remainder of the twentieth century.

And it's good business.

REFERENCES

Banks, Louis. "Here Come the Individualists." *Harvard Magazine*, September–October 1977.

Drucker, Peter F. *Concept of the Corporation.* New York: The John Day Company, 1946/72.

Dunn, Angela Fox. "How Fit Are Our Top Executives?" *California* (PSA Flight Magazine), September 1977.

Paluszek, John L. *Business and Society: 1976–2000* (AMA Survey Report). New York: American Management Association, 1976.

Rosow, Jerome M. *World of Work Report.* Scarsdale, N.Y.: Work in America Institute, Inc., October 1977.

Appendix

EMPLOYEE ATTITUDE SURVEY
QUESTIONNAIRE

This model questionnaire can help to assess the attitudes of the employees, including managers, in an organization concerning factors important to their job satisfaction, health, and well-being. These 25 questions should provide a picture of what's going on in the organization as a sociotechnical system sufficient to allow top management to decide what corrective changes, if any, are necessary. You may decide to add other questions to explore specific features of your own organization.

Here are some pointers on using an attitude questionnaire like this in a typical business organization:

1. Don't make it a mysterious process; let everyone know what the questionnaire is and why you are asking them to fill it out. Make the results public or at least freely available to any employees who want to know them.

2. Make the returns completely anonymous. Be sure any employee can feel free to answer as he sees fit without apprehension.

3. Don't insist on 100% compliance. You can't get it without jeopardizing anonymity, and you don't need it anyway.

4. Don't jump to conclusions in interpreting the results. You can seldom safely base any actions solely on questionnaire data. Feed the results into your normal channels of management thinking, planning, and decision making.

5. Plan on repeating *exactly* the same questionnaire at intervals of six to 12 months. Keep baseline data so you can spot trends.

6. Be careful not to imply inadvertently any future actions or problems merely because you are taking an attitude survey; be careful not to "shop" for preconceived answers or results in administering the questionnaire.

This model questionnaire offers multiple-choice questions, most of which are keyed to five discrete choices to facilitate processing the data and expressing the results of all questions in bar graph form for the work force as a whole. It is also possible to separate out managerial responses as well as those of other kinds of employees on the basis of the job-category question. Notice that a number of the questions can help to assess the relative level of life stress the employee is experiencing, as well as current perceptions of the quality of his overall life.

EMPLOYEE ATTITUDE SURVEY QUESTIONNAIRE

To the employee:
Please answer the following questions as thoughtfully and accurately as possible. This information will help to create a picture of working conditions and social climate in our organization that will be useful to managers at all levels. After answering the

multiple-choice questions, feel free to add any comments you like at the bottom of the last page.

Classification Factors:

1. Which of the following categories most nearly describes your job?
   1) Manual job, unskilled or semiskilled.
   2) Manual job, skilled.
   3) Clerical.
   4) Managerial.
   5) Professional.

2. What is your age range?
   1) 20-29.
   2) 30-39.
   3) 40-49.
   4) 50-59.
   5) 60 or over.

3. What is your sex?
   1) Male.
   2) Female.

4. What is your educational background?
   1) Less than high school diploma.
   2) High school diploma.
   3) 1-2 years college.
   4) 2-4 years college.
   5) 4 years or more of college.

5. How long have you worked for the organization?
   1) Less than 1 year.
   2) 1-5 years.
   3) 5-10 years.
   4) 10-20 years.
   5) More than 20 years.

Job Factors:

6. What is your overall level of satisfaction with your day-to-day work on the basis of factors such as difficulty, challenge, variety, interest, workload, sense of accomplishment, and so on?
   1) I hate my job.
   2) My job is generally unpleasant.
   3) It's just a job to me.
   4) I enjoy my job.
   5) I find my job very satisfying.

7. To what extent do you consider your pay and other benefits to be fair and equitable for the work you're doing?
   1) Not at all fair.

2) Somewhat unfair.
3) Adequate.
4) Better than average.
5) Very favorable.

8. How effective do you consider your immediate supervisor?
   1) Very poor.
   2) Poor.
   3) So-so.
   4) Fairly effective.
   5) Very effective.

9. How well do you get along with your co-workers?
   1) Very poorly.
   2) Poorly.
   3) So-so.
   4) Well.
   5) Very well.

10. To what extent do you feel "in" on the important aspects of your unit's operation?
    1) Not at all.
    2) Mostly left out.
    3) Moderately involved and included.
    4) Usually feel a part of things.
    5) Very involved; I feel I'm an important member of the group.

11. To what extent do you feel your work and contributions are generally appreciated by your supervisor?
    1) Not at all.
    2) Not very much.
    3) To some extent.
    4) Mostly.
    5) Very much.

12. How would you rate your own relative job security?
    1) Very low.
    2) Low.
    3) Moderate.
    4) High.
    5) Very high.

13. What is your opinion about opportunities for advancement in the organization?
    1) Nonexistent.
    2) Poor.
    3) Fair.
    4) Good.
    5) Excellent.

14. How would you evaluate your own physical surroundings on the job?
    1) Extremely unpleasant.
    2) Unpleasant.
    3) Acceptable.
    4) Pleasant.
    5) Very pleasant.

15. To what extent do you consider upper management loyal to you and your co-workers?
    1) Not at all.
    2) Not very.
    3) Moderately.
    4) Usually loyal to us.
    5) Very loyal to us.

Individual Factors:

16. How much physical exercise do you get, on the average?
    1) Little or none.
    2) Occasional.
    3) Moderate.
    4) Frequent.
    5) A great deal.

17. How do you evaluate your bodyweight?
    1) Obese.
    2) Very heavy.
    3) Moderately overweight.
    4) Mildly overweight.
    5) Not overweight at all.

18. To what extent do you smoke cigarettes?
    1) More than a pack a day.
    2) A pack a day.
    3) Less than a pack a day.
    4) Only occasionally.
    5) Not at all.

19. How much liquor do you drink?
    1) Too much for my own good.
    2) Daily.
    3) Socially only.
    4) Seldom.
    5) Never.

20. Are you currently seeing a psychiatrist, psychologist, or other therapist/counselor?
    1) Regularly.

2) Frequently.
3) Occasionally.
4) Seldom.
5) Not at all.

21. Are you currently taking any mood-leveling medications (e.g., tranquilizers, sedatives, sleeping pills, blood pressure medication, etc.)?
    1) Regularly.
    2) Frequently.
    3) Occasionally.
    4) Rarely.
    5) Not at all.

22. Do you currently use drugs for "recreational" purposes?
    1) Regularly.
    2) Frequently.
    3) Occasionally.
    4) Rarely.
    5) Not at all.

23. Would you describe yourself as relatively tense, nervous, anxious, or unable to unwind? (Consider also the impressions other people have of you in deciding.)
    1) Very tense most of the time.
    2) Frequently tense.
    3) Often moderately tense.
    4) Only occasionally tense.
    5) Seldom tense, except for serious problem situations.

24. How would you rate your overall health?
    1) Very poor.
    2) Poor.
    3) Fair.
    4) Good.
    5) Excellent.

25. How would you rate your relative enjoyment of your life lately?
    1) I'm miserable.
    2) I'm mostly unhappy.
    3) I have my ups and downs.
    4) I'm mostly happy.
    5) I'm enjoying my life very much.

Please add any comments you have below:

SCRIPT FOR RECORDING YOUR OWN
DEEP RELAXATION INSTRUCTIONS

General Procedure

1. Allow a 30-second "leader" of silence on the cassette before beginning to speak.
2. Speak in a soft, soothing, slightly authoritative voice directly into the microphone. Speak slowly in a singsong pattern, elongating your vowel sounds slightly.
3. In the following script, the cue, " . . ." means to pause for two or three seconds; make these pauses natural, not mechanical.
4. Don't rattle the microphone or otherwise introduce startling sounds into the recording.

Relaxation Instructions
(To Be Read Into The Recorder)

This recording will help you learn the skill of deep relaxation, which is so important for stress reduction, stress management, and overall health and well-being . . . sit comfortably, in a relaxed position, and concentrate your mind fully on these instructions . . . take a deep breath, and as you let it out, allow your eyes to fall shut . . . let your body begin to relax and unwind . . . take another deep breath, and as you exhale let it carry all the tension out of your body . . . allow a feeling of peacefulness to descend over you . . . A pleasant, enjoyable sensation of being comfortable and at ease . . . now turn your attention to your body, and begin to pay close attention to the sensations and signals you can detect . . . find the place or the muscle that is most strongly tensed or exerted and allow it to let go of its hold . . . begin to let all your muscles, all over your body, give up their hold and begin to go limp . . . now direct your attention to the top of your head and allow a feeling of relaxation to begin there . . . allow it to spread downward through your body . . . let the small muscles of your scalp relax . . . let the muscles of your forehead relax . . . devote special attention to your forehead and *feel* the muscle there giving up its hold . . . feel your eyebrows sagging down and let your eyelids become very heavy . . . let all the muscles around the back and on the sides of your head relax completely . . . imagine that your ears are even drooping under their own weight . . . now let your jaw muscles relax and allow your jaw to drop slightly . . . don't deliberately open or close your jaw, just let it float freely . . . Allow the muscles of your cheeks and lips to relax and grow limp . . . now, all the muscles of your face and head have given up their hold and are very relaxed . . . now, let the muscles of your neck relax slightly, keeping them exerted only enough to hold your head upright and balanced easily in position . . . let your shoulders become heavy and sag downward as you relax the muscles that come down from the sides of your neck to the shoulders . . . let the feeling of relaxation continue to spread downward to the muscles of your chest and upper back . . . command those muscles to release their hold . . . you have no need of them for the time being . . . let your shoulder muscles go completely limp, and let your arms rest heavily with your hands in your lap or on your thighs . . . feel your arms growing very heavy . . . relax all the muscles of your forearms, hands, and fingers . . . you have no desire whatever to move any single muscle in your entire body . . . pay attention to your breathing for a few seconds, and notice how it has become regular and shallow . . . now let the feeling of deep relaxation spread fully down into your chest, down through the muscles of your back, and down into your arms . . . allow your stomach muscles to relax completely . . . your stomach will probably sag just a bit as the muscles release their hold . . . relax the muscles of your sides, shoulder blades, and the small of your back . . . let the muscles of your spine relax — the ones on either side of your spine that run from the base of your skull down to the tip of your spine . . . keep them exerted only enough to keep your back in position . . . now relax the large muscles in your thighs . . . let them go completely limp . . . feel *all* your muscles so relaxed that they begin to feel as though they're turning to jelly . . . your entire body is becoming profoundly relaxed . . . relax the muscles of your buttocks and the muscles underneath your thighs . . . let the muscles of your calves relax . . . be sure to relax the muscles on the front of your lower legs and shin muscles . . . let your ankles feel free and loose . . . now wiggle your toes once or twice and let all the little muscles of your feet give up their hold completely . . . now your whole body is extremely relaxed, and we're going to concentrate on certain areas in order to increase this feeling of profound relaxation even more . . . pay close attention to the sensations in your arms . . . by now, your hands and feet will have become somewhat warm, due to the increased circulation of blood in them . . . tune in to this feeling of slight warmth and allow it to increase . . . don't try to *make* it happen . . . allow your arms to feel extremely heavy and completely limp . . . feel this growing sensation of warmth spreading out to your fingertips . . . concentrate closely on your hands and arms . . . allow the feeling of pleasant heaviness and warmth to increase by itself . . . simply observe the process and encourage it . . . now, let those same feelings of heaviness and warmth spread through your legs . . . concentrate closely on the sensations in your legs and let them become very, very heavy . . . very heavy and very warm . . . arms and legs becoming *so* heavy and *so* warm . . . your entire body is profoundly relaxed, and you feel only a pleasant overall sensation of heaviness, warmth, and absolute peace . . . now turn your attention to your breathing, and without interfering with your breathing in any way, simply begin to observe it . . . feel the slow, peaceful rise and fall of your stomach as the breath moves slowly in and slowly out of your body . . . don't try to hurry it up or slow it down . . . just act as a casual observer, taking a curious interest in this slow, steady process . . . imagine you have just discovered this steady rising and falling of your stomach, and you are observing it with curiosity and respect . . . wait patiently for each breath to arrive and notice its passing . . . notice the brief periods of quiet after one breath passes and before the next one arrives . . . now continue to observe this breathing process and begin to count your breaths as they arrive . . . as the first one comes, watch it closely and hear yourself say "one" . . . wait patiently for the next one and count "two" . . . continue until you've counted 25 breaths, not allowing *any* other thoughts to distract you . . . (pause here long enough to count 25 of your own breaths and add an extra five or so) . . . [gently, so as not to startle the listener] now you are deeply relaxed, and you can return to this peaceful state whenever you want to . . . take a few moments to pay close attention to this relaxed feeling all over your body and *memorize* it as carefully as you can . . . store the entire feeling of your whole body in your memory, so that later you can retrieve it and relax yourself at will . . . now, before you return to full alertness and activity, take plenty of time to wake up your body and bring it back up to its usual level . . . [here, make your voice stronger and more definite] wiggle your fingers and toes . . . shrug your shoulders, move your arms and legs a little bit . . . keeping your eyes closed for a few moments longer, make sure you can sense all parts of your body . . . use your hands to massage your thigh muscles and the muscles in your arms . . . move your head around a little bit . . . now, take a nice, deep breath and allow your body to feel fully alive and flowing with plenty of energy . . . and now open your eyes.

Index